ROLE OF THE MIDDLE CLASS IN NATIONALIST MOVEMENT

ROLE OF THE MIDDLE CLASS IN NATIONALIST MOVEMENT (1912-1947)

RAN VIJOY KUMAR

Commonwealth

Role of The Middle Class in Nationalist Movement (1912-1947)

ISBN : 81-7169-030-0

Edition : 2024

Published by :

JANAKI PRAKASHAN for

COMMONWEALTH PUBLISHERS (P) LTD.

4831/24, Govind Lane,
Ansari Road, Darya Ganj,
New Delhi - 110002
Ph. : 23272541, 23242541
e-mail : commonwealthpublishers2016@gmail.com

Distributed by :

ARJUN PUBLISHING HOUSE

4831/24, Govind Lane,
Ansari Road, Darya Ganj,
New Delhi - 110002
Ph. : 23272541, 23242541
e-mail : arjunbooks2001@gmail.com

Laser Typesetting by :

Dimple Computers

Delhi

Printed at :

Balaji Offset

Delhi

Acknowledgements

I am greatly indebted to my esteemed teacher and guide Dr. V.A. Narain, Professor of Modern Indian History, and Dean Faculty of Social Sciences, Patna University (at present Principal, Patna College) for giving me all possible help in this work. I am grateful to Dr. S. Gopal for his various suggestions. I am also grateful to Dr. P. Dutta and Dr. R. Ram for their co-operation and help in this work.

I express my deep sense of gratitude to the authorities of the National Archives, New Delhi, the State Archives, West Bengal, Calcutta and the Central Records Office, Government of Bihar, Patna as also the Divisional and District Record Offices in Bihar for allowing me to consult relevant records in their custody for my work.

I am very much grateful to the authorities of the National Library, Calcutta, Sinha Library, Patna, Patna University Library, Patna, Library of the Department of History, Patna University, Patna for allowing me to use their collections in course of my work.

Ran Vijoy Kumar

Abbreviations

A.I.C.C.	All India Congress Committee
A.I.S.A.	All India Spinners' Association
Cr. P.C.	Criminal Procedure Code
M.L.C.	Member of the Legislative Council
M.E.	Middle English
N.C.O.	Non-Cooperation
P.S.	Police Station
P.C.C.	Provincial Congress Committee

Contents

Acknowledgements v

Abbreviations vi

Introduction ix

1. Growth and Composition of the Middle Class in Bihar 1
2. The Middle Class and the Nationalist Movement in Bihar 51
3. The Nationalist Movement Between 1919 and 1929 and the Middle Class in Bihar 98
4. The Civil Disobedience Movement and the Middle Class in Bihar (1930-34) 172
5. Revolutionary Nationalism and the Middle Class in Bihar (1912-1933) 217
6. The Middle Class and the Nationalist Movement Between 1935 and 1941 in Bihar 239
7. The Nationalist Movement Between 1942 and 1947 and the Middle Class in Bihar 278

Conclusion 317

Bibliography 327

Index 335

Introduction

In this study an attempt has been made to examine the role of the middle class of Bihar in the Indian National Movements between 1912 and 1947 A.D. Bihar played a significant and inspiring role in the various phases of the national movement. The Home Rule Movement, the Champaran Movement, the Non-Cooperation Movement, the Civil Disobedience Movement and the Quit India Movement, had been important stages to which Bihar made its unique contribution. In these events of the national movement the middle class in Bihar played a pivotal role and made its presence felt. Bihar had the unique historical privilege in getting inspiration from Mahatma Gandhi since the year 1917. Mahatma Gandhi came to Champaran in response to the appeals of down-trodden peasants subjected to all sorts of torture under the British Indigo planters. He was asisted in his mission of deliverance of the peasants from the grinding socio-economic anomalies by a band of Bihari co-workers like Rajendra Prasad, Brajkishore Prasad, Gorakh Prasad, Anugraha Narayan Sinha, Shambhu Sharan, Janakdhari Prasad and others. These great personalities belonged to the educated middle class of Bihar. It was under their influence that Bihar played a marvellous role in the successive phases of India's battle for liberty.

Much has been written on the history of the freedom movement in India and the role of the various provinces in it. Dr. K.K. Datta's *History of the Freedom Movement in Bihar*, in three volumes, is a monumental contribution to the study of the history of the freedom struggle in Bihar. Dr. Datta has dealt in detail with Bihai's participation and role in India's freedom struggle since 1857, but in this work the role of the middle class has not received adequate attention. Similar is the case of the *Indian Middle Classes* by B.B. Misra. *Bihar Through the Ages* makes no reference to this valuable theme. It is the first chance that an attempt has been made to examine this theme under the perspective of modern historical developments.

The present study begins with the year 1912 which marks a landmark in the history of Bihar for two reasons. In the first place it witnessed the creation of Bihar as a separate province, and secondly, it was also the year when the Indian National Congress, for the first time, held its twenty-seventh session at Bankipore (Patna). The study ends with the year 1947 when India attained independence from the British colonial rule.

The creation of Bihar as a separate province was the result of a movement for the separation of Bihar from Bengal which gained momentum with a growing awareness to the Government's discriminatory policy against the Biharis. The educational development had created a social and political consciousness among the educated Biharis who could foresee the benefits of the separation of Bihar. The problem of their employment in the public services had become acute. The members of the middle class educated Biharis took keen interest in organising the movement and dedicated themselves to the cause of separation of Bihar. It was an urge of objective historical forces that the leadership to this movement was given by the persons belonging to the educated middle class, whose interests were clashing with those of their counterparts in Bengal. Eminent leaders belonging to the middle class justified through their speeches and writings that on cultural, historical, geographical, sociological and ethnological grounds, Bihar had a separate and distinct identity as the constituent force of Indianism.

The movement for the separation of Bihar was carried on jointly by the Hindus and Muslims. Educated Muslims like

Mazharul Haque, Ali Imam, Hasan Imam and Mohammad Fakhruddin were closely associated with the movement. Other prominent men of the educated middle class who played the leading role in the movement were Sachchidanand Sinha, Mahesh Narayan, Bisheshwar Singh, Shaligram Singh, Nand Kishore Lal, Brahmadeo Narayan, Parmeshwar Narayan Mehta, Taj Narayan Singh, Gajadhar Prasad and Krishna Sahay. The joint efforts made by the leaders of both the communities led to the fruitful results and ultimately the new province of Bihar came into existence on the 1st April 1912.

The present study is spread over in seven chapters—Growth and Composition of the Middle Class in Bihar, The Middle Class and the Nationalist Movement in Bihar between 1912 and 1918, The Nationalist Movement between 1919 and 1929 and the Middle Class in Bihar, The Civil Disobedience Movement and the Middle Class in Bihar (1930-34), Revolutionary Nationalism and the Middle Class in Bihar (1912-33), The Middle Class and the Nationalist Movement between 1935 and 1941 in Bihar, The Middle Class and the Nationalist Movement between 1942 and 1947 in Bihar.

In the first chapter discussions over the concept of class, the definition of the middle class, British impact and social change in India and growth and composition of the middle class in Bihar have been made.

In the second chapter an attempt has been made to explain the role of the middle class in the agitation leading to the establishment of the Patna University, in the Home Rule Movement and in the Champaran Movement under the leadership of Mahatma Gandhi.

The third chapter deals with the role of the middle class in the Satyagraha of 1919, the Khilafat and the Non-Cooperation Movements, the formation of Swarajya Party and its activity and with organising its vehement protest to the Simon Commission. The constructive programmes proposed by Mahatma Gandhi form a new ground for the treatment of this theme.

The role of the middle class in the celebration of Independence Day, the Salt Satyagraha, the militant activities for the boycott of foreign cloth and boycott of intoxicants and non-payment of chaukidari tax, anti-untouchability campaign, observing successful hartals and other national and constructive programmes have been examined in the fourth chapter.

The role of the middle class in the revolutionary nationalism has been discussed in the fifth chapter.

The sixth chapter throws light on interesting aspects like the role of the middle class in the constructive programmes, the celebration of the Golden Jubilee of the Indian National Congress and other national occasions, the elections to the Provincial Legislature and the formation of the Congress Ministries, the Kisan Movement, the propaganda against Government's War Policy, holding the session of the Ramgarh Congress, the Satyagraha Camp at Sonepur and the Individual Civil Disobedience Movement.

In the seventh chapter issues like the role of the middle class in educating and preparing the people for irresistible struggle against the British imperial rule, launching the call of the Quit India Movement, organising the underground revolutionary activities, an outburst of the communal politics, the elections to the Provincial Legislature, the constructive works and celebration of the Independence Day and other national occasions have been thoughtfully considered in the light of the present theme of middle class role.

Present study is based on reports of the All India and Provincial Congress Committee, Government reports, unpublished records of the National Archives of India, New Delhi and the State Archives of Bihar, Patna, and of the West Bengal, Calcutta and the Divisional and District records, memoirs of the leaders of the period, biographies. A select bibliography has been given at the end of the book for an advanced reading.

1

Growth and Composition of the Middle Class in Bihar

The inauguration of the social change through occasional reforms in Bihar was made by the new ruling class, the British rulers.[1] As a result of the British rule the Indian society, which had been largely based on birth-status and tradition, had been in a flux, moving towards a new status system determined by economic-occupational achievements, education and economic forces of competition. Alongside the traditional caste categories there had emerged the classes which cut across the traditional caste stratification and represented constellations of cross-sections of castes.[2]

1. The Concept of Class

Before discussing the newly emerged classes, it is necessary to discuss the concept of class. Plato was not very wrong when he said that class rests on the foundations of individual 'differences and aptitudes' and class-structure is the ranking of such aptitudes by their social values. But no discussion of the class is complete if it stops with Plato. After Plato it was Karl Marx who made the most important contribution to the concept of class. Marx made an economic approach to the study of class phenomena. The fundamental determinant of class is the way in which the individuals co-operate with other in the satisfaction of his basic needs of food, clothing and shelter. If two men are carpenters, they belong to the same occupation, but one may run a small shop of his own while another works in a plant manufacturing pre-fabricated housing. Thus the two belong to the same occupation, although to different social classes.[3]

There is another concept known as the Weberian concept based on the notions of prestige and status which are universal but variable. Max Weber declared that the distribution of power (e.g. economic) in any legal order is influenced by the structure of the order and "class" is a phenomenon of distribution of power within its community. He defines class as a group of persons "occupying the same class-status" or "in the same class-situation." Class-status or class-situation denotes the possession or lack of power to exchange "goods or skills for the sake of income in a given economic order. Such a group of persons, is then, a class in Weberian sense.[4]

Joseph Schumpeter further points out an important fact when he says that such a class is something more than an aggregate of numbers. It is a special social organism with a set of generalised interests derived from, and based upon, the amount of 'power' (in Weberian sense) that the group possesses or lacks. This similarity of situation unites these people, though differing individually, into a single living entity having certain social attitudes in common.[5] One essential characteristic of the phenomenon of class is that class members behave towards one another in a fashion characteristically different from their conduct towards members of other classes.[6] They are unconsciously eonscious of their ownness. While there is an easy social intercourse within the bounds of the same class, the easiness tends to disappears as we move away from the centre of one class towards the boundary and beyond that into another.

In this way in his attempt to define and study class phenomenon Weber makes an economic approach. In his view the concept of class-status has arisen out of market-economy which is the main plank of capitalism. Property and lack of property are, therefore, the basic categories of class situations. He differentiates class-status from social status. The latter term signifies a claim on negative or positive privileges with respect to social prestige resting on a formal process of education, a corresponding mode of life or the prestige of birth or of an occupation. Both these concepts are related though not identical. Social-status may be based on class-status and conversely social status may determine class-status without being identical.[7]

W. Loyd Warner's conception of class is an alternative to that of Marx. He believes that class is not a phenomenon necessarily of a capitalist base. Rather it is a multifactored phenomenon. According to him, a class refers to "two or more orders of people who are believed to be, and are accordingly ranked by all the members of the community, in socially superior or inferior position."[8] It is an all inclusive hierarchy which ranks all the members of society into a vertical series of horizontal layers.

Social status may be said to provide the key or main to one's true social class. According to MacIver and Page a social class is any portion of a community marked off from the rest by social status.[9] Ogburn and Nim Koff further point out that a social class is the aggregate of persons having essentially the same social status in a given society.[10] Nevertheless, all the individuals of any group in a society are not of equal or similar status but their interests may be same. E.A. Hoebel is correct in stating that a social class is a group within a society, whose members hold a number of distinctive status develop awareness of their like interests as against the different traits and interests of other groups.[11]

Another fundamental determinant of class is occupation.[12] Occupations are a system of regulated social relations in as much as they are necessarily approved aspects of the structure of communities. A person is ascribed a particular status—high or low—in society because his work is a response to a claim upon him by the society, in return of which he acquires a particular set of reciprocal rights. The greater the amount of trust laid in an individual, the higher are his reciprocal rights and his status in society. We can say that vocational or occupational status involves "Standardized remuneration" and contains "elements of respect, honour, ascendency and domination". It involves prestige.[13] Accordingly class may be defined as a group of persons possessing the same occupational status. Thus, when we speak of the "occupational structure" of the society as a whole or of a particular limited class or section what we mean is a "*hierarchical* organisation of individual behaviour responses to key stimuli or rank, title or privileges."[14] We mean that society is arranged in a series of layers based on prestige, both economic and social.

According to Lewis and Maude, "family may be said to be the key" to one's true social class. The style of life and social participation refer, nearly always, to families and not to individuals. If the society is not a very rigid caste society, or if there is an open education system on democratic lines, there is bound to be a movement on the vertical plane of social structure. This movement in social space "makes the question of social classification a matter of family rather than of individual."[15]

Social mobility may be recognised as a basis of class concept. It meant equality of opportunity to improve one's lot in society. It was a dynamic concept which left the individual to move freely in social space. It became a principle of economic law and social philosophy which guided the conduct of the Western middle-class societies.[16] It was due to this social mobility, which followed the Renaissance and the Protestant movements of Europe, and the American and the French Revolutions that man achieved his natural and political rights. The revolutions introduced laissez-faire as the principle of trade and broke the monopoly of political privileges which the owners of feudal estates enjoyed before.

The new groups of people, for example, the elite and the business classes who came to share these rights did so from no religious sanction. They rose into higher social and political grade merely by virtue of their wealth, education and power.

An important element that emerged out of the eighteenth century revolutionary situations was that of self-consciousness. It was a result of the intellectual thinking and progress of secular education that preceded these revolutions. It emphasized the importance of the political rights of man regardless of the 'estate' to which he might belong. It was the principle of human dignity which formed the basis of struggle against feudalism. It signified adherence to certain liberal values which received the general acceptance of the nation in time.[17] Thus while element of social mobility was conducive of progress, the factor of socially accepted consciousness involved fulfilment of conditions precedent to that progress. While one was dynamic, the other was static. Together they constituted an important principle of social mechanics and it was under the influence of this principle that the social history of the democracias proceeded.[18]

To look at the question of class from these different view-points does not mean that those views are exclusive. As working concept in social research both can be effectively employed. We can say that the one is based on economic factors, such as, income, economic functions or relation to a system of production which render class a socio-economic aggregate and the other is based on the subjective considerations of class-consciousness which *changes* the class into a socio-psychological phenomenon, and both are inter-related and mutually inclusive.[19] Thus, 'Class' seems to be bound together by occuaptional, economic and stratificatory bonds.

2. Definition of the Middle Class

Professor Hexter insists on a sharp and meaningful definition of the "Middle Class" and castigates those who sweep into it every one who did not either work as a wage-labourer or come over with William the conqueror. Merely to insist on such a definition is a salutary exercise. Merchants and town-dwellers (the true bourgeoisie), employers of industrial labour, middling and smaller land owners, graziers and Yeomen farmers, lawyers and public officials, did not form a single articulated social group.[20]

A study of the various groups or classes in a society is, thus, a necessary part of the natural history of mankind, since groups have been existing in all societies and at all times.

Plato judged men in terms of their inherent capacities. He divided the population into three groups: those who laboured; those who performed administrative and military duties, and those who ruled. We can say that these were the three main layers of social relationships in his ideal republic which constituted the three main social classes.

Karl Marx presents a dynamic theory of social stratification taking into consideration an all-time evolution of forces at work in the economic field. He maintains that different periods of history are characterised by different modes of production and a class-structure; the all-time common point of the latter is that it always consists of two antagonistic groups—the haves and the have nots that is to say, the bourgeoisie and the proletariat. Other groups according to him do not constitute real classes and therefore calls them as obsolescent.

The bourgeoisie is the owner and controller of the means of production. They exploit the working class and very subtly influence their moral and intellectual life. The workers are exploited because they are paid less than the value they produce. Not all workers are exploited in this way because they do not "create" value as goods but are engaged in distribution or commerce or services. Their remunerations are decided by higgling and bargaining. Such workers are petite bourgeoisie[21] in Marxian terminology.

Warner does not agree with Marxian capitalism bias in the theory of classes. He adopts an essentially subjective approach and is concerned primarily with the prestige—dimension of stratification. He further claims that the classes he describes are empirically existing entities. Says Warner "These social levels are not categories invented by social scientists to help explain what they have to say, they are groups recognised by the people of the community. . . . The designations of social levels are distinctions made by the people themselves in referring to each other."[22] He claims that he "worked out empirically . . . the existence of six stratified social classes:[23] Upper-upper, lower-upper, upper-middle, lower-middle, upper-lower ,lower-lower. The first or the upper-upper is the "aristocracy of birth and wealth" proud of their 'old ancestry'. The lower-uppers are mostly like the upper-upper but they lack ancestry and do not have "long traditions of upper class behaviour". The upper-lower are 'honest workmen'. This group consists mostly of semi-skilled workers plus a few small tradesmen. They are semi-skilled and unskilled workers and from the "level below the common man." The upper-middle class is composed of substantial businessmen and professional people. These are respected members of the community who often act as civic leaders. Members of the lower middle classes are almost frequently small businessmen, clerical workers, other lower level white collar workers and a few skilled workers."

When the feudal economy was crumbling down, a growing gulf was created between the producers of raw materials and the manufactures and their productive activity gravitated towards the towns. This gave birth to an 'intermediate social and functional group of people called Mittelstand"[24] and it was this group who were responsible for the transformation of the medieval economy into modern. This was a cohesive group knit by a new 'civic spirit', ready to revolt against the feudal land owner. This group was later known as the middle class and was also spoken of as the bourgeoisie.[25] It was a middle group between the privileged and the peasants. As capitalist economy developed and mercantilism gave place to liberal and monopolistic industrialism, new ideologies and new theories developed and these rendered this cohesive group heterogeneous. Marx, for the first time, changed the entire concept of this group when he called it "a privileged upper minority feeding on surplus value and state favouritism."[26] Molier in his famous work *La Bourgeoisie Gentil homme Uses* the word bourgeoisie as suggestive of niggardliness and stupidity, the old foils of the supposed generosity and refinement of feudal aristocracy.[27] In contrast to this the middle classes are a group possessing certain attitudes, distinct from the other classes between which they are placed.

In order to define social classes Max Weber speaks of social class structure, in between which an "inter-change of individuals on a personal basis or in the course of generations is readily possible and typically observable." It consists of a plurality of class statutes. On the one hand there is a negatively privileged class and on the other there is a positively privileged class. The latter comes into existence when a group of persons through economic activity and market succeeds in monopolising certain "positive privileges" in respect to property, while the former class comes into existence when a group of persons acquires certain "negative privileges" in respect to property, i.e. (most commonly) they themselves are the objects of ownership and are unfree and out-castes. In between the two extremes, maintains Weber,[28] stands another group known as the middle classes.

These middle classes include "Groups who have all sorts of property or marketable abilities through training, who are in a position to draw their support from these sources. Some of the groups belonging to the middle classes may be from amongst those forming acquisition classes. When the class-situation of the class-members is "primarily determined by their opportunity for the exploitation of services on the market", they constitute an acquisition class. Just as the social class structure, so also the scale of acquisition classes consists of a positively privileged class and negatively privileged class. The first category consists of merchants, industrial and agricultural entrepreneurs, bankers and financiers and the second category consists of workers—skilled, semi-skilled and unskilled.[29]

Thus according to Max Weber the middle classes "float over acquisition classes and social classes. If one sells his labour he belongs to the proletarian class, but if he . . . sells his ability in the form of labour commodity acquired through training, vocational or otherwise, he belongs to the middle class, no matter whether he belongs primarily to acquisition class or social class structure. In other words, they may be described as consisting of various occupational and economic groups which are associated with the development and marketable ability of the human beings received through training.

Weber lists the following occupational and other groups in the middle classes : (a) entrepreneurs, (b) executives and managers, (c) intelligentia, (d) men from liberal professions, (e) small businessmen, (f) skilled and semi-skilled workers. But these must be viewed in the light of (1) marketable ability, (2) income, and (3) status as determined by income and occupation. In contrast to this Christopher Hill suggests that "we should not think merely in economic terms."[30] Income was not and income is not, a complete guide to social status.[31]

The middle class is a social class resting between the aristocracy and the proletariat on the social scale.[32] According to the Encyclopaedia of Social Sciences, it constitutes: "the smaller industrial and commercial capitalists, the artisans, the small shopkeepers and tradesmen, the peasants and the petite bourgeoisie on general and bureaucratic officials and private employees working on salary."

According to S. Aaranovitch,[33] the concept of the middle class today is not what it was a hundred year ago. At that time the capitalist was the middle class and the aristocracy and nobility constituted the upper class. Today these two have become fused with the capitalist class to form the upper or ruling class. The middle class today is generally thought of as including small capitalist and traders, the workers on own account, the professional sections and the "white collared" worker.

The constituent elements of the old middle class may be counted as follows: the artisans, the small shopkeepers, the tradesmen, the peasants and the smaller industrial and commercial capitalists.[34]

However, we must emphasize that no objective criterion of ranking "necessarily coincides with social and civic prestige" which the various members of one rank enjoy. An examination of the images which the people of each level have of the people of other levels reveals one major fact: Small business (and white collar) people occupy the most ambiguous positions. It is as if the city's population were polarised into two groups, big business and labour, and every one else were thrown together into the nondescript middle class.[35]

Besides income and occupation, we must also take into consideration education. More University education changes the style of life of a member of the lower classes and pushes him up to the middle classes. Therefore we are lead to conclude that the term "middle classes" denotes a way of life based on occupation, income, education and social status which, in turn, is determined by the extent of social participation.[36]

One more significant fact to bear in mind is the position from which point of view we judge the members of middle class. In smaller cities and 'town-areas' the middle class people are "above" anyone else. In big cities and industrial towns like Jamshedpur or Calcutta they are the junior executives, the clerks and the petty traders. His position is explained in terms of the prestige ascribed to him by the lower groups but denied by the upper.[37] According to E.P.W. de costa,[33] "The middle classes are defined largely by a process of elimination. It is really a question of excuding agricultural labourers and the servant class." Pandit Jawaharlal Nehru speaking at the Council of Vocational Training at Delhi said: "I am, of course, a middle class person. I am not an industrial worker or a peasant."[39] Further they comprise groups of people which exclude the 'manual lábourers and ordinary hawkers and factory operatives' at the one end and the big propertied men forming the upper class at the other.[40]

It is amply demonstrated by the class theories discussed above that no two authors agree on the meaning, implication and dimensions of the term middle class. To some the term represents a distinctive section of population, to others it is merely an adjective designating those in the middle. Some speak of the middle classes as bourgeoisie, some as petite bourgeoisie. Some say that there is one single middle class while there are others who maintain that it is better to speak of the middle classes. And there are those also who deny that this group of persons can be given the name of class. It is clear that from the Marxian criterion of relationships with the means of production, this group exhibits different relationships for different individuals. "It is more accurate therefore to speak of the middle strata rather than of a middle class."

As newer and newer groups are coming into existence generated due to developments in economic systems—and are merging with the old middle class, it is now customary to speak of the middle classes as in the plural.[41]

The concept of the middle class, whatever it is, is imprecise. It is rather doubtful that the different groups constituting this class have common interests. The old middle class consists of small and independent property owners, small entrepreneurs in the field of industry and business and finance. The new middle class consists of technical-managerial, professional and clerical employees—the "typical class-product of large scale collective economic activity."[42] These groups who have sometimes interests opposed to one another render the middle class a heterogeneous class. "While, therefore, it is not possible to isolate a middle class which will satisfy the . . . definition of a social class, it is somewhat less difficult to isolate the middle classes from the remainder of the nation.[43]

At one extreme of the social scale, are the workers who earn wages, who are paid less for their utility occupations. They are manual workers and their payments are the only incentive for their work. Their occupations do not carry any prestige with them. At the other extreme is the "upper" class, the landed aristocracy, who have appropriate manners and their resources and amount of wealth gives them a sense of "aboveness". They are "high families".[44]

The remainder of the population would therefore comprise the middle classes. They are the professional men, businessmen, and managers, most farmers, the majority of "white collared" and "black jacketed" persons, most shopkeepers, clerks—except the very low diffusing into the lower classes—and some of the independent craftsmen. This is a rough and somewhat arbitrary list but it embraces a vast field though in it are included some of those who move properly belong to other classes. And that is because no single set of characteristics can be applied satisfactorily in order to identify the members of the middle class.[45]

Some distinction has also been made between bourgeoisie and the middle class. The bourgeoisie can be visualised as a "body of citizen ascertaining independence of a social system dominated by feudal power based on land-holding and the services attached to it. Marxian petite bourgeoisie is bound to be dragged down into the proletariat during the struggle of the two antagonistic classes— the grande bourgeoisie and the proletariat in between which it is placed. But the modern middle class, the equivalant of petite bourgeoisie on the social scale shows no signs of decline or diminution. Instead it is expanding and there is constant movement upwards on the social ladder.[46]

G.D.H. Cole points out another distinction between bourgeoisie and the middle classes, tracing their relationship with the institution of family when he says that the conception of class, historically speaking, is very closely connected with that of family status. "Where the family loses its clan character ... a middle class may still be held to exist "in the adjective sense ... " but a bourgeoisie in the sense historically attaching to the term, cannot."[47] Thus though the petite bourgeoisie and the modern middle class are similarly placed on the social scale, they differ fundamentally as far as their present social predilections are concerned and also as far as the trend of future events can be visualised.

Thus, the middle class is a composite intermediate layer, occupying the central position between the extremes of the capitalists and the workers,[48] consists of a wide range of occupational interests but bound together by a common style of living and behaviour pattern. Ideologically the new order stood for intellectual freedom and social mobility, liberal individualism and political democracy. A middle class, thus became identified with a stratified social order representing a new standard of values which its members or groups impressed upon the entire societies in which they lived.

3. British Impact and Social Change in India

The acquisition of Diwani of Bengal by the English East India Company in 1765 was an historic event. It marked the beginning of the British rule which, in course of time, came to cover all the Indian sub-continent. For the Indian masses it might have meant, as had been the case in the past,[49] just another change of political masters. Actually it turned out to be much more than that. The British shook the old Indian society to its very foundation[50] and introduced into it elements of Western society which, as time passed, became an increasingly important part of the Indian society itself. British rule thus proved to be the catalytic agent for the transition of India from tradition to modernity.[51]

The political conquest turned India into a colony of

England with all economic implications that such a relationship carried with it. That British rule proved ruinous for Indian industry and trade and that Indian revenues helped to finance the industrialisation of England in the initial stages of the Industrial Revolution are widely known and well acknowledged factors of history.[52] That was the fulfilment of Britain's destructive role in India. Here, our concern is with the second, what Marx called the 'regenerating' role that Britain played in 'laying of the foundations of Western society'[53] in India. This was done not as a part of a deliberate plan but was the indirect result of the British administration and the related measures necessitated by the establishment of British imperial relations with India. All those influences which helped in the introduction of some of the features of Western social organisation in India and the transition of the country's traditional society may be grouped, for the purposes of study, under three headings : (i) Land settlement and property rights in land; (ii) Structural and institutional changes in Indian economy; (iii) Western education.

The new land system introduced by the British destroyed the structure of rural society. By introducing the concept of private property in land, by changing crop production for subsistence into production for the market, and by turning the former administrators-cum-contractors of state revenues into landlords, the British caused a revolution in the agrarian system.[54]

The period immediately following the Permanent Settlement, and indeed for three or four decades thereafter, was one during which the Zamindars were struggling for their existence against the Sale law. There was a large portion of agricultural lands in Bengal lying uncultivated[55] due to paucity of labour caused by the Famine of 1770. The competition for tenants was keen and very few Zamindars managed to meet the annual demand of the government with the result that more than half of the Estates in Bengal were sold for arrears of revenue; many of the large Zamindaris were dismembered; and most of the original Zamindars were reduced to poverty.[56] The Zamindaris thus came to be subdivided into *patnis*. *The patnidars*, finding themselves in a similar situation after sometime, further sold lots of their *patnis* to *dar patnidars*. Thus was started the process of subinfeudation which created a chain, in some cases, of as many as 150 intermediaries between the original landlord and the tenant.[57] Buchanan found in his travels in the first decade of the 19th century that new landholders belonging to the class of merchants, agents of government officials and Calcutta "*banias*" (the modern mercantile class) were rapidly displacing the old Zamindars on account of the rigours of the Sale law.[58]

The resumption of rent-free lands, in 1828, was another measure that ruined the old land holding classes of "Brahmins and Rajputs of Gaya, Sahabad and Saran, and the Mussalmans of Patna . . .[59]

The new land tenures necessitated changes in the system of administration of revenues and dispensation of civil justice. The process of change was started by Warren Hastings but it was left to Cornwallis to lay a durable foundation of the British system of civil administration in India. Apart from collection of revenues, the Zamindars during the Mughal rule had exercised a number of judicial and administrative functions. Civil disputes between villagers were resolved and decided be village panchayats which, though considerably weakened, had not been completely eclipsed in Bengal when the English came on the scene.[60] In the south their position was still very strong.

For the ryotwari areas of the south, the court of directors recommended the adoption of a judicial system which would preserve in large measure the indigenous system of judicial administration. This included "the authorization of village and district panchayats to hear and determine suits, the appointment of certain grades of Indian judges like munsiffs and sadar amins with power to settle suits of higher values under the control of district and city judges, the vesting of certain limited civil and criminal jurisdiction in the heads of villages called munsiffs and the union of magistracy with the office of the Collector exercising certain judicial powers also.[61] These reforms were adopted in Madras in 1816 and in Bombay in 1819. This, however, failed to prevent the break-up of the ancient social institutions and disintegration system of the agrarian system in these two presidencies.

During the period of the company's rule, India's trade and industry underwent changes that had far-reaching effects on her economy and the structure of her society. In the earlier part of its rule, the interest of the company centred on providing its "investments" or making purchases of Indian manufactures for export abroad. In every centre of production, weavers had their own guilds and a head weaver who dealt with the merchants on behalf of the guild.[62]

The first dent made in this form of organisation was the replacement of dadni merchants, through whom purchases had been made earlier, by the system of direct purchases by the company either through their own servants or through gomasthas appointed by it. Instead of making advances to dadni merchants, the company began to deal directly with the weavers, thus, dispersing with intermediaries of all types. The guild chiefs, who offered resistance to oppression of the weavers,[63] perpetrated by the company's servants and their gomasthas, were swept aside.[64] The company set up a number of collecting depots, called factories for procurement of goods from the producers and shipment abroad. Private European merchants, as also the company's servants who freely engaged in private trade, organised themselves into agency houses to perform those very functions that the "factories" performed for the company. Thus came a radical transformation of the form of commercial and industrial organisation in India.

Changes also occurred in the banking and financial organisation of the country. The well-organised indigenous banking system broke down under the impact of structural changes in India's trade and industry and banks modelled on European lines began to be established by the European agency houses as a part of their business. The Bank of Hindustan was the first European bank started in 1770 by the then well known agency house, Messrs Alexander and Co.[65] The Bengal Bank was the earliest of the European banks unconnected with any agency house and started specifically to do only banking business. The General Bank of India, started in June 1786, was "the first joint stock Bank in India with limited liability."[66]

The industrial ventures by the new class of Indian businessmen in Bengal and Bombay Presidencies were solitary instance and did not represent a trend. By and large, the interest of the new class remained commercial and landed and did not become industrial till the end of the company's rule. Destruction of native manufacture and the effects of the permanent settlement had combined to produce a sizeable body of landless labourers. Apparently the time seemed ripe for an industrial revolution in Bengal, under British management, financed by joint resources of the British and native capitalists which open avenues of employment to the middle class, divert capital from land to industry, and take off the increasing pressure of population on land.[67]

Among the influences responsible for the social revolution wrought in India by the rise of British power, Western education occupies the central position. It was the famous Minute of Macaulay in February 1835 that laid foundation of the official policy on English education in India in which William Bentick found a means of raising in this country a class of persons who would be "Indians in blood and colour, but English in tastes, in opinions, in morals and in intellect," or in short, Indians with modern Western mind.[68]

Some Indians learnt English through their commercial and business contacts with Englishmen. Some learnt it in private schools started and maintained by Englishmen. The deserters from company's army, chaplains, and English merchants taught many Indians.[69] But the largest contribution to the spread of English, before official patronage came to be extended to this task, came from the Christian missionary schools.[70] As Duff put it : "The English language...is the lever which, as the instrument of conveying the entire range of the knowledge, is destined to move all Hindustan."[71] The first to avail of the educational facilities thus afforded were the old upper class Hindus. In Bengal, the Brahmins and Kayasths formed the majority; in Bombay, the Brahmins, Kayasths and Parsis; and in Madras, the Brahmins alone.[72] The Muslim upper class remained, on the whole, aloof.[73]

To the new middle class, which itself was the product of the British rule, "English promised to be the talisman which could open new vistas of wealth and influence, of material gain, and, therefore, of advancement in social status and personal dignity.[74]

Thus we see that the inauguration of the social change was made by the new ruling class, the British rulers. It was the East India Company and its officers and servants that led the way. The initial push was given by the new land laws, the new system of judicial and revenue administration, the company's "investments" and commercial activities in the country before 1813, the private enterprise of the company's servants in trade, finance, and plentation industries, and the Western system of education. From the very beginning a section of the Indian population grew up in these presidency towns of Calcutta, Bombay, and Madras which themselves owed their commercial and later political importance to the British. This section which gradually assumed the character of a new social class was the first to be affected and influenced by the social change wrought by the new rulers. This social class was the Indian Middle Class, which, in relation to the rest of the Indian population at the time, occupied the elite positions in all spheres of social life and activities—economic, political, cultural and religious.

Several social groups and streams from social life contributed to the composition of this class. Socially and economically, all these groups constituted a single class though occupationally they constituted so many distinct groups or "classes". B.B. Misra prefers to eall each of these groups as a "class" by itself for tracing the history of the development of each one of the several occupational groups constituting the middle class. The phrase "Middle Classes" may be innocuous and its use may be justified, but if this is to be used as an analytical tool for the study of the forces that shaped the course of history, as is intended to be done here, all these occupational groups may be treated as constituting one single class. Thus it can be called middle class.

The origin of the new class in India bore some resemblance to the development of its European counterpart in the 16th and 17th centuries. The European class had its origin in the opportunities of trade thrown up by the discovery of the New World and the East by Columbus and Vosco-da-Gama respectively in the closing decade of the 15th century. The Indian middle class likewise was the product of the new opportunities of making money and amassing riches from working as agents of European traders in the latter half of the 17th and first half of the 18th century. The Indian Middle Class differed also from the middle class or the bourgeoisie of the West. Whereas the European middle class was independent, the new Indian middle class was dependent; whereas the former, on exhaustion of opportunities for investment and employment in the commercial field, turned to industrial enterprise, the latter, faced with a similar situation, turned to purchase of landed estates and thus failed to lead the development of capitalistic enterprise on any significant scale.

In the political field also, the development of the middle class in India was along different lines from that in the West. The national bourgeoisie in Europe first allied itself with the monarchs to destroy the power of the feudal lords. Later they set themselves up as the ruling class using democracy as a cloak for the class rule[75] and reducing monarchy to symbolic headship of the State as in Britain, or destroying it completely as happened in the present century in several countries of Europe.[76] In India on the other hand, since the new middle class owed its origin and prosperity to European commercial enterprise in this country, it helped in the first phase of its evolution in the establishment of British power and promotion of European Commerce and enterprise in India. It was only much after the Revolt that it assumed the role of competitor for political power[77] and came to constitute a serious challenge to the continuance of British political supremacy. The credit for spreading national consciousness among the masses of the people, organising the national liberation movement and ultimately emancipating the country from foreign rule must go to this class.

4. The Middle Class in Bihar—its Growth and Composition

From the very beginning, a section of the Indian population grew up in the three presidency towns of Calcutta, Bombay and Madras which themselves owed their commercial and political importance to the British East India Company. This section, which gradually assumed the character of a new social class, the middle class was the first to be affected and influenced by the social change, a tradition rather than a revolution,[78] wrought by the new rulers.

Calcutta was in fact the first among the presidency towns to be effectively influenced by Western ideas and institutions. These filtered downwards to provincial and district levels through the media of civil servants and commercial residents, who operated through the agency of the company's courts and factories.[79] To these must be added Christian missionaries, free merchants and European merchants and European planters, who likewise carried liberal traditions to the interior of the Bengal Presidency. Schools and colleges came later. These constituted the various nuclii[80] for the growth of modern middle class on the basis of money, economy and Western education. As the middle class started emerging under the British rule in such fields as trade and commerce, industry, land and education, a suitable study of this class warrants a study of its different social groups such as the commercial middle class, the industrial middle class, the landed middle class and the educated middle class.

5. The Commercial Middle Class

After the establishment of political supremacy on the fertile soil of Bengal and Bihar as a result of the mid-eighteenth century political upheavals, the English concentrated on Bihar for commerce and trade. It was due mainly to her economic importance. Bihar was a centre of trade for cotton cloth, silk goods, opium, sugar and, most important of all, for saltpetre,[81] which was used as principal ingredient in the manufacture of gunpowder.

In the early part of its rule, the interest of the Company centred on making purchases of Indian manufactures. This cotton-weaving industry and silk industry were organised on domestic basis. The weavers seldom did the marketing of their products themselves. This function was done by the merchants who very often gave advances to weavers for purchase of raw materials, etc. for the goods ordered for manufacture. Later on, the Company made purchases directly through its servants or gomosthas appointed by it.

It was mostly from Bihar that European trading companies exported saltpetre in large quantities. After several attempts from 1720, the English East India Company established a factory at Patna in 1657-58.[82] Saltpetre was a chief manufacture of Champaran district which contained saliferes earth.[83] Muzaffarpur was another important producer of sultpetre. During 1876-77 nearly 16,486 licences were issued for its manufacture.[84] Besides, saltpetre was produced in Sahabad and Bhagalpur. In the latter its trade was increasing steadily.[85] The great importance attached to saltpetre trade is apparent from the fact that boats carrying saltpetre from Patna to Calcutta were put in charge of the military.[86]

There emerged a commercial middle class as trade in saltpetre was also done through Indian agents, through whom the English gave advances for the manufactured goods.

Some of the principal industries connected with agriculture were those of indigo, opium, sugarcane and jute etc. Indigo industry was the leading industry in Bihar. Though indigo had been cultivated from ancient times, F. Grand, the Collector of Tirhut (1782-87) was the pioneer of modern indigo industry in Bihar. He started his own model farm and factory.[87] The example of Grand was followed by many others in Bihar. Consequently indigo factories were started in Muzaffarpur, Purnea, Darbhanga, Bhagalpur, and Saran districts. In Champaran, the first factory was established at Nilganj before the introduction of reformed methods by Grand.[88] The largest producer of indigo was Champaran. About 10,000 mounds of indigo was exported from Champaran. In 1872 the outturn of indigo was 8000 cwt. which soon arose to 11,982 cwt. in 1882-83.[89] After improving the quality of production the company left European planters in 1785 to carry on the trade and made advances to them to put them on their feet.[90] The application of European skill and capital raised the quality and quantity of its production to such an extent that Bengal and Bihar alone could supply the entire need of Europe.[91]

The large scale production of indigo created in rural areas a group of contractors or agents whose business was to distribute advances and make supply of plants. Thus emerged the commercial middle class or bourgoeisie in rural areas.

Another commercialised agricultural product was sugar. The cultivation of sugarcane was introduced into Champaran from Gorakhpur in the beginning of the 19th century.[92] Its cultivation received more attention after the decline of indigo industry towards the close of the 19th century. With the opening of the 20th century more attention began to be paid to the cultivation of sugarcane. Madhubani in Darbhanga and Nasriganj in Sahabad contained a large number of refineries and carried on a large trade in sugar. Several factories under European management were started in Champaran, Saran and Tirhut.[93]

With the growth of refineries and factories there emerged a commercial middle class of contractors, agents or employees of the English, whose responsibility was to supply sugarcane for sugar production.

Jute was another most important commercial crop in India. In Bihar also jute was grown in some districts. The districts where jute was grown were Bhagalpur, Champaran, Darbhanga, Muzaffarpur, the Santhal Parganas, and Purnea, where it was grown on a large scale. Eighty-six per cent of the total cultivation of jute was grown in this district. After 1867 its cultivation received an impetus from the great demand for gunny bags. The principal marts in Bihar were Kishanganj and Farbesganj in Purnea district.[94] The cultivation of jute led to the emergence of the commercial and trading middle class, who purchased it from village markets and carried to the larger bazars for being exported to Calcutta.[95]

India was by far the greatest producer of lac. In fact 50% of world's output of lac came from India and at least half of India's produce came from Chhotanagpur. The principal factories were in the districts of Ranchi and Manbhum. Two factories were at Bundu.[96] The class which in fact stood to gain from this industry was the commercial middle class of agents or contractors employed by the British.

The impact of the Industrial Revolution in Great Britain was soon felt on the mineral industries of Bihar. Coalmines were worked along the banks of Damodar river and other places.[97] Besides working in coal mines, iron manufacturing industry was widespread in Bihar. The working of the iron mines was a profitable business at Ramgarh from where iron was exported to other parts of Bengal.[98] Development of Mica mining in the second half of the 19th century and after, and of copper industry in the first of the present century encouraged the growth of the commercial middle class. Alongwith mineral industries there grew a commercial middle class of traders, smaller transporters, agents of commercial supply and stockists.

The increase in number of joint stock companies may be another yardstick to measure the progress of economic and commercial development. Of the early examples of joint stock business was the Union Insurance Company established in Calcutta in 1828, with Rustomji Cowasjee as one of the four members of its committee of management, and with its agency offices spread over the whole of Bengal, Bihar, Assam and the North-west Provinces.[99] Besides the district headquarters in the provinces, its branches included even small places like Revilganj and Allynganj in Siwan district of Bihar which were important from commercial point of view. The number of joint stock companies operated in Bengal, which included Bihar also, between 1902-03 were 407 in number.[100] The beginning of a large-scale commerce and import industry was tending towards managerial revolution. The emergence of joint stock companies had not only begun to separate the managerial and proprietary functions of business but introduced a pattern of commercial organisation which, on account of increasing specialisation, gave rise to a multiplicity of employment. It called for special education and training without which commerce could not grow into a recognised profession. The new commercial class was in fact taking the lead in English education, and the traditional gulf between learning and trade had thus gradually begun to narrow.[101]

The new middle class, which owed its birth as well as its prosperity to European commercial enterprise in Bihar, originally was purely commercial in character. It was the exigencies of trade of the Europeans who neither knew their languages nor customs and trade practices, that forced them to seek the mediation of such local people who could help them secure supplies of local merchandise from producers and sometimes financial accommodation from local bankers to finance their commercial activities. Thus there emerged a commercial class of agents, gomasthas, munims, brokers, paikars, dalals, money-lenders, banyas, shroffs, poddars or cashiers, who constituted the spring-board of a rising middle class in the latter part of the eighteenth century. Since the Europeans engaged the local people in the transaction of most of their business, the middle class commercial interest increased in Bihar with an increase in the number of European companies and firms after 1858. And tha commercial middle class elements, who began as the agents or intermediaries or "banyas" of the Englishmen, had accumulated fortunes to establish themselves as independent businessmen such as traders, merchants and also as landlords.

6. The Industrial Middle Class

The emergence of industrial middle class took place slowly. The poverty of the industrial workers and their social disabilities operated as serious handicap to the growth of an industrial society. Unlike the clothiers who heralded the Industrial Revolution in England, the Indian weavers had no marginal savings to subsist on. They were mere wage-earners receiving about two or three rupees a month, and a man with an income of 48 a year was deemed a middle class man even in 1830's.[102] Moreover, an industrial occupation was not a respectable one. Thus, both economic and social factors precluded the growth of an industrial middle class on European lines.[103] The middle class in India and also in Bihar operated as an agency of commercial supply, not of superintendence and direction.[104]

The manufacture of saltpetre, a major industry of Bihar, represented more or less similar personnel organization. The local element of industrial superintendence was ill-supplied. The same state of affairs obtained in the manufacture of opium in Bihar.[105] The application of European skill and capital raised the quality and quantity of indigo production. The large-scale production of indigo created in rural areas a clerical and supervisory group of persons called 'amlas' who constituted a class of persons who might be called rural industrial bourgeoisie.[106] Same set of clerical and supervisory group of middle class industrial interest emerged as a result of saltpetre and opium industry.

The abolition of the trade monopoly of the East India Company in 1833 and the end of its rule in 1858 saw the real beginning of the era of laissez-faire of free enterprise in commerce and industry. The end of the company's rule also saw a steep and steady rise in external trade, which created capital resources for industrialisation. The flow of British capital and skill contributed to the agricultural and manufacturing industries and also led to the introduction of the managing agency system, which provided a pattern of industrial organisation. The exigencies of large-scale production in economic or other fields caused the emergence of new functional groups as well as expansion of the existing ones. Together they added to the number of the industrial middle class.[107]

The main field for investment of private European capital was the plantation industry, particularly indigo, jute and sugar. Indigo industry remained in a flourishing condition till the second half of the 19th century.[108] In 1885 the success of the German experiment in manufacturing synthetic dyes ruined the Indian indigo market and there was almost a ninety per cent drop in the production of indigo in Champaran and Muzaffarpur.[109] But the outbreak of hostilities in 1914 practically closed the market of the world to German synthetic dyes and revived the foreign demand for Indian indigo. As a result factories in Bihar began the indigo cultivation a new.[110]

Sugar industry, which was flourishing in Bihar especially in Bettiah Sub-division[111] and in the districts of Sahabad and Tirhut,[112] received a setback after the commencement of the first World War. There was a decline of nearly 30% in the out-turn of sugar.[113] But after 1920, there was swing of the pendulum. By 1922, the sugar industry was fairly well established. Towards the close of the period under study there were nearly 30 sugar factories in Bihar.[114] Although jute was grown in Purnea in fairly large quantities, and in Tirhut to some extent, no thought was given to the establishment of jute mills.

in these areas.[115] So jute cultivation did not lead to the emergence of middle-class industrial interest.

The demand for saltpetre in Great Britain gave impetus to this industry and in the last quarter of the 18th century the company had saltpetre factories at Fatwah in the Patna district and at Chapra, Mow and Singhia in North Bihar.[116] Its production grew with the passage of time and in 1903-04 nearly 10,533 tons was produced in Saran. The World War brought an active demand for saltpetre and the government took special steps to encourage its manufacture.[117]

Besides these lac manufacture showed noticeable progress in Chhotanagpur and Santhal Parganas, particularly in Ranchi and Manbhum.[118] There were iron mines in Singhbhum, Manbhum and Palamau. Iron mining gave impetus to gun manufacture at Monghyr, Jhalda in the Manbhum district.[119] Coal-mining began in the district of Hazaribagh in the last quarter of the 19th century.[120] Coal-mining in the Jharia fields started in 1893.[121]

Unfortunately industrial development in Bihar, as in other parts of India, was due prominently to the capital and enterprise of Europeans. The ownership and management of the indigo and sugar factories, of saltpetre and lac industries, and of the mines, was almost in their hands. The unwillingness of the Indian capilalists to invest in industrial ventures was a stumbling-block in the path of real progress. The increas in industrial units increased the avenues and scope of industrial employment. Every industrial unit maintained a separate staff—supervisory, clerical and other subordinate staff. Thus middle-class industrial interest grew with the growth of industrial units. Want of proper technical knowledge and skill, and lack of sufficient state encouragement hampered the scope of industrial employment covering managerial and technical elements till the first decade of the present century.

During the decade following the formation of the

province in 1912, however, there was one welcome development, namely, that the Government came forward to encourage industrial development in a number of ways. At first the encouragement came in the shape of state assistance for technical education and research. In 1920 a Directorate of Industries was constituted, and the control of all technical and industrial institutions was transferred to the Director. There were by this time two state-managed technical institutions in the province, the Bihar Engineering School at Patna and the Ranchi Industrial School, besides a number of other state aided institutions. Within the next decade, the Engineering School at Patna became an Engineering College, and new institutions were opened, such as the school of mines at Dhanbad and the Technical Institutes at Jamshedpur and Jamalpur, followed shortly by the Tirhut Technical School at Muzaffarpur. Steps were taken also to assist private enterprises.[122] This gave fillip to the growth of industries in Bihar.

The Peninsular Tobacco Company at Monghyr, a big tannery at Motihari and several small tanneries in different places, the Rohtas and Dalmianagar cement works and the Silk Institute at Bhagalpur, may be mentioned as important development in the field of industry in Bihar.[123] Besides these, the Government Lac Research Institute at Namkum near Ranchi was opened in 1924.[124] In 1913 the Cape Copper Company opened a mine at Rakha.[125] Other firm doing excellent work was the Cardova Copper Company. Besides these, about fifty small industries were carried on by independent artisans on their own initiative. Government also offered assistance to the industry by starting the Bihar Cottage Industries at Gulzarbagh. Before long many private technical institutes were set up for the manufacture of various handloom fabrics.[126]

The most striking achievement was the establishment of the Tata Iron and Steel Company at Sakchi in the district of Singhbhum in 1907-08.[127] The E.I.R. Locomotive workshops were established early in the second decade at Jamalpur and by 1920 over 10,000 men were employed. The next considerable progress was made in the coal mining industry. As early as 1913, the Jharia coal-fields afforded employment to more than 71,000 persons.[128] Another industry, which recorded marked progress, was mica mining in the three districts of Bihar—Hazaribagh, Gaya and Monghyr.[129] Throughout the 19th century, mica mining industry of Bihar was chiefly in the hands of Indian miners and mahajans.[130] In the beginning of the present century there was a sharp competition in the mica industry of Bihar. Consequently, the number of small prospectors, who had been mostly Indians, gradually decreased. This was so mainly in the Hazaribagh district. Most of the mica mines passed into the hands of the Europeans.[131] The number of mines rose from 18 in 1901 to 168 in 1910.[132]

The establishment of institutions imparting technical knowledge and skill and the impetus it gave to industrial development increased the avenues and scope of industrial employment covering directional, managerial, technical, supervisory and clerical elements constituting the industrial middle class. Emergence and growth of small but independent industrial entrepreneurs also added to the number of the industrial middle class in Bihar.

7. The Landed Middle Class

The general effect of British rule was to weaken the landed superstructure which throve under the Mughal. This was done chiefly in two ways: first, by creating a strong political authority with a network of judicial and executive apparatus which left no room for a Zamindar to exercise any public responsibility or function; and secondly, by defining or recognising the right of under-tenures, which reduced his power to subject them to his observance. The second mode was directly responsible for the growth of the landed middle class, which was constituted out of agrarian landlords, small zamindars and peasant proprietors.

The farming out of the revenue collection by auction to the highest bidders under Warren Hastings was an opportunity for banyas or commercial brokers to develop a middle class landed interest which their English masters also shared with them.[133] The system of farming seriously injured the prestige of the old aristocracy in Bihar and affected dislocation in the ownership of landed property in favour of the rising commercial middle class.

Besides this, the recognition of the rights of Taluqdars, an order of landed interest inferior to a Zamindar or Jagirdar in Bihar,[134] of smaller zamindars and holders of under-tenures called Mukarraridars in Bihar[135] by a settlement of revenues direct with them also threatened the existence of the old aristocracy.

But more serious was the famine of 1770. In the words of G.G. Ducarel, the Supervisor of Purnea in 1771, the ravages of famine caused 'the greatest mortality of the inhabitants, which continued almost twelve months in a degree of severity hardly to be paralleled in the history of any age or country'.[136] More lands then were available than were tillers to cultivate. In a revenue consultation of 5 November, 1776, Philip Francis stated "In the present state of the country, the Ryot has in fact the advantage over the Zamindar where so much land lies waste, and so few hands are left for cultivation, the peasant must be courted to undertake it."[137]

The scarcity of tillers reduced a number of old zamindars to a state of impoverishment. They fell into arrears and had to loose the direct management of their zamindars. In these circumstances the non-resident ryots, who had previously formed an insignificant and degraded order, became the most prominent feature in the rural system of the Bengal Province for thirty years.

A gradual decline in the land revenue figures brought the system of farming by auction to a dismal end. Hastings' failure to restore the collections to the farmer level then brought him discredit. The hostility of zamindars of Bihar which followed the Chait Singh's affair at Benaras in 1781 (and the Company's wars with the Marathas and Mysore) dictated the expediency of a fixed and equitable land policy which Cornwallis was called upon to execute in 1786. The approval of the Court of Directors reached Cornwallis in 1793 when what was known as the Permanent Settlement was affected, on the basis of a net revenue amounting to Rs. 28,800,909.[138] The Zamindars and other proprietors were deemed to have heritable and transferable property rights subject to the payment of a fixed annual sum to the Government.

Cornwallis's policy was simply to have the land revenue settled, with the zamindars or with other proprietors. But he emphasised that landed property should come into the hands of the most frugal and thirfty class of people who might improve their lands, protect their cultivators, and promote the general prosperity of the country.[139]

It is thus clear that Cornwallis had in view the interests of a new class of zamindars consisting of the company's regular revenue farmers, its banyas as well as inferior zamindars and Taluqdars who formed a rival group different in habits and characters from the zamindars descending from old families. It is against the background of his regard for the interest of the new landed middle class that some of Cornwallis's other measures which weakened the old aristocracy, can better be explained. Although generally supposed to have been partial to big land-holders, he recognised taluqdars and mukarraridars as separate from and independent of, their overlords. The abolition of the custom introduced under the native government by which most of the principal Zamindaris in the country were made to descend entirely to the eldest, or next heir of the last incumbent, also led to the disintegration of estates[140] through partition among heirs. The abolition of the zamindars' police authority in 1792, and the removal of all kinds of duties previously levied by him on the internal movement of trade, tended further to reduce his influence and resources.

Thus the statutory recognition of zamindaris as property transferable without the permission of Government and a simultaneous provision for the partition of estates among heirs led to a great multiplication of the number of estates among heirs with a corresponding reduction in the average size of each. The number of landholders, which did not exceed 100 in the beginning of Hastings' administration in 1772, rose in the course of a century to 154,200. In 38 districts of Bengal proper and Bihar, out of total number of 154,200 estates 533 or .34 per cent, only were great properties with an area of 20,000 acres and upwards, 15,747, or 10.21 per cent, ranged from 500 to 2000 acres in area; while the number of estates of less than 500 acres was no less than 137,920, or 89.44 per cent, of the whole.[141]

In Bihar a number of petty estates sprang from the settlement of such rent-free lands as were resumed under Regulations II and III of 1819 and 1828. The number of resumptions in Bihar was much greater than in Bengal, for whereas the total revenue of Bihar rose from Rs. 53,09,181 in 1790-01 to Rs. 97,04091 (exclusive of Purnea) in 1871-02, the increase in revenue in Bengal proper since the decennial settlement was Rs. 25,80,179 only.[142]

To secure a timely collection of the revenue, the British enacted what is known as 'the sunset law' which required landholders to pay their revenue by a specified date and time. Within twenty years of the Permanent Settlement more than one-third of the landed property of Bengal was sold for arrears of rent. And the new moneyed class especially banyas and brokers, agents and creditors found in land a source of investment and social prestige.

Thus there was the growth of sub-infeudation comprising a number of intermediate proprietary layers of under-tenure holders known as mukarrari tenure in Bihar. The middle-class landed interest thus grew both from the disintegration and partition of old estates as well as from the increase of under-tenure holders.

On the termination of the Company's rule in 1858, however, emphasis on the creation of a landed midde class was renewed. The Crown could not undo the work of the company. Sir Charles Wood, the Secretary of State, desired the growth of a landed middle class, but 'without dispossessing the peasant proprietors and occupiers'.[143] He clearly pointed out that in spite of their comparative poverty many of the peasant proprietors and resident cultivators possessed 'great intelligence, public spirit, and social influence',[144] which they could best use in the improvement of their condition if the public demand on their land were limited. The post-mutiny concept of a landed middle class was thus richer in its economic content and broader in social basis. The concept of the middle class connected with land was no exclusive. It included the intelligent, public spirited and enterprising section of all such classes as engaged in agriculture.

8. The Educated Middle Class

The establishment of the new administrative system and the spread of Western education generated the growth of new social class in Bihar as elsewhere in India. The educated middle class signifies a group of persons who received English education and engaged in various professions. This class comprised of lawyers, barristers, doctors, teachers, writers, newspaper editors, public servants, clerks, assistants and university students. The role of new education introduced by the English in bringing about social changes in the nineteenth century cannot be denied. But in Bihar the case was quite different. Here the Biharis were not so enthusiastic as the Bengalis to learn English.[145] English education in Bihar was in fact misconstrued as an attempt on the part of Government to proselytise the people. A rumour was spread that those who took to English education would be deported to Mauritius and other British colonies for employment there.[146]

Contrary to the general belief that efforts for spreading English education was made in Bihar after the historic Resolution of Bentinck of 7 March 1835, there are references to prior existence of some schools where instruction was given in English language and also of some individuals making private arrangements for tuition of their wards in English. Adam has referred to the establishment of an English school for Ramgarh Kols. From a different source it is known that about the year 1831 two British officers of Ramgarh district, Cuthbert and Neave, had made strenuous efforts for the establishment of a "College" for the Kols there which had a very short life.[147] The other institution which had made provision for English education was the school at Gaya maintained by Maharaja Mitrajit Singh of Tikari.[148] Similarly, the fact that the reports on the progress of students of Patna, Chapra and Arrah schools make mention of certain boys having some knowledge of English before joining the school clearly proves that they had acquired it from private tuitions.[149]

Institutions for English education began to spring up at different places. According to Adam, one school for English education had already been started at Purnea early in 1835. An English School at Patna came into existence on 10 August 1835 after a meeting of European and local gentlemen.[150] The Arrah school was opened on 24 April 1837 and a school at Chapra was established in early 1839. But both schools failed to attract children of the upper classes of the people and consequently were closed.[151] The Bhagalpur school was established in the latter half of the year 1837. In 1844 the Patna school was upgraded into a central college. But it was not a college in the modern sense of the term. The main idea was to centralise the education of Bihar with a view to providing efficient instruction by attracting meritorious students from all over the province by means of scholarships.[152] Two private Anglo-Vernacular schools came into existence. One of the two had been established in December, 1861 at Darbhanga and the other was established at Barh. There were eight Zila schools in 1862 with 1135 students.[153] In 1863, Zila schools were sanctioned for Deoghar, Motihari, Hazaribagh and Chaibasa. In Bihar two educational circles were started, one in Bihar and the other at Bhagalpur.[154]

The effect of the introduction of English in the Chief Appellate Court and the opening of the rail to the chief city in Bihar made Bihar as ready as any other province to take English education upto the demand for public appointments. It had been proved by the rise in the number of pupils during the year from 1085 in April, 1862 to 1396 in 1863.[155]

Yet the number of Bihari students in the Zila schools of Bihar remained less than Bengali students for many years. Considerable difficulties were experienced by different administrators posted in districts and sub-divisions in the educational administration. Difficulties were experienced even in the extension of primary education owing to the prejudices of the people, people did not view with favour the new education but passively resisted as much as possible.[156] The Patwari class opposed the new system because many feared that an extended system of education would affect their particular business. The Zamindar class also failed to give assistance to the educational development.[157]

But the seventies of the 19th century witnessed a greater consciousness on the part of the people towards education particularly in the field of secondary education. By 1880 there were five government High Schools where the number of students was above 400. The Director of public instruction thus observed in his annual report, "The last two or three years have witnessed a surprising development of the demand for English education in Bihar, quite unprecedented in that province and unparalleled in any other part of Bengal. The movement is as yet most conspicuous in the headquarters stations, and not as heretofore half of them Bengalis. But the same desire has begun to manifest itself in the interior of districts among the Rajputs and Babhans."[158]

Thus gradually, there came about a change in the attitude of the higher classes in society towards education. By the end of the nineteenth century the Government Zila schools were filled with Bihari students.[159] To keep pace wit the increasing enthusiasm of the people secondary education after the creation of the province was expanded. The first quinquennial report (1912-17) shows that there were 100 High schools with 34,734 pupils and 226 M.E. schools with 23,415. The High Schools specially suffered most owing to political upheavals of the later years. In 1930 there were instances of picketing and concerted absence from English schools on various special occasions. Yet the number of secondary schools went on increasing. By 1936-37 the number of High schools rose to 196 with 57,043 students and M.E. schools to 637 having 83,009 students on the roll.[160]

In 1859 there was no college in Bihar nor there was any political organisation. An educated middle class which had sprung up elsewhere with the growth of English education, was yet unborn in Bihar.[161] As early as in 1861, W.S. Atkinson, the Director of Public Instruction of Bengal traced the educational backwardness of Bihar for want of proper employment opportunities here.[162]

Atkinson's endeavour led to the foundation in 1863 of the Patna college which was raised to the degree standard in 1865-66 and which eventually turned out to be the nerve centre for the spread of English education in Bihar. New Bihar had been to a very large extent the creation of its accomplished alumni.[163] In the beginning the Biharis were more averse to higher collegiate education. Out of five that passed the B.A. Examination in 1876-77 only two were sons of Bihar. The principal observed: "The Biharis hold back partly from caste prejudices and scruples about eating."[164] But the history of the Patna college in the last quarter of the nineteenth century shows a gradual change in their attitude. The figures for this period reveal a gradual increase in the number of Bihari students. In 1899 there were 85 Bengalis as compared to 150 Biharis in the Patna college.[165]

The question of employment for Biharis in Bihar was considered by the Government of Bengal at the instance of the Commissioner of Patna Division, R.P. Jankins, who had recommended "that a certain number of opportunities in the subordinate judicial and executive services be annually reserved for natives of Bihar."[166] On the ground of political expediency the Government ordered that at least a certain portion of probationary appointments to ministerial posts should in each district of Patna Division be given to persons who had received education in Bihar.[167]

As regards the subordinate executive service the Government promised favourable consideration and in their case the standard qualification in English was relaxed. The High Court of Calcutta which controlled the appointments of Munsiffs and subordinate judges was at the same time requested to consider favourably the Government's proposal: "to reserve a certain number of appointments in the subordinate Judicial and Executive Services for natives of Bihar."[168]

As such an order was issued on 28 December, 1880 directing that the orders of 3 October, 1871, regarding the employment of Biharis in Bihar should be strictly observed in all Government and Semi-Government offices in Bihar including those of the Commissioners, District Offices, Court and Police, where they were supposed to be already in force.[169]

While employment opportunities were still very limited for Biharis by the last decade of the nineteenth century, English education had produced a band of spirited and ambitious youngmen who were not to be satisfied with reservations of a handful of clerkships here and there. They had their eyes fixed on higher appointments under Government, such as respectable share in the provincial Executive and Judicial Services for the people of their province. These youngmen were mostly from the Kayastha and Muhammedan classes, which had long supplied men for Government service and learned professions.[170] They converted the old agitation for employment of Bihari in Bihar into a movement for separation of Bihar from Bengal.

It were the politically and culturally motivated elites

who reinforced the process of qualitative social change already proceeding from an interaction between Indian society and British administration. The motivation of these elites, who were moving up to replace the aristocracy, was both power and ideology. While the former was reflected in their demand for representative government, the latter found expression in the movement for religious and social reform.

Socio-religious reformation movement had been directly or indirectly, the motive force in bringing about a social awakening and even political consciousness among the masses. Of all the religious movements of the nineteenth century the Brahmo Samaj was the most influential. The appeal of the Samaj was limited to the intellectual classes. At Patna the Brahmo Samaj was founded by Sri Prakash Chandra Roy and his wife Aghore Kamini. Aghore Kamini worked among the women of Patna bringing a new outlook among them.[171] The Brahmo Samaj at Patna was the pioneer of female education in Bihar. It was through the initiative and exertion of the Brahmo Samaj that Bankipore Girls' High School was established. As Bihar had been backward in female education the opening of a High school for girls in Bihar was a significant event pregnant with weighty consequences.[172] Besides this the Sadharan Samaj sect of Brahmos established Ram Mohan Seminary, a secondary school for boys at Patna, which became a source of positive moral influence amongst the rising generation of Bihar. The Brahmo Samaj at Giridih was doing the most useful work; it ran a girls' boarding school. Another school for girls established was a mission school at Ranchi.[173] The Brahmo Samaj movement, however, had never taken deep root in this province. But in the realm of ideas the contribution of the Samaj was much more important than the number of Brahmos.[174]

The second most important was the Arya Samaj of Swami Dayanand Saraswati. Its impact on life of the Hindus in Bihar was felt from the very beginning.[175] Its influence was comprehensive steadily reaching every aspect of social and individual life.[176] Baidnath Prasad as head of the Arya Samaj was mainly associated with the educational activities. He was instrumental in the establishment of several Arya Samaj schools and orphanages in the province. In Dinapur a school named Ved Ratna Vidyalaya was established in 1915. The most important educational institution of the Samaj in Bihar was "Gurukula Mahavidyalaya at Deoghar established by the efforts of Lakshmipati besides other Gurukulas and orphanages.[177] In Bihar it had a strong appeal for low castes such as Kurmis, Gowalas and Mushars. Many important leaders in different walks of life in Bihar in spite of their low caste owed their elevation to Arya Samaj. They got their education through Arya Samaj and raised their status through it.[178]

The first attempt to organise all sections of educated class was initiated by the Theosophical Society.[179] The Bihar Theosophical Federation was established in 1900. Its tenth annual session, held at Chapra in August 1910, collected a good number of educated men. Purnendu Narayan Sinha, a great promoter of education in Bihar presided.[180]

Ram Krishna Mission, one of the main currents of social reform movement, was inspired by the tradition of mysticism and devotion and by Western philanthropy and social welfare work.[181] In Bihar there are seven centres—at Patna, Jamshedpur, Ranchi, Jamtara, Deoghar, Dungri and Katihar. Chronologically the first centre to be started in Bihar was at Jamshedpur. Its chief activity was educational. It managed five high schools, four middle schools, three upper primary and two lower primary schools. In these institutions emphasis is laid on the cultivation of moral virtue, regard for higher values of life, development of a Catholic outlook and growth of the spirit of self-help. The Ram Krishna Mission Centre at Patna came into existence in June, 1922 in a rented house on the Govinda Mitra Road. The nucleus of the students' house was formed here in 1927, twelve college students being accommodated in the Ashram.[182]

Thus the Brahmo Samaj, the Arya Samaj, the Theosophical Society and the Ram Krishna Mission played a remarkable role in spreading education, the ideas of nationalism and enlightenment of modern Bihar.

Several caste organisations were organised with the object of spreading education, introducing social reform and advancing the material prosperity of their members. Of all the Hindus the Kayasthas had shown a greater sense of adaptability. Peary Lal of Sahabad set up an organisation, called the Sadar Anjuman-i-hind, for the propagation of his ideals. A branch of the Anjuman was established at Arrah in 1866 with the support of a brilliant Kayastha lawyer, Harbans Sahay of the same place.[183] The Kayastha Conference which was established in 1887 held its third Conference at Bankipore on 5 and 6 November, 1889.[184] Within decade local sabhas were set up in most of the towns. Bihar had also a provincial sabha at Bankipore. A Kayastha Pathshala was established there and steps were taken to set up a large Boarding House with 100 rooms. A Kayastha Trading Company was established at Arrah and a Kayastha Messenger Co. at Gaya with a view to encouraging the community to undertake commercial and other professions. A national fund for helping the poor and meritorious students was started. The Muslim community was also organised by the efforts of Syed Ahmad and other Muslims. Syed Ahmad, in his efforts to dispel the prejudices of his community towards English education, had established a Scientific Society at Muzaffarpur due largely to the efforts of Syed Imdal Ali, a subordinate judge of the district.[185] These attempts of the Muslims and the Kayasthas inspired others to organise themselves on caste lines. Thus a number of caste Sabhas came into existence in quick succession. In 1889 the Pradhan Bhumihar Brahman Sabha was formed at Patna "to improve moral, social and cducational reforms of the community and to represent the wants of the community to the government."[186] The Sabha set up Boarding Houses at Muzaffarpur, Banaras, Tikari and other places. It was followed by the establishment of The Sarjupuri Brahman

Sabha (1905), The Rajput Sabha (1906), The Revani Kahar Sabha (1906), The Marwari Youngmen's Association (1907), The Khatri Youngmen's Association (1907), The Dusadh Sabha (1911), The Gope Jotiya Mahasabha (1912), The Keot Sabha (1912), The Kurmi Sabha (1912) and others. The contemporary government records show that Knyvett, the Superintendent of Police, Patna, was instrumental for the caste movement among Dusadh and Gowalas.[187] Thus there existed several caste Sabhas in Bihar which had for their object the encouragement of learning and material prosperity. Addresses were delivered at their meetings on education and other subjects.[188]

The rise of the educated middle class synchronised with the phenomenal upsurge of the press, both English and Vernacular, which helped to accelerate the pace of social reform and national consciousness.[189] Many Vernacular journals in Hindi and Urdu were started. A periodical in Hindi, *The Behar Bandhu,* came out first in 1874. The two brothers, Bisheshwar Singh and Saligram Singh, founders of the B.N. College started the first Bihar organ in English under the name of *The Indian Chronicle.* The publication of *The Bihar Times* was started in 1894 under the editorship of Mahesh Narayan.[190] In April 1906, the journal was reconstituted and its name was changed to *The Beharee.* Another organ was *The Behar Herald* started by Guru Prasad Sen in 1893.

In the last decade of the nineteenth century big Zamindars of the province came forward to champion and promote higher education. The Tej Narayan Jubilee College was established by Tej Narayan Singh of Bhagalpur with the cooperation of the Banaili Raj, while the B.N. College was founded by Bisheshwar Singh, the Zamindar of Kulharia. Tej Narayan Jubilee College was made a first grade college in 1890 and the B.N. College in 1892. In 1897 was established the D.J. College, Monghyr. In 1899 was established the G.B.B. College at Muzaffarpur by a liberal donation of public spirited Zamindar Langat Singh. In the same year was founded the St. Columbas' College at Hazaribagh. Thus at the close of the nineteenth century there was one government and five unaided Colleges in Bihar, with a total number of 776 on the roll.[191]

Several enlightened Zamindars of Bihar had helped higher education in Bihar towards the end of the nineteenth century. Many of them responded enthusiastically to the proposal of Lt. Governor Andrew Frazer in 1904 to open a college at Ranchi. A subscription of Rs. 312897 was deposited by the leading Zamindars of Bihar.[192]

To facilitate higher education connected institutions were separated from the parent institution, the Patna College. The Government Law College was started in July 1909. The Bihar College of Engineering became separate institution in 1909 and it was raised to the status of a college in July 1924.[193]

These attempts led to the emergence of a group of educated persons, who was eager to adopt modern way of life. This educated Bihari middle class became the most vocal element in the society. A look at its composition explains its motivations. It was wholly upper caste, and predominantly upper class. The scions of the landed aristocracy or the Kayastha community contributed to its numbers.

Even so, the creation of Bihar and subsequent inauguration of a separate University for Bihar and Orissa gave an impetus to higher education. All colleges except the Diamond Jubilee College made a steady progress. This college still remained weak. Its working was not satisfactory in the years 1917-18. A new block at St. Columbas' College was opened by the Lt. Governor in November 1917.[194] After the establishment of the University in the province the number of students went on increasing. But till 1937 only two more new colleges came into existence. The Nalanda College was established at Biharsharif in July 1920 as a result of an endowment made by Rai Bahadur Edal Singh. In 1926 Intermediate classes were opened in Ranchi Zila school. By 1937 the total number of students in the colleges of Bihar rose to 3620.[195]

Post-graduate classes in various arts subjects were started at Patna college in July 1919 and those in Physics and Chemistry in 1921. The Science College was established as a separate institution for higher scientific teaching in 1927.[196] By 1938-39 two new colleges, namely the Chandradhari Mithila College at Darbhanga and the Rajendra College at Chapra were established. Two arts colleges for females also came into existence in 1941. In 1946 the number of colleges for males was 18 with 10,096 students on the roll. The number of students in the two women's colleges in the same year was 240.[197]

Thus the spread of education brought a stimulating process of social change and a group of educated middle class emerged, who came to assert Bihar's interest. Demands for higher appointments and Government's liberal attitude towards the demands increased the scope for appointment in provincial civil service, a middle class organisation.[198] The creation of Bihar and subsequent establishment of a separate University and a separate High Court increased avenues of government services and learned professions which swelled the educated middle class, the vanguard of social and political movements in Bihar.

Members of the new middle class moved into the social space which the aristocracy was being obliged gradually to vacate. This class started emerging under British rule in such fields as trade and commerce, land, industry, education and the learned professions. This growth proceeded in the main from a change in the political system and its institutional arrangement based on the supremacy of law and legislative authority. Spread of Western education also brought a process of social change.

In terms of caste the new middle class was multicaste in Bihar. Every community such as the Bania, the Babhan, the Brahmin, the Rajput, the Kayastha, the Muhammedan, etc. contributed to the bulk of the middle class in Bihar. But there was domination of specific caste on specific group of the middle class. The Vaishya or Bania community dominated the commercial middle class and the industrial middle class. The Rajputs and the Babhans formed the main body of the landed middle class, while the English educated middle class was dominated entirely by the Kayastha community and the higher strata of the Muhammedan community or by the immigrant Bengalis.

Notes

1. Bhatia, B.M., *History and Social Development*, Vol. I, p. 122.
2. Chhibbar, Y.P., *From Caste to Class*, p. 3.
3. *Ibid.*, pp. 9-10.
4. Max Weber, *Economic and Social Organisation*, p. 380.
5. Joseph Schumpter, *Class, Status and Power*, p. 76.
6. *Ibid.*, p. 77.
7. Max Weber, *Op. cit.*, p. 393.
8. Warner and Lunt, *Social Life of a Modern Community*, p. 82.
9. MacIver and Page, *Society*, p. 348.
10. Ogburn and Nimkoff, *A Handbook of Sociology*, p. 210.
11. Haebel, E.A., *Man in the Primitive World*, p. 715.
12. If a person "regularly engages" in any activity with a view to achieving a "Standardized utilitarian award", we may describe that activity an occupation. (Hiller, E.T., *Social Relations and Structure*, p. 479).
13. *Ibid.*, pp. 479-480.
14. Fairchild, H.P., *Dictionary of Sociology*.
15. Lewis and Maude, *The English Middle Classes*, p. 13.
16. Misra, B.B., *The Indian Middle Classes: Their Growth in Modern Times*, p. 3.
17. *Ibid.*, p. 4.
18. *Ibid.*
19. Page, C.H., *Class, Status and Power*, pp. 47-48.
20. Davies, K.G., Review Article—'The Mess of the Middle Classes', *Past and Present*, July 1962.

21. Cole, G.D.H., *Studies in Class Structure*, p. 12.
22. Kornnauser, R., *Approach to Social Stratification*, p. 226.
23. *Ibid.*, p. 230.
24. *Encyclopaedia of Social Science*, Vols. IX-X, p. 1407.
25. The Word Bourgeoisie according to *Chambers' 20th Century Dictionary*, 1952, means Middle Class Citizen.
26. *Encyclopaedia of Social Sciences*, Vols. IX-X, p. 1407.
27. *Ibid.*, Vols. I-II, p. 654.
28. Max Weber, *op. cit.*, p. 390.
29. *Ibid.*, pp. 390-91.
30. *Puritanism and Revolution* (London, 1958), p. 30.
31. Davies, K.G., Review Article—'The Mess of the Middle Class', *Past and Present*, July 1962, pp. 77-78.
32. Fairchild, H.P., *A Dictionary of Sociology*.
33. Aarnovitch, S., Monopoly : *A Study in British Monopoly Capitalism*, p. 18.
34. If the peasant pursues his vocation independently, he possesses marketable capacity and belongs, according to Max Weber, to this assembly of heterogeneous group (Max Weber, *Social and Economic Organisation*, p. 390).
35. Mills, C.W., *White Collar*, p. 47.
36. Chhibbar, Y.P., *Op. cit.*, p. 52.
37. *Ibid.*, p. 53.
38. Quoted in *Caste and Class* by Y.P. Chhibbar, p. 53.
39. *The Tribune* (Ambala Cantt.) dated August 2, 1957, p. 1.
40. Singh, Baljit, *Urban Middle Class Climbers*, p. 3.
41. Chhibbar, Y.P., *Op. cit.*, p. 18.
42. Lewis Corey, *Class, Status and Power*, p. 375.
43. Lewis and Maude, *The English Middle Class*, p. 15.
44. Chhibbar, Y.P., *Op. cit.*, p. 19.
45. *Ibid.*
46. *Ibid.*, p. 17.
47. Cole, G.D.H., *Op. cit.*, p. 100.
48. Ghurye, G.S., *Caste and Class in India*, p. 276.
49. James Mill, *History in India*, Vol. III, p. 365.
50. Marx-Engels, *Collected Works*, Moscow, 1950, p. 313.
51. Rudolph and Rudolph, *The Modernity of Tradition*, pp. 3-4.

52. Tara Chand, *History of Freedom Movement*, Vol. I, Chapter X; Fredrick John Shore, *Notes on Indian Affairs*, 1837, Vol. I, for the ruination of Indian's nobility and other elites as a result of East India Company's rule.
53. Marx, Karl, *A Contribution to the Critique of Political Economy*, Moscow, 1970, p. 320.
54. *Calcutta Review*, 1863, 'Land System in India', p. 124.
55. *Floud Commission*, 1943, Report, Para 50.
56. *Ibid.*, See also W.W. Hunter, *Introduction to Bengal Ms Records*.
57. *Friend of India*, 17 January 1839, p. 34.
58. Quoted in *History and Social Development*, Vol.I, by B.M. Bhatia, p. 88.
59. Letter by 'Legion' to the Editor, *Friend of India*, 7 May 1846, p. 297.
60. Henry Maine, *The Early History of Institutions*. Also Holwell, *India Tracts*, pp. 203-204.
61. Misra, B.B., *The Central Administration of East India Company*, 1773-1833, pp. 269-270.
62. Martin, *Eastern India*, Vol. II, p. 282; Buchanan, *A Journey From Madras*, Vol. I, p. 212 and Baines, *Cotton Manufactures of India*, p. 56.
63. William Bolts, *Consideration on Affairs of East India Company*, pp. 192-194.
64. *Bengal Board of Trade* (*Commercial*) *Consultations*, 29 June 1784, 4 July 1794, and 11 Nov. 1800.
65. Sinha, H., *Early European Banking in India*, 1927, p. 4.
66. *Ibid.*, p. 9.
67. Tripathi, Amlesh, *Trade and Finance in the Bengal Presidency* (*1793-1833*), p. 266.
68. Trevelyan, C.E., *On the Education of Peoples of India*, London, 1838, p. 9.
69. Tara Chand, *History of Freedom Movement in India*, Vol. II, p. 184.
70. *Ibid.*, p. 182.
71. *Speech of Alexander Duff at the general assembly* (*Christian Mission*), 25 May 1835, Quoted in P. Sen, *Western Influence in Bengal Literature*, Calcutta, 1932, p. 75.
72. Tara Chand, *Op. cit.*, Vol. II, p. 209.
73. *Parliamentary Paper 48* (*20*) *of 1847-48*: *House of Commons Return on Education in British India*.

74. Tara Chand, *Op. cit.*, Vol. II, p. 180.
75. Stanley, W. Moore, *The Critique of Capitalist Democracy*, New York, 1957, p. 88.
76. *Revolution and Counter Revolution being a collectinn of Karl Marx's articles*, New York, Tributung, 1851-52.
77. Misra, B.B., *Bureaucracy in India*, p. 315.
78. Bhatia, B.M., *Op. cit.*, Vol. I, p. 122.
79. Misra, B.B., *Op. cit.*, p. 75.
80. *Ibid.*
81. Diwakar, R.R. (ed.), *Bihar Through the Ages*, p. 578.
82. *Ibid.*
83. *Imperial Gazetteer of India*, 1855, Vol. III, p. 343.
84. *Ibid.*, 1886, Vol. X, p. 81.
85. *Ibid.*, 1885, Vol. II, p. 350.
86. *Ibid.*, 1902, Vol. XXII, p. 89.
87. Roychoudhary, P.C., *Inside Bihar*, p. 112.
88. Houlton, Sir J., *Bihar—The Heart of India*, p. 116.
89. *The Imperial Gazetteer of India*, 1885, Vol. III, p. 341.
90. *Mins. of Ev. II, Sel. Com. HC, 1831-2* (735-11), p. 93.
91. *Sketch of Commercial Resources and a Monetary and Mercantile System of British India (1837)*, p. 35.
92. *Imperial Gazetteer of India*, 1885, Vol. III, p. 342.
93. *Report on The Administration of Bihar and Orissa*, 1911-12, p. 13.
94. O'Malley, *Bengal District Gazetteer (Purnea)*, 1911, p. 89.
95. *Imperial Gazetteer of India*, 1885, Vol. XI, p. 328.
96. *Ibid.*, 1886, Vol. VII, pp. 484-5.
97. Datta, K.K. (ed.), *The Comprehensive History of Bihar*, Vol. III, Part I, pp. 506-7.
98. *Ibid.*, p. 508.
99. *Bengal Directory*, 1835, Commercial.
100. *Moral and Material Progress Rep.*, 1902, p. 47.
101. Misra, B.B., *Op. cit.*, p. 106.
102. *Sketch of Commercial Resources*, p. 28.
103. Misra, B.B., *Op. cit.*, p. 109.
104. *Ibid.*, p. 112.
105. *Ibid.*
106. *Ibid.*, p. 87.
107. *Ibid.*, p. 214.

108. Houlton, Sir J., *Op. cit.*, p. 116.
109. Diwakar, R.R., *Op. cit* , p. 775.
110. *Ibid.*, p. 779.
111. *Imperial Gazetteer of India*, 1885, Vol. III, p. 342.
112. *Report on the Administration of Bihar and Orissa*, 1911-12, p. 13.
113. *Ibid.*, 1914-15, p. 58.
114. Diwakar, R.R., *Op. cit.*, p. 779.
115. *Ibid.*, p. 774.
116. *Ibid.*, p. 770.
117. Gadgil, D.R. *Industrial Evolution in India in Recent Times*, p. 2.
118. Datta, K.K., (ed.), *The Comprehensive History of Bihar*, Vol. III, Part I, p. 503.
119. Diwakar, R.R. *Op. cit.*, pp. 776-76.
120. *Moral and Material Progress of India 1889-90*, p. 149.
121. Diwakar, R.R., *Op. cit.*, p. 776.
122. *Ibid.*, p. 778.
123. *Ibid.*, p. 780.
124. *Bihar and Orissa in 1923*, p. 62.
125. *Quinquennial Review of the Mineral Production of India*, 1914-18, p. 257.
126. Diwakar, R.R., *Op. cit.*, p. 780.
127. Elwin, V., *The Story of Tata Steel*, p. 12.
128. Diwakar, R.R., *Op. cit.*, p. 778.
129. *Memoir, Geological Survey of India*, Vol. XXXIV, Part II, 1902, p. 45.
130. Ball, V.A., *Manual of The Geology of India*, p. 529.
131. Ghosh, D.R., *The Industrial Guide*, pp. 752-53.
132. O'Malley, *Report on the Census of India*, Vol. V (Bengal, Bihar, Orissa and Sikkim), 1913, Part I, p. 79.
133. *4th Report Com. Sex HC*, 1772-73, p. 116.
134. Misra, B.B., *Op. cit.*, p. 120.
135. *Ibid.*, p. 121.
136. *Controlling Council of Rev.*, *Murshidabad*, Proc. VIII.
137. *6th Report*, *Sel. Com. HC*, 1782-3, p. 943a.
138. Hunter, *Bengal*, *M.S. Records*, p. 107.
139. *Forest*, *Selections*, II, 75 (18 Sept. 1789).
140. *2nd Rep. Sel. Com. HC*, 1808-12, p. 100.
141. *The Bengal Administration Report of 1872-3*, p. 73,

142. Misra, B.B., *Op. cit.*, p. 131.
143. *I.O. Coll. to Rev. Desp.*, No. 14 of 9th July 1862, Para 48.
144. *Ibid.*
145. Misra, B.B., *Op. cit.*, p. 154.
146. *Ibid.*, p. 54.
147. Jha, J.S., *Education in Bihar* (1813-1859), p. 6 fn.
148. Datta, K.K. (ed.), *The Comprehensive History of Bihar*, Vol. III, Part II, p. 408.
149. *Ibid.*, p. 409.
150. Jha, J.S., *Op. cit.*, pp. 121-124.
151. *Ibid.*, p. 188.
152. Datta, K.K. (ed.), *Op. cit.*, Vol. III, Part II, p. 417.
153. *Ibid.*, p. 424.
154. Diwakar, R.R., *Op. cit.*, p. 717.
155. *Bengal Education Report*, 1862-63, Appendix 'A', p. 194.
156. Roychaudhary, P.C. (ed.), *B.R.D.G. Champaran*, p. 446.
157. *Ibid.*, p. 444.
158. Quoted in *The Comprehensive History of Bihar*, edited by K.K. Datta, Vol. III, Part II, p. 427.
159. *The Behar Times*, 12th February 1897.
160. Datta, K.K. (ed.), *Op. cit.*, Vol. III, Part II, pp. 428-29.
161. *Ibid.*, Part I, p. 191.
162. *Bengal General* (*Education*), *A. Proceedings*, August 1861, Nos. 40-45.
163. Diwakar, R.R., *Op. cit.*, p. 718.
164. Jha, J.C., *History of Patna College*, p. 64.
165. Pandey, S.N., *Educational and Social Changes in Bihar* (1900-21), p. 157.
166. *Bengal General* (*Education*), *A. Proceedings*, October 1871, Nos. 8-10.
167. *Ibid.*
168. *Ibid.*, (Letter to the High Court, 3 October 1871).
169. *Bengal Appointments*, *A. Proceedings*, January 1881, Nos. 21-22.
170. Datta, K.K. (ed.), *Op. cit.*, Vol. III, Part I, p. 226.
171. Sastri, Sivanath, *History of the Brahmo Samaj*, Vol. II, 1912, p. 536.
172. *Ibid.*
173. *Ibid.*, p. 530.

174. Karunakaran, K.P., *Religion and Political Awakening in India*, p. 50.
175. Diwakar, R.R. (ed.), *Op. cit.*, p. 678.
176. *Ibid.*
177. Vachaspati, Indira Vidya, *Arya Samaj Ka Itihas*, Vol. II, pp. 225-26.
178. Srinivas, M.N., *Social Changes in Modern India*, p. 101.
179. *The Beharee*, 20 January 1910.
180. *Ibid.*, 2 September, 1910.
181. Heimsath, Charles, H., *Indian Nationalism and Hindu Social Reform*, pp. 44-45.
182. Datta, K.K. (ed.), *Op. cit.*, Vol. III, Part II, p. 46.
183. *Ibid.*, p. 230, *Bihar Regional Records Survey Committee's Report for 1965-67.*
184. *Report of the Tenth National Social Conference held in Calcutta on 1 January 1887.*
185. Datta, K.K. (ed.), *Op. cit.*, Vol. III, Part II, p. 449.
186. *Political (Special) File No. 64 of 1912.*
187. *Political (Special) File No. 9 of 1915.*
188. *General Administration Report*, Patna Division, Para 139.
189. Verma, Kamla Prasad, *Bhulti Bhagati Yaden (Hindi)*, p. 170.
190. Sinha, S., *Some Eminent Bihar Contemporaries* (Introduction, XI-XII.
191. Datta, K.K. (ed.), *Op. cit.*, Vol. III, Part II, pp. 416-17. Pandey, S.N., *Op. cit.*, pp. 160-61.
192. *Proceedings Government of Bengal, General Department (Education)*, May 1906, No. 7, p. 98.
193. Diwakar, R.R. (ed.), *Op. cit.*, pp. 719-20.
194. *Report on The Administration of Bihar and Orissa, 1917-18*, p. 101.
195. Datta, K.K. (ed.), *Op. cit.*, Vol. III, Part II, p. 419.
196. Diwakar, R.R. (ed.), *Op. cit.*, p. 720.
197. Datta, K.K. (ed.), *Op. cit.*, Vol. II, Part II, p. 420.
198. *Note by Mackenzie, Home Secretary, on Statutory Civil Service, 24 July, 1884, Home (Public) Proceedings, September 1884, Nos. 162-210*, pp. 65-84.

2

The Middle Class and the Nationalist Movement in Bihar

(Between 1912 and 1918)

The beginnings of modern political consciousness can be traced in Bihar from the early Congress days, and some here were also attracted by the socio-cultural movement in the first decade of the twentieth century. The motto and programme of the Servants of India Society attracted Rajendra Prasad,[1] Sri Krishna Prasad and Ramdayalu Singh. The inauguration of a Youths' Club, called the "Boys' Association", on the 3rd March 1809, which derived inspiration from some revolutionaries of East Bengal,[2] marked a turning point in the rise of political consciousness.

The Bengal Partition agitation had its echo in different parts of Bihar. On the 16th October, 1905, 'Rakhi Bandhan Divas' was celebrated at Darbhanga under the inspiration of Satish Chandra Chakravarty, Assistant Head of the Saraswati Academy. established in January, 1901 at Darbhanga under the patronage of Kameshwari Charan Sinha. Feelings of nationalism were gradually influencing many youths in this area and in other parts of Bihar. Youths of Bihar were also inspired by the ideals of the Swadeshi movement.[3] Surendra Nath Banerjee came to Monghyr in 1906 and delivered a fiery speech which made a deep impression on the minds of some, including Shri Shrikrishna Sinha and Shri Tejeshwar Prasad, who were then in the youthful stage of their career as students. The Behari Students' Conference, destined to play a highly significant role in the history of nationalism in this province, was established by Rajendra Prasad in 1906 and began since then to serve its interests enthusiastically.[4]

In the earliest days of the Congress there "used to be a great deal of enthusiasm in Bihar about it, and a large number of delegates used to attend the sittings of that body."[5] At the Sonepur fair in 1908 an important meeting was held under the Presidentship of Nawab Sarfaraz Hosain Khan Bahadur at which a Bihar Provincial Congress Committee was formed.[6] The first session of the Bihar Provincial Conference met at Patna early in 1908 with Ali Imam as its President.[7] Largely through the efforts of Deep Narayan Singh the Bihar Provincial Conference held its second session at Bhagalpur on the 9th and 10th April, 1909, with Sachchidananda Sinha in the Chair. A special feature of this session was the presence of G.K. Gokhale. Shri Gokhale rightly pointed out that the Bihar Provincial Conference occupied "a unique position among the political institutions in the country, in the sense that it has given body and shape to the ideas which ruled in other conferences by working together of Hindus and Muhammadans side by side taking part in its deliberations with equal enthusiasm."[8]

The year 1912 is memorable in the history of Bihar for two reasons. It saw the creation of a separate province of Bihar in response to the legitimate demands of the local people, and it was also the year when the Indian National Congress in its twenty-seventh session met for the first time in this historic land, hallowed by the scared traditions of a glorious past, with R.N. Mudholkar as its President. The Chairman of the Reception Committee was Mazharul Haque, and there were twenty Vice-Chairmen including important public workers and representative zamindars. Sachchidananda Sinha was General Secretary and Kuar Nandan Sahay, Joint General Secretary. There were ten Assistant Secretaries, headed by Parameshwar Lal, who was also captain of the Congress volunteers.[9]

In his welcome address Mazharul Haque, after referring to the past history of Bihar as a source of inspiration, observed : "We yield to none in our love for mother India and we share with the Congressmen of the whole country, the Congress ideal, the ideal which is throbbing in the heart of the Indian people."[10] The President thus spoke about Bihar : "Foremost among those who have been devoting themselves to unite in brotherly relations, the Mohammedans and Hindus, you, men of Bihar, have before you not only that task but the higher one of resuming the work of your forefathers to carry to all parts of this great continent rejuvenated faith, of universal fraternity and love."[11] The following gentlemen from Bihar now went to the All-India Congress Committee. Mazhar-ul-Haque was ex-officio member, and the elected members were Maharaj Kumar Gopal Saran Narayan Sinha of Tikari, Sachchidananda Sinha, Brajkishore Prasad, Gopi Krishna, Rai Krishna Sahai Bahadur, Ras Behari Mandal, Dasrath Lal, Maheshwar Prasad, Parmeshwar Lal, S.M. Ismail, Chaudhuri Karamat Hussain, Sant Prasad, Rajendra Prasad, and Kuar Nandan Sahai.[12]

The fifth meeting of the Bihar Provincial Congress Committee was held at Bankipore on the 10th April, 1914, under the Presidentship of Braj Kishore Prasad.[13]

In fact, new Bihar began to play an active role in the successive phases of Indian nationalism. In 1914 two eminent Beharis, Mazharul Haque and Sachchidananda Sinha were elected to serve on a deputation sent to England by the Congress along with Bhupendra Nath Basu, M.A. Jinnah, N.M. Samarth, B.N. Sharma and Lajpat Rai.[14] In presiding over the seventh session of the Bihar Provincial Conference, held at Chapra on 3rd April, 1915, Nand Kishore Lal referred to it in glowing terms. Lal delivered a long presidential address in which he discussed various topics of public interest and national importance in the light of those days.[15]

Thus we see that from the early Congress days Bihar witnessed modern political consciousness and national awakening under the leadership and guidance of the middle class Rajendra Prasad, Sri Krishna Sinha, Ramdayalu Singh, Satish Chandra Chakravarty, Kamleshwari Charan Sinha, Sachchidananda Sinha, Deep Narayan Singh, Mazharul Haque, Sarfaraz Husain, Ali Imam, Kuar Nandan Sahay, Parmeshwar Lal, Braj Kishore Prasad, Nand Kishore Lal and others, who played a leading role in arousing national consciousness and organising institutions and organisation furthering the cause of the nationalist movement, constituted the bulk of the middle class. Most of them belonged to the landed middle class families and later on turned professionals after taking Western education.

In this chapter I have to review also the role of the middle class in the agitation leading to the establishment of the Patna University, the Home Rule Movement and the Champaran Movement under the guidance and leadership of Mahatma Gandhi.

Agitation Leading to the Fstablishment of Patna University and the Middle Class in Bihar

The creation of Bihar as a separate province opened a new chapter in the history of educational development in Bihar. This new province needed certain important institutions, such as, University, High Court, etc. It had been an ardent desire of the educated middle class elites of Bihar to make their province a self-contained unit of administration. For that it was necessary to furnish it with two institutions in particular, viz., a High Court and a University.

On the formation of Bihar and Orissa as a separate province the educated middle class became more vocal in their demand for a separate University. They pleaded that their dependence on a University outside the province did not cater to their educational needs. The chief organ of educated middle class of Bihar, *The Beharee* which had worked strenuously for the creation of a separate province caused a similar campaign for the establishment of a University in Bihar. In a series of editorial comments and articles by many prominent public figures it emphasised the need of establishing a University in Bihar. It put very convincing arguments in favour of a University : "We have materials for our University at hand. We have 84 high schools and 6 colleges already at work. We have 811 students actually passing through them with University certificates and degrees each year. What we want is to incorporate them into a body distinct from the Calcutta University in which they are revamped and merged beyond all recognition."[16]

In the new province of Bihar and Orissa, 1989 candidates appeared for the Matriculation Examination, 98 for the Intermediate and 68 for the B.A. examination in 1912. These numbers at different stages of examination were sufficient feeders for a new University.

Public opinion in Bihar was unanimous in demanding the establishment of a separate University for the province. The educated men sorely felt the need of a separate University. There was a strong desire among them to build up modern Bihar, and for the advancement of the new province the educational progress was absolutely necessary. Therefore, the demand of a University was made with great vehemence.

A large and representative meeting of the citizens of Patna consisting of the educated professionals and businessmen was held in February, 1912. In this meeting Mazharul Haque proposed that the new province of Bihar and Orissa should have a separate University of its own as soon as practicable and that in the meantime there should be proportionately adequate representation of the people of Bihar in the Senate and the Syndicate of the Calcutta University. Purnendu Narayan Sinha seconded this resolution.[17]

The agitation for the establishment of a University spread throughout Bihar. The residents of Saran district assembled in a public meeting, under the Presidentship of Durga Prasad Vakil on 26 June, 1912 and passed a resolution demanding a University for the new province.[18] Another crowed public meeting under the presidentship of Giddour Maharaja was held on 19 July, 1912 at Monghyr. This meeting was attended mainly by the leading Zamindars, traders, merchants and pleaders who formed the middle class of the district. Deep Narayan Singh moved a resolution for the establishment of a University at Patna which was adopted with great enthusiasm.[19] Such meetings were held in other towns as well.

An extraordinary session of the Bihar Provincial Conference held on 19 February, 1912 under the presidentship of Tekari Maharaja advanced the following arguments for establishing a University at Patna: "In ancient times Nalanda, which is not far from Patna was probably the most famous seat of learning in all India. It is needless to refer to the great fame of Mithila for learning. In more recent times, under Mohammedan rule, Patna was famous centre to which students used to come from distant quarters to learn the various branches of learning prevalent in those times. Why should not Patna then be once again the centre of learning that it used to be?"[20]

The practical advantage of having a University in Bihar could not be doubted. Such a University would develop Bihar's education a great deal more than a University situated at a considerable distance from the province and subject to influence which did not respond to Bihar's wants and wish.[21] Many speakers including Purnendu Narayan Sinha, Kedarnath of Gaya and Dwarkanath of Muzaffarpur, who belonged to the middle class educated elites, pointed out that the establishment of a University was the crying need of Bihar.

According to *The Beharee* a University, specially adopted to the requirements of Bihar, would usher in a new era in the history of education, helping the recruitment of the public service "from the sons of the soil and the dissemination of knowledge among the masses." The creation of a University at Bankipore was not an intellectual but a social and moral lever for the people.[22] This newspaper pointed out to the public as well as to the Government the absolute necessity of expediting the establishment of the Patna University. Besides the Press, other forums were also utilised for putting weight to the demand.

In 1912 Sachchidananda Sinha raised the issue of establishing a University at Patna in the Imperial Legislative Council. Harcourt Butler replied that Government was aware of the necessity of providing a University to the new province, but the opinion of the local Government in the matter was awaited. Bihar's Lieutenant Governor-in-Council was convinced that there was a strong and growing demand for a separate University for the province. He agreed that time had come for a thorough examination of the case. He proposed to constitute a representative committee with a view to the formulation of a definite scheme. The Committee's report would be examined and submitted for the consideration of the Government of India.[23]

The Government of India approved of the proposal to appoint to a committee to consider the question of establishing a University at Patna. On 19 May 1913 the Government of Bihar announced the following resolution: The Government of India have, on several occasions, explained the necessity which has arisen for circumscribing the limits of Universities in India and the desirability of the teaching and residential system of university life may be enjoyed. With the growing demand for a separate University, the local Government proposed to constitute a representative committee with a view to formulate a definite scheme. The Lt. Governor announced at the meeting of the Legislative Council held on 12 Februry, 1913, that a Committee would be appointed to enquire into and report on the whole subject. This announcement was received most favourably, and a cordial desire to cooperate in the execution of the project was expressed on all sides.

This resolution of the Lieutenant Governor-in-Council constituted the Patna University Committee to frame a scheme for the establishment of a University at Patna. The following gentlemen were appointed members of the Committee:[24]

1. R. Nathan—President
2. J.G. Jennigs, Principal of Muir College, Allahabad, officiating D.P.I.
3. A.G. Wright, Director of Public Instruction Central Province
4. W.A.J. Archbold, Principal, Dacca College
5. C. Russel, officiating Principal of Patna College
6. R.W.F. Shaw, Principal of Rovenshaw College, Cuttack
7. S.L. Thompson, Principal, St. Columbas' College, Hazaribagh
8. D.N. Sen, Principal, Bihar National College
9. U.H. Jackson, Professor of Chemistry, Patna College
10. K.S. Caldwell, Professor of Chemistry, Patna College
11. Rajendra Narayan Bhanj Deo of Kanika, Orissa
12. Sheo Shankar Sahay Bahadur
13. Madhu Sudan Das, M.A., B.L.
14. Saiyid Muhammad Fakhruddin, B.A., B.L.
15. Dwarkanath, B.A., L.L.B.
16. Saiyid Nurul Hudda, M.A., L.L.M.
17. Sachchidananda Sinha, Barrister-at-law
18. P.C. Talleuts was appointed to act as Secretary of the proposed Committee. The Indian members of the committee such as D.N. Sen, Sheo Shankar Sahay, S.M. Fakhruddin, S.N. Hudda, Dwarkanath and Sachchidananda Sinha belonged to the educated middle class of Bihar.

The Lt. Governor desired to leave the committee unfettered in the execution of the important task entrusted to it. But he made a few observations for general guidance, which fixed the nature of scheme. The following conditions were laid down:[25]

1. The University being intended for the benefit of the whole province, the needs of all parts of the country and of all sections of the people should receive careful attention.
2. Provision should be made for a University at Patna or at some convenient place in its neighbourhood, of the teaching and residential type, and for the affiliation to the Central institution of cóllege situated in other places.
3. The scheme should not involve any such additional cost to the students, as it would discourage them from taking full advantage of the facilities to be offered.

It was decided that the report of the committee would be published and circulated for comment and advice before any definite action was taken.

Rajendra Prasad who, as the barrister of the High Court, was then practising at Calcutta wrote a long letter in *The Beharee* on this occasion: "The question of the proposed University of Patna is naturally engaging the attention of all the thoughtful people of our province. Various rumours are afloat, and some of them at any rate are of a very disquieting nature. On an occasion like this it is absolutely necessary that the people of the province should express their opinion so that the Government as well as the non-official members of the University Committee may be in a position to gauge the public feeling. . . . I venture to think that if there was any time in the history of Bihar under the British regime when a conference was needed to give expression to the public feeling on any important topic, the present is such a time."[26]

The Committee met at Bankipore from 16 to 23 July 1913 to settle the main outlines of the project. The report of the Dacca University Committee served as a basis of discussion. The President and several members of the committee visited Muzaffarpur, Bhagalpur and Cuttack where schemes for local colleges were prepared with the aid of local advice. The committee held its last meeting on 15th and 16th December and outlined its final report.[27]

The Committee submitted its report in March, 1914. The Government of Bihar and Orissa resolved on 19 March, 1914 that the report of the committee which had been received and published should be circulated for comment and advice. Copies of the report were forwarded to newspapers, the leading associations of the province and interested persons. Comments were solicited by 31 May, 1914.[28]

The Committee's scheme envisaged a central institution at Patna which would undertake the higher branches of instruction, conduct the examinations, supervise the general life and training of the students, and regulate the teaching and organisation of a number of incorporated colleges. Some of these colleges would be in the University area and others would be situated in different parts of the province. In the Central University, laboratories, lecture halls, and seminars, library and a museum, and other similar facilities would be provided for the common use, while ample accommodation and opportunities would be afforded for all kinds of games and for the various associations and social amenities which a University should encourage.[29]

Commenting on the object of this scheme, it said, "the aim of a University should be in the first place to discover students of merit and the net must be cast as widely as possible. From this point of view the existence of the various local colleges is all to the good as they will connect all parts of the province with the central University."[30]

The Committee recommended that the University of Patna should contain departments of Arts, Science, Sanskrit

Studies and Law, and a department for the training of teachers.[31]

The management of the University was to rest with a Chancellor, a paid whole-time Vice-Chancellor, a convocation of 160 members and a Council of not less than 24. The Chancellor, who was to be the Lt. Governor of the Province, was to nominate 50 college or University teachers and 31 other members of the convocation and 6 of the council and the election of other members was to be subject to his confirmation. He was to appoint the external members of the governing bodies of the colleges to select professors and assistant professors from amongst the members of the staff and to confirm proposals for the grant of honorary degrees. The Vice-Chancellor as the Deputy of the Chancellor and the Head of Executive, would preside over the council and more important Boards and Committees and be one principal visiting and inspecting officer of the university for both external and internal colleges.[32]

All important executive matters were to come before him and he was to be responsible for the general working of the University. The convocation was to consist of 16 ex-officio members besides all principals of the colleges, senior professors and professors, so senior lecturers and 31 other persons nominated by the Chancellor and 25 elected graduates. It was to deal with legislative matters and questions of principle only and to have no power to revise the executive matters of the council. It was to be open to the convocation to initiate legislation, development or reform. Such resolutions, if carried, were to be forwarded to the council and the latter was to be required to inform the convocation in due course of the action taken.[33]

If the convocation was not satisfied it was at liberty to address the local Government on the subject. The council was to be the supreme executive authority of the University, responsible for its general and financial administrations. It was to consist of 3 'ex-officio' members all principals of colleges and the Dean of the non-collegiate students, 6 teachers appointed by the Chancellor and 7 Fellows elected by the convocation.[34] In the words of Committee the Government of new University was to be entrusted mainly to its principals and teachers but the graduates were also to be given a share in its managements and a sufficiently strong outside element was to be introduced to ensure due weight and popular opinion and sentiment.[35]

The report of the Committee was published in the local Government Gazette followed by criticism which mainly centered on the following points.[36] The amount of Government control, the proposed position and duties of the Vice-Chancellor, the constitution and relative functions of the convocation and the Council, the omission of courses in medicine and engineering and other professional subjects, the limitation of the courses of study in external colleges, the absence of any provision for the opening of external colleges other than the four already in existence.

The local Government considered the criticism and submitted its reports to the Government of India on 28th May, 1915. The local Government desired to provide the province a University as soon as possible because the eagerness of the people of Bihar to have its own University had increased much. The new conditions made heavy expenditure. So when the draft bill was prepared, it incorporated into the University only the colleges already in existence.

The Patna University Bill was introduced in the Imperial Legislative Council by C. Sankaran Nair, Member of Education in the Viceroy's Executive Council on the 27th September, 1916, after the due examination of the scheme by the education department of the Government of India and the Secretary of State-in-Council.

In the Bill the Chancellor was empowered to nominate 4 out of 16 members of the syndicate. Of the ordinary Fellows 12 were to be elected and the remainder (40 to 60) nominated by the Chancellor. The Vice-Chancellor was to be the Principal

Executive Officer of the University.[37] The council was replaced by a Syndicate of 16 members of whom 3 were to be appointed 'ex-officio' while the remainder 9 were to be elected by the Senate and 4 to be nominated by the Chancellor. The Syndicate was to have the entire management of and superintendence over the affairs and property of the University. The convocation was replaced by smaller Senate which was to be constituted on the lines of Act VIII of 1904 and to include 8 'ex-officio' Fellows besides 40 to 60 ordinary fellows. The senate was only a deliberative body. Its resolution would not be binding on the Syndicate. The new senate thus differed from the one constituted under the Universities Act of 1904.[38]

The bill laid down that no college should be affiliated except five approved existing centres, namely one in each division. The diamond jubilee college was left out. The select committee had added a provision that intermediate college might be opened without restriction.[39]

Many members participated in the debate on the Patna University Bill in the Imperial Legislative Council. Sri Krishna Sahay, a member from Bihar expressed his sincere gratitude on behalf of the people of Bihar. He refrained from making any observations on the Bill. Pandit Madan Mohan Malviya speaking on the Bill welcomed the creation of this University. But he considered the proposal to make the Syndicate practically independent of Senate, retrograde and objectionable. C.H. Setalvad also pinpointed the retrograde character of the Bill, which would turn the University into a department of the Government. Tej Bahadur Sapru condemned its retrogade character and called it most backward.

Mazharul Haque, Bihar's representative, expressed satisfaction at the fulfilment of Biharis' demand. "It was the long cherished desire of the people of Bihar to have a University of their own, and that desire is on the point of fulfilment." He did not like some of the provisions of the Bill which was elucidated by the education member in the council. However, he observed that the time for a detailed criticism would come after some time at Delhi. He was not prepared to call it a retrograde measure and reserved his criticism for a future occasion.[40]

Thus, many of the provisions of the Bill were criticised as 'retrograde and reactionary' on the day it was introduced. In fact, this became the most controversial Bill in the Legislative Council. The newspapers and journals, not only of Bihar but of the whole country commented on it. The Bihar Provincial Association[41] took a very active part in educating public opinion on this Bill. It published pamphlets and collected comments. Rajendra Prasad, the Joint Secretary of Bihar Provincial Association, published two pamphlets which were called the 'Bihar Provincial Association' Tracts. The object of these pamphlets was to provide those interested, the views expressed in different parts of the country. The Bihar Provincial Association tried to place the text of the Bill and comments on it within easy reach of the public. The two Bihar representatives in the Imperial Council enclosed a letter to some persons in the province asking their opinions and suggestions. Braj Kishore Prasad was actively organising public opinion against the retrograde provisions of the Bill.

A. Caste Organisations and the Establishment of Patna University

Caste organisations also opposed the bill tooth and nail. The Bhumihar Brahman Sabha, for example, described most of the provisions of the bill as unsatisfactory.[42] It passed into an Act, if imagined, it "would prove highly injurious to the cause of education."[43] An ideal University of Bihar, it thought, should have an adequate representation of educated people from every community in the different University bodies. Moreover, there should be a provision for starting and fostering of a network of colleges and schools all over the province.

The Bihar Provincial Muslim League also described the bill "a highly retrograde measure", aiming and preventing the spread of education by restricting the opening of external colleges and of lowering the quality of education in the external colleges.[44]

Similarly, the Orissa Association of Cuttack opposed the bill on the ground that the Rovenshaw College without proper equipments would gain nothing from the change in jurisdiction.[45]

Citizens of some towns also passed resolutions condemning the new bill, for example, the citizens of Muzaffarpur criticised the principle underlying the bill, demanding the modification of its "stringent and retrograde provisions."[46]

B. Journals and Establishment of Patna University

The Leader of Allahabad considered the Patna University Bill retrograde. Its proposal not to allow honours and post-graduate instructions at any centre outside Patna was not commendable. This newspaper advocated that doors for future development in education should be kept open.[47]

Special attention was paid to the comments of *The Times of India* of Bombay which was one of the foremost organs of Anglo-Indian public opinion. This paper was as strong in its condemnation of the Patna University Bill as any of its counterparts. It commented: "The powers to be conferred on the Chancellor, to begin with, are unprecedented in the annals of Indian Universities Legislation....The Bill, as it is drafted, is far from satisfactory. We have worked up in India to a certain standard of independence and public spirit in University administration. Nothing can be more detrimental to the growth of higher education in this country than that anything should be done to debase that standard."[48]

The Express of Bankipore regretted the exclusion of Diamond Jubilee College of Monghyr from the pale of the University. It was indeed a matter of surprise. Monghyr was one of the most important districts of the province and the college had been supplying the educational needs of a large number of youngmen of Bihar. It was badly damaged and badly equipped. It should have been the duty of the University authorities to make it as efficient as other colleges. It further criticised the restriction that colleges would not be recognised if they were not located either in Muzaffarpur, Bhagalpur, Cuttack, Hazaribagh or within one mile of the Senate House. But there were other towns which needed a college. There were four H.E. schools in the town of Gaya and five in its sub-divisions including those lately established. Thus, Gaya urgently required a college. There was a demand for it. The district of Chapra had ten H.E. schools, and it required a college. The effect of the Act would roughly be to check the growth of educational institutions in the province.[49]

A very lengthy article published in *The Modern Review* of Calcutta analysed the draft bill in detail and put forward its own opinion on the needs of Bihar. It was pointed out that a province like Bihar should equip itself with technical institutions. But the Bill had ignored this requirement. The number of colleges provided in it was inadequate for a big province comprising Bihar and Orissa. The omission of a college for worker was most regrettable. The most astonishing feature of the Bill was that it practically made University education stationary in the province. It quoted Professor Jadunath Sarkar's presidential address at the Bihari students' conference saying that Bihar had been 50 years behind the other provinces in taking to English education, and must make more exertion than they to come to the front line and take her legitimate place in the march of national life.[50] The article in *The Modern Review* concluded with the following comment: "We have written at some length on the Patna University Bill as we think the educational interests of not only the province of Bihar and Orissa but of the whole of India may be prejudicially affected by it....The course of high education in India would suffer most seriously if the existing Universities were fashioned after the model of the Patna University."[51]

The Bengali of Calcutta regretted that the proposed Patna University would not be an improvement on the existing universities in India. *The Amrit Bazar Patrika* thought it impossible to conceive of a more retrograde and reactionary measure. In fact, no journal published in any part of the country shirked from commenting on the proposed Bill. The Patna University Bill became an all India topic. *The Hindu* and *The Indian Patriot* from Madras, *The Punjabi* from Lahore, *The Marhatta* from Poona and *The Indian Social Reformer* from Bombay joined in condemning the provisions of the Bill.

The Bihar Provincial Conference held a special session to examine the provisions of the Bill under the Presidentship of Purnendu Narayan Sinha. A Note on the Bill specially prepared by a committee was laid before the Conference. It was resolved that unless timely measures were taken to remove the retrograde character of its provision, the University would not serve the cause of education in Bihar. The Congress session of 1916 held at Lucknow also sharply reacted to the restrictions provided in the Patna University Bill. Ambika Charan Majumdar, the President of the Congress, said in his address: "The Patna University Bill which empowers the Chancellor to deal with any matter connected with the University in any manner and that may seem to him to be fit and proper places the University education in a large province entirely under the authority of the Lt. Governor of Bihar and it makes the spread of high education impossible by practically prohibiting the establishment of a new college."[52]

Principal R.P. Paranjapey of Bombay moved that, "this Congress places on record its emphatic protest against the highly retrograde character of the Patna University Bill, and strongly urges that it should be so amended as to make it a thoroughly liberal and progressive measure."[53]

Sachchidanand Sinha who subsequently rose to be the Vice-Chancellor of Patna University, said that Bihar was opposed to the unprogressive and reactionary measure embodied in the Patna University Bill.

The Beharee which had led movement for the creation of Bihar as a separate province and demanded a University by publishing many articles, now took up the cause of educating the people of Bihar on the draft Bill. It had the following comment: "We will be failing in our duty if we do not give vent in unmistakable terms, to the great disappointment that the Bill has caused in the province and already many amongst our countrymen are wondering if it would not be better to continue the old regime rather than enter the new one which seems certainly to usher in an era of a more or less officialised University. We know with what lively interest the ruler of our province has been working for the realisation of our wish for a University of our own; and we now look up to him to intercede on our behalf and guarantee that the Bill in its present form would not be passed and shall be thoroughly liberalised before it becomes Act."[54]

Thus, the objections raised against the Patna University Bill were mainly with regard to the undue power vested in the local Government, to the peculiar and unlimited powers given to the Vice-Chancellor and to the constitution of the syndicate and the Senate.

The Bill was modified in certain respects in response to public criticism. But it is note-worthy that for more than twenty years after the passing of the Act, Orissa had to be satisfied with only one college, Chotanagpur with one first grade and one second grade college each and the Patna Division with only three—one first grade and two second grade institutions.[55]

The Patna University Bill was referred to a select committee which modified the draft, especially in the direction of increasing popular control in the Senate. On September 23, 1917 the Bill as amended by the Select Committee, was passed unanimously by the Imperial Legislative Council. Thus, Patna University Act came into force on 1 October, 1917.[56]

The regulations of the new University were drafted on the lines of those in force in Calcutta, but were substantially modified from time to time.[57] Two important changes were the abolition of the age limit for matriculation and the institution of a system of supplementary Examination.[58]

Thus, as a result of the persistent zeal and efforts of the middle class the Patna University came into existence. Inauguration of a separate University for Bihar gave an impetus to higher education in Bihar. Now it became easy to take higher education to those who were unable to go to Calcutta or elsewhere and as a result of it the number of students went on increasing in this province. The inauguration of the new University added equally to the enthusiasm of the students and teachers.[59]

Thus we see that role of the middle class in the wake of national agitation also touched the issue of education as is evident from its role in the agitation leading to the foundation of the Patna University in 1917. The educated middle class became more vocal in their demand for a separate University and their chief organ, *The Beharee*, campaigned for the establishment of a University in Bihar. Public meetings, which passsed resolutions demanding a University for the new province, were organised and attended largely by the middle class. For example, Mazharul Haque and Purnendu Narayan Sinha (Pleaders) were the chief force in organising the meeting at Patna in February 1912. Such a meeting was also held under the Presidentship of Giddour Maharaja on 19 July, 1912 at Monghyr. Though it was presided by a personality from outside the middle class, the main participants of the meeting were members of different groups of the middle class. The Bihar Provincial Conference, which passed resolutions in favour of the establishment of a University, was mainly a middle class organisation.

Besides, there were several persons of significance who pleaded for the establishment of a University in Bihar. Such were Mazharul Haque, P.N. Sinha, Kedarnath Sinha, Dwarkanath, Sachchidanand Sinha, Rajendra Prasad, Sri Krishna Sahay, Braj Kishore Prasad, Jadunath Sarkar and others who came from the educated and landed middle class. The Committee appointed to frame scheme for the establishment of a University at Patna consisted of 8 Indians. Members from Bihar were mainly from legal profession and D.N. Sen, one of the members, was principal of the B.N. College. Thus it may be concluded that Bihari members of the committee were mainly from the middle class educated elites.

We cannot ignore the role of the Bihar Provincial Association and Bihari Students' Conference in educating public opinion on the Patna University Bill. And both the organisations were organised by the men of the middle class. The Bihar Provincial Conference, which met under the Presidentship of P.N. Sinha and resolved to remove the retrograde provisions of the Bill, was also dominated by the middle class.

To conclude, it can be said that the establishment of the Patna University was the work of middle class. Agitation for it was organised and kept alive till its establishment by the men of learned professions who came from the land owning families of Bihar. But after its establishment the leaders took least interest at their own in creating an atmosphere of academic awareness among the general mass. They did not campaign for educating the masses as was being done in neighbouring states. This shows the typical class character of the middle class leaders of the Bihari landlord bourgeoisie society dipped in the old social institutional hurdles and in the ideas of social disabilities for lower social orders. It appears, the middle class in Bihar could not rise above its own class interest in spite of the general discontent and revolutionary gestures against the British rule.

The Home Rule Movement and the Middle Class in Bihar

With the onset of the year 1914 began the World War I a highly critical period in human history. Mankind everywhere was subject to the ordeals of the volcanic cataclysm of 1914-18, and it had profound repercussions on India in various ways. There was considerable ferment in Indian political life with a new turn in the history of nationalism. Mahatma Gandhi remarked through a speech delivered at Karachi on 29th February, 1916, "In the course of my tour in India, I have been particularly struck with one thing and that is the awakening of the Indian people. A new hope has filled the hearts of the people, hope that something is going to happen which will raise the Motherland to a higher status."[60] The All India Muslim League began to give up its exclusive attitude from 1913, when at its annual session held at Lucknow on the 22nd of March it declared its aim to be "the attainment of self-Government for India along with the other communities."[61] As the President of the All-India Muslim League, held at Bombay in 1914 Mazharul Haque delivered a remarkable address : "by the same breadth of views, the same fearless independence, the same undaunted courage of conviction and unselfish patriotism that had ever been the distinguishing features of his active public life."[62] He emphasised that sincere cordiality between the Hindus and the Muslims was essential for the fulfilment of the cherished national aspirations. Muslim sentiments in India were also deeply stirred by war of Britain against Turkey, particularly since 1916 when the Shariff of Mecca had rebelled against his overlord the Sultan of Turkey who was the Khalif of all the faithful and in "Moslem eyes had become England's tool." This facilitated co-operation between the Indian Muslims and the Indian National Congress. Both the Congress and the League held their annual sessions at Lucknow in December, 1916, and concluded "The Lucknow Pact", according to which the Congress agreed to separate electorates and both the organisations jointly formulated a scheme of reforms, known as the "Congress-League Scheme".

In moving the Resolution for Self-Government on the third day of the Lucknow session of the Congress (29th December 1916), Surendra Nath Banerjee remarked : "Today is a red letter day in our history. Today Hindus and all ranks of the National Party are united on this platform inspired by a common resolve and a common purpose. May the memory of this day be embalmed in the recollections of posterity by the inauguration of a new campaign for the attainment of Self-Government."[63]

On the same day Mazharul Haque of Bihar, who rose amidst scenes of profound enthusiasm and observed on the resolution for Self-Government : "All my political life, I have been of opinion that our motherland cannot advance without the unity of the Hindus, Mussalmans and other races. Having been of this opinion, I have worked for the attainment of that unity and that unity has been achieved this year in this town of Lucknow.…The time for action has come. Remember, you are demanding Self-Government and Home Rule for India. Do you for a moment believe that you get it by asking ? Unless and until, as Mrs. Besant has told you, you make your rulers believe that you are in earnest, and that you are serious in your demands you will never get anything. I am sure of it. So my advice to my countrymen is this : Try to work now. I believe that there is going to be a meeting of the Subjects Committee today and a resolution is going to be placed before you for a machinery which you could work up for the attainment of Self-Government. We must have a propaganda throughout the country and let our rulers see for themselves that every man, every woman, and every child of India is determined to have Self-Government."[64]

The Lucknow session of the Congress was also important for affecting union between the Moderate and Radical sections of the Congress. The two great leaders of the Moderates, G.K. Gokhale and Pherozeshah Mehta, had passed away from this world on the 19th February, 1915 and in November, 1915 respectively. Annie Besant and Lokamanya Balgangadhar Tilak now came to the forefront as leaders of a new political life in the country. This year, 1916, is memorable for the starting of two Home Rule Leagues, one by Lokamanya Tilak in Poona in April and the other by Annie Besant in Madras in the month of September. The two began to carry on a vigorous national propaganda in support of the Congress-League Scheme.

The influence of the Home Rule Movement was felt in different parts of India including Bihar.[65] At a meeting, held at Bankipur under the leadership of the middle class on the 16th December, 1916, it was decided to start a Home Rule League at Bankipur, and Mazharul Haque was elected its President; Khan Bahadur Sarfaraz Hussain (zamindar of Patna City) and Purnendu Narayan Sinha were elected Vice-Presidents and Chandra Bansi Sahay and Baijnath Singh (Pleaders) were elected Secretaries. Shri Mazharul Haque delivered an illuminating speech stressing the need for the formation of this League. He observed that "Home Rule means Self-Government. The object of our League will be to educate and organise the people and popularise the idea of Self-Government the length and breadth of our motherland. Our procedure within will be certainly constitutional and unobjectionable but the propaganda will be carried on with a perseverance and determination which will lead us to final victory."[66]

At another meeting held at Patna on the 17th February, 1918, office-bearers of the Provincial Committee of the Home Rule League were elected. It was decided to organise village campaigns and to collect subscriptions during February, 1918.[67] Besant came to Patna on the 18th April, 1918, and she was escorted from the station in a triumphal procession with Arati on the way to the residence of Purnendu Narayan Sinha at the Bhikhna Pahari Mohalla of Patna.[68]

This procession was thus described in a contemporary official Report:

"Mrs. Besant visited Patna on the 18th instt. arriving at Patna City at 5 a.m. and after being received at this early hour by some 200 people headed by the Hon'ble Rai Bahadur Purnendu Narayan Sinha and other local celebrities of the Home Rule party proceeded in a triumphal procession to the latter's house reaching it at 9 a.m. She entered a tandam belonging to Badshah Nawab with Purnendu Babu's son Nalini Ranjan Sinha and Babu Chandra Bansi Sahai acting as grooms, the former holding a silver umbrella over Mrs. Besant while the crowd dragged the tandam through the streets. At 3 places the Arati ceremony was performed about her person. Some 5000 people collected and cheered her. Flowers were showered at her and streets were decorated. At one place it was proposed to wash her feet and she was offered a glass of Sherbat.

"At Chowk Bazar the Hon'ble Mr. Mazharul Haque was found waiting for her. At the house of Babu Balgovind Malviya where she was taken to see the Barahmihir Library she was wrapped in a costly Benaras Chaddar by the owner of the house. Mr. Mazharul Haque delivered a short ovation, and a small purse on behalf of the Biparni Rakshak Sabha was handed over to her to spend for the good of the country. K.B. Sarfaraz Hussain Khan and Balgovind Malviya delivered short eulogistic speeches to which Mrs. Besant replied saying the ovation she received was given to her as one upholding the cause of the country and any one else doing the same was entitled to a similar ovation. Large number of students, both Hindus and Mohammedans, lined the streets and house-tops, and women-folk at some places also saluted Mrs. Besant. She was greeted with cries of 'Bande Mataram', 'Bharat mata ki jai', 'Swaraj Mata Ki jai.' At 4.30 p.m. she visited the Anglo-Sanskrit School, Purnendu Babu's institution, and at 5.30 she delivered a lecture at Ali Manzil and then left for Madras via Calcutta on receipt of an urgent telegram, instead of going to Benaras as originally arranged. Her speech[69] was much on the lines of those delivered in Calcutta recently. About 5000 people were present, K.B. Sarfaraz Hussain Khan being in the chair."[70]

At the meeting, held at the Ali Manzil, the local Home Rule leaders, Hasan Imam (Pleader), Purnendu Narayan Sinha, and Sarfaraz Hussain Khan signed the latest public manifestoes. All these caused anxiety to the Commissioner of Patna. Besant paid at flying visit to Patna again on the 25th July, 1918, to ascertain the views of the local Home Rulers regarding the Reforms and she met among others Hasan Imam and Sachchidananda Sinha.[71]

At Champaran, the associates of Mahatma Gandhi kept aloof from the Home Rule activities under his instructions. Referring to this Rajendra Prasad observes : "Throughout the country a large number of workers were going on about delivering lectures and rousing and organizing the people. Bihar too had its share of political agitation. We used to read reports in the papers how many of our friends and co-workers in other districts were busy going about holding meetings and delivering lectures, and sometimes felt tempted to follow the same course in Champaran also. But Mahatma Gandhi had sealed his own as well as our lips and we were not permitted to deliver public speeches either on the Champaran situation or in connection with the Home Rule movement. We expressed our desire to take part in the movement which was convulsing the whole country, particularly after the internment of Mrs. Besant. He used to tell us that by our very silence we were doing the highest kind of Home Rule work."[72]

However, Shri Janakdhari Prasad, a co-worker of Mahatma Gandhi, started a Home Rule League in Muzaffarpur region in co-operation with some members of the local Bar and businessmen and was elected its Secretary.[73]

There were participants of Home Rule also in the Saran District, where several meetings were held. Shri Manindra Nand of Arrah was active in addressing these meetings.[74] It is evident from the letter of L.F. Morshead, Commissioner of Tirhut Division reported from Sonpur that Home Rule was quite popular in Saran (Letter No. 671 dated 27th November, 1917). It was addressed to H. McPherson, Chief Secretary to the Government of Bihar and Orissa, that "Village to village Home Rule meetings were being held in the district of Saran."[75]

In a note, addressed to the Chief Secretary, the Lieutenant Governor of Bihar and Orissa dated the 28th November, 1917 observed that "the Maharani of Hathwa also told me this morning that there is a tendency in Saran for the ryots to withhold their rent because of the unrest caused by Mr. Gandhi and the Home Rule propaganda. It is worth considering whether it would not be well to issue proclamation to ryots enjoying the payment of their lawful rents and pointing out that they will themselves be the sufferers if they withhold payment."[76]

Mahatma Gandhi visited Chapra on the 27th January, 1918, and in this meeting Home Rule badges were sold and subscriptions worth Rs. 800 were collected from the people there.[77]

The District Magistrate, Saran, Mr. F.M. Luce, wrote to the Commissioner of Tirhut Division on the 7th June, 1918, that "I have frequently drawn your attention during the last years to the activities of the so called Home Rulers in this district. They consist mainly of a number of second rate pleaders of Chapra Bar, and for some time they have been concentrating their efforts on starting a trouble between the Manager and Raiyats of Mareais.[78]

In the course of his speech delivered in the Theosophical House at Gaya in July, 1917, Surendra Nath Banerjee advised the members of the Home Rule League to publish booklets in Hindi on the subject of Home Rule and to circulate these in the villages.[79] A pamphlet, entitled *Swaraj Katha* (Hindi) by Balmukund Bajpai, a leader of Home Rule Movement was prosecuted by the Government of Bihar and Orissa as also by the Governments of U.P. and the Punjab. Bajrang Sahai of Hazaribagh, a prominent political worker of Bihar and a pleader at Patna, paid his respects to Annie Besant in 1917 at Calcutta where he was then a student.[80] He came into contact there with Tarini Prasad Sinha, who originally belonged to village Deokuti in Gaya district, and after having received his education at the Banaras Central Hindu College, went out of India to Japan and America on the eve of World War I and served as a Lieutenant in England during this war. On his return to India, he closely associated himself with the Home Rule Movenent and was interned[81] along with some others.

One significant event in the history of nationalism in Bihar about this time was that Rai Puranchand of Patna City, Joint Secretary of the Patna Home Rule Leage, mooted the idea of starting the worship of Bharat Mata on the Vijaya Dasmi Day. He himself could not give effect to the idea immediately, as he died in August, 1918. But it materialised soon through the efforts of his two sons, Rai Baldeo Prasad and Rai Damodar Prasad. On an occasion like this prominent public men and patriots were invited to deliver lectures and national songs were sung. Such functions continued till 1930. A Bulletin of the Patna Hindi Sabha contained the following notification about worship of Bharat Mata :

"Worship of Bharat Mata will be solemnized on the occasion of Vijaya Dashmi. All communities, Hindu, Mussalman, Christian, Buddhist, Sikh, and Parsi had cordially invited to join hands in the performance of the function."[82]

In course of the Home Rule Movement in Bihar we see that the new social class, the middle class, comprising members of trading society, agrarian community, legal and other professions, dominated the political scene in leadership and participation. Prominent persons, who organised and propagated the Home Rule Movement in Bihar, were : Mazharul Haque, Purnendu Narayan Sinha, Chandra Bansi Sahay, Baijnath Narayan Sinha, Hasan Imam, Sachchidanand Sinha, Rajendra Prasad, Janakdhari Prasad, Bajrang Sahay, Khan Sarfaraz Hossain, Tarini Prasad Sinha, Manindra Nand, Balmukund Bajpai and Puranchand. All except last five, were pleaders. On the basis of leadership and participation it can be said that the Home Rule Movement was predominantly a movement of pleaders. Yet it cannot be denied that this movement attracted the middle class peasantry and landlords in rural regions of Bihar and middle class urban members comprising traders, businessmen, students and men of other professions. This fact is evident from the above description of the course of the movement.

In Bihar the Home Rule Movement attracted a suitable number of the members belonging to the middle class hailing from all castes as is evident from the persons enumerated above. The class essence of this movement, to a great extent, was free from self-centred caste bickerings and social prejudices. In comparison to the extent and speed of the movement in other provinces of India, in Bihar it was slow and limited because of illiteracy of the people. In this connection the leaders hailing from the middle class society of Bihar may be held partly responsible for not taking care to educate the masses in course of driving them to the course of the Home Rule Movement in Bihar. Certainly, this course was deliberately adoptd by the members of the middle class men of Bihar for safeguarding their socio-economic privileges amounting to their political importance.

An Appraisal of Home Rule Movement in Bihar

However, some amazing changes in the political views of Annie Besant took place. In a public lecture under the joint auspices of the Home Rule League on 10 June 1918 she maintained that nothing sort of the Congress-League system would satisfy India. Even as late as 3 August 1918 she said that the Montford Report established the continuation of the machinery of Autocracy in India with shreds and patches of local freedom. But in course of a few months her views were changed. She had a good following and abundant influence at the special Congress of Bombay (September 1918), but she became a back number at Delhi Congress (December 1918). She incurred great unpopularity by supporting the Rowlatt Bill and she sank very low in the popular estimation when she wrote on 18 April 1919 that "when the mob begins to pelt them (soldiers) with brickbats, it it is more merciful to order the soldiers to fire a few volleys of buck shot".[82A]

Later there came a mysterious riddle in the vision of theosophists under the leadership of Annie Besant that while taking inspiration from Fabian socialism of England they at the same time were dipped in spiritualism, mystic religionity involved in organising weekly meetings, holding religious discourses and were dragging the suffering people of Bihar to their vague Vedic and Puranic past. In fact Bihar was burning in the brutal and barbaric economic measures taken by the Indigo planters in Champaran. Theosophists in Bihar with Annie Besant became prey to their internal contradictions because of their class essence connected with the ruling class of the time. Annie Besant became a legend out of Indian politics after 1920. Home Rule League refused to elect her President and chose Mahatma Gandhi in her place in 1919 due to her reactionary attitude in regard to the ghastly incident of the Jallianwalla Bagh masssacre of the Indian freedom fighters by the British militia. Soon on the recommendation of a sub-committee duly appointed by Gandhiji, the name of Home Rule League was alterted to Swaraj Sabha, which also lost its separate identity and unconsciously merged into the Indian National Congress by the end of October 1920.[82B] Finally even echoes of Home Rule movement became extinct in the wake of Mahatma Gandhi in Champaran and the middle class ethos seen in the beginning in the Home Rule fed away.

Gandhiji's Champaran Mission and the Middle Class in Bihar

Champaran has a unique importance in the history of Indian freedom. It was here that Mahatma Gandhi after return from Africa, made for the first time on Indian soil a bold and successful experiment of the new weapon of Satyagraha he had forged abroad. It was a unique method in social dynamics, based on what he loved to call soul-force, developed through service and sacrifice, with truth and non-violence as the sheet anchors. It was aimed at 'curing all human ills', the awakening and salvation of downtrodden masses, the eradication of economic inequities, and the purification of society.[83] Rajendra Prasad rightly observed in 1949: "...what happened in Champaran has been repeated, as I had hoped, on a vast scale in the country as a whole. Champaran became free from planter's tyranny, India today is free from foreign rule."[84] Gandhiji's advent imbued the people of this area with a consciousness and moral faith in the righteousness of their cause, which are supremely important factors for the progress and successful consumption of a creative and constructive revolution.

European indigo planters in North Bihar carried on indigo cultivation under two systems, (a) Zerait and (b) Assamiwar. Under the Zerait system, indigo cultivation was under their direct management. They engaged tenant-labourers who were always ill-paid and were discontented. According to the Assamiwar system, the factory chiefs have the indigo lands cultivated by tenants. The most prevalent method under this system was known as Tinkathia or the system of three cottah, i.e. 3/20 of a bigha.[85] The other methods were Khushki and Kurtauli. The Kurtauli method, though not extensively prevalent in Champaran, was highly prejudicial to the interests of the ryots. The Commissioner of Patna observed in 1885: "The Kurtauli lease is a new institution dating from a very few years back....There is growing up in our midst and in spite of our efforts at beneficient legislation, a system under which the ryot mortgages his entire holding including even the very site of his house for a period probably extending beyond his own lifetime, redemption being contingent on the repayment of a loan; the ryot, to use the common expression, is selling himself body and soul into hopeless servitude."[86] In the Khushki method, rather uncommon in Champaran, agreements were executed by ryots who were not tenants of the factory.[87]

Under the Tinkathia method, a tenant had to cultivate indigo on three kathas per bigha of his holding or the factory lands during a long period (20 years, 25 years or even 30 years) and was formally entitled to get a price for it, according to the Sattas or written agreements. It was calculated to promote the maximum interests of the planters at the cost of tenants.

Coercion on them for converting their lands into indigo-producing fields, extortion of forced labour from them under all kinds of threats, extremely meagre payment and sometimes even no payment, inflictions of heavy fines for failure to grow indigo for any reason whatsoever, were some of the notorious features of this oppressive and grinding system.[88] Their occasional protests and cries for protection against the harsh treatment of the planters were wasted on the air. At last their deliverance was wonderfully affected through the efforts of Mahatma Gandhi and some of his Bihari co-workers belonging to the middle class, such as Rajendra Prasad, Braj Kishore Prasad, Gorakh Prasad (all lawyers)[89] who were in the vanguard of the movement.

Gandhiji's mission to Champaran was undertaken at the request of the people of Bihar, some of whom, who came from the middle class, had the privilege of contacting him at Lucknow during the thirty-first session of the Indian National Congress, which met there in December, 1916, with 2,300 delegates from all parts of India. Bihar also sent a number of delegates[90] to this session of the Congress, because two important resolutions were to be moved there on behalf of this province—one about the Patna University Bill and the other on the relations between the planters of Champaran and their tenants. Rajkumar Shukla (Peasant), who had felt the full brunt of indigo planers' tyranny and who, in the words of Gandhiji, was "filled with a passion to wash away the stain of indigo for the thousands who were suffering as he had suffered,"[91] went to the Lucknow Congress as a representative of the tenants of Champaran. Brajkishore Prasad proposed the following resolution before the Congress:

"The Congress most respectfully urges upon the Government the desirability of appointing a mixed Committee of officials and non-officials to enquire into the causes of agrarian trouble and the strained relations between the Indigo ryots and the European Planters in North Bihar and to suggest remedies therefor."[92]

After the Congress had unanimously passed this resolution, the Bihar delegates requested Gandhiji to come to Champaran. Rajkumar Shukla, in particular, urged him to visit Champaran personally and witness the miseries of the ryots there. Gandhiji promised to tour Champaran about the next March or April. He went to Kanpur, where also some Bihar people and Rajkumar Shukla followed him and were assured by him about his visit to Bihar.

In the company of the simple but resolute peasant-leader, Rajkumar Shukla, Mahatma Gandhi started from Calcutta on the 9th April, 1917, and reached Patna in the morning of the next day. Rai Krishna Sahay also saw Mahatmaji at the house of Mazharul Haque (lawyer). The same evening Gandhiji, accompanied by Shuklaji, took the train for Muzaffarpur and reached there at 10 o'clock in the night. He had already sent a telegram there about his journey. J.B. Kripalani, who was a Professor at the G.B. College, Muzaffarpur, received Mahatmaji at the railway station with a crowd of students of the same college along with others. The people gave a reception to Mahatmaji at the station, took his arti and the students dragged him in a closed carriage[93] of Shyam Nandan Sahay, a student of G.B. College.

In the morning, some local vakils saw Mahatmaji, some of them were Ramnavami Prasad, Bindeshwari Prasad Verma, Ramdayalu Singh, Janakdhari Prasad and others.[94] At his request, Mahatmaji went to the house of Gaya Singh, a well known pleader there. Soon Brajkishore Prasad came to Muzaffarpur from Darbhanga and Rajendra Prasad from Puri. This time the former impressed Gandhiji "with his humility, simplicity, goodness and extraordinary faith, so characteristic of the Biharis"[95] and Gandhiji felt himself "becoming bound to this circle of friends in life-long friendship."[96] Brajkishore Babu and his companions promised all possible co-operation in his work there.

Gandhiji's object in coming to Bihar "was to enquire into the condition of the Champaran agriculturists and understand their grievances against the indigo planters."[97] This, he had previously thought, would take him only two days, but after his conversation with the vakil friends at Muzaffarpur he realised that the "work might take even two years"[98] for it would be necessary to meet thousands of the ryots.

Mahatmaji told his vakil friends: "I want clerical assistance and help in interpretation. It may be necessary to face imprisonment. We cannot afford to pay for this work. I should be all done for love and out of a spirit of service."[99] The vakils gave assurance to Mahatmaji that they would do whatever he "may ask". "The idea of accommodating oneself to imprisonment was a novel thing" to them, and they said that they would "try to assimilate it."[100]

Before starting his inquiry, Mahatmaji wanted to meet the Commissioner of the Tirhut Division and the Secretary of the Planters' Association. Both of them unfortunately "misunderstood and misinterpreted"[101] Mahatmaji's object. On the 11th April, 1917, Mahatmaji saw J.M. Wilson, the Secretary of the Planters' Association, and after explaining to him why he had come there asked him to extend his co-operation in his work. In reply the Secretary of the Planters' Association first told Mahatmaji that he would say nothing in this respect on behalf of the Association but might give whatever help he could in his personal capacity. On the 12th April, Mahatmaji informed L.F. Morshead, the Commissioner of the Tirhut Division, of his arrival there. The same day J.M. Wilson intimated to Mahatmaji that there was no need of any enquiry, and that being an outsider he had "no business to come between the planters and their tenants." Gandhiji politely replied that he did not regard himself as an outsider, and that he had "every right to inquire into the condition of the tenants if they desired me to do so."[102] When Mahatmaji called on the Commissioner on the 13th April, the latter "proceeded to bully"[103] him, enquired as to who had brought him there and asked him "forthwith to leave Tirhut."[104]

In fact, the hard attitude of the Divisional Commissioner and the Secretary of the Planters' Association not only deepened his conviction about the injustice of which he had heard, but also made him realise that he would get obstruction from the Government. He felt that he "might be arrested" earlier than he expected, and if he was to be arrested, "it would be best that the arrest should take place in Motihari or if possible in Bettiah."[105]

"I know that these people (planters and Government officials) would act harshly towards me and a warrant for my arrest may come any moment. I am therefore anxious to reach Champaran as quickly as possible, so that whatever action they may have to take against me may be taken in the midst of the ryots of Champaran."[106]

By the midday train on the 15th April, 1917, Mahatma Gandhi started for Motihari with Dharnidhar (Pleader) and Ramnavami Prasad in his company. When the train reached Motihari at 3 p.m., he was taken straight to the house of Gorakh Prasad,[107] a local pleader, which became "a caravanserai."[108] On hearing that a respectable tenant of village Jasaulipatti had received harsh treatment, Mahatma Gandhi at once decided to proceed there on the next day, and the tenants who had come to Motihari were asked to turn up on Thursday next for getting their statements recorded. At 9 a.m. on the 16th April, Mahatma Gandhi started for this village with his two interpreters (Dharnidhar and Ramnavami Prasad) on an elephant without caring in the least for the fury of summer in the month of Baisakh, as in his "heart there was burning a fire to see and to redress the miseries of the ryots, compared with which the outward heat of the sun, and the dust and sand were nothing."[109]

The Government, however, did not like Gandhiji to probe into the hardships of the downtrodden peasants. The Magistrate ordered him not to enter the villages and leave Motihari immediately. But Gandhiji insisted on his right to see things for himself despite orders under section 144. Mahatma Gandhi kept awake the whole night writing letters and "giving necessary instructions to Brajkishore Prasad."[110] He prepared for a plan of work to be followed by others after he had been imprisoned and gave a copy of it each to Dharnidhar and Ramnavami Prasad on their return to Motihari from Jasaulipatti.

The news of the notice and the summons served on Mahatma Gandhi "spread like wild fire", and Motihari "witnessed unprecedented scenes" on the 17th April, when a vast crowd of peasants had reached there and recording of their statements began. The people had for the moment lost all fear of punishment and yielded obedience to the powers of love which their new friend exercised.[111] Thousands of peasants were baptised by Mahatma Gandhi's love. It was a miracle—a great triumpth of moral force. "It is no exaggeration, but the literal truth, to say", observes Mahatma Gandhi, "that in this meeting with the peasants I was face to face with God, Ahimsa and Truth."[112] Very soon the summons came calling upon Mahatma Gandhi to appear before the Sub-divisional Officer of Motihari at 12.00 noon on the 18th April, 1917. Gandhiji appeared before the court with his two interpreters, Dharindhar and Ramnavami Prasad, who had made up their mind to follow Gandhiji to jail.

It was a decision of great significance. "The 18th of April, 1917, is a memorable day in the history not only of Champaran, but of the whole of India. It was on this day that Mahatma Gandhi was preparing himself to go to jail for the sake of the poor and suffering people of the province of Bihar. On this day the whole of India was to get her first lesson and her first modern example of Satyagraha which was to open new floodgates of light and of vision before her."[113]

The Government pleader must have thoroughly prepared himself on points of law for the case. But when the trial began, "the Government pleader, the Magistrate and other officials were on tenterhooks. They were at a loss to know what to do."[114] The Government pleader pressed the court to postpone the case. But Mahatma Gandhi intervened and requested the Magistrate not to postpone it, as he "wanted to plead guilty to having disobeyed the order to leave Champaran."[115] Thousands of people surrounded the court to have a 'Darshan' of Mahatmaji. The court could give no verdict against Mahatmaji rebutting his bold statements and Gandhiji was released. In the afternoon of the 18th April, 1917, Polak, Mazharul Haque, Rajendra Prasad, Brajkishore Prasad,

Anugraha Narain Sinha (Lawyer) and Shambhusaran Verma (Pleader) came to Motihari from Patna.

In the night, Haque, Polak and Brajkishore Prasad left Motihari. After Polak had returned to Patna, a meeting of the Bihar Provincial Association was held there with Rai Krishna Sahai (Lawyer) as its President. Polak spoke about the situation at Champaran. The Association decided to render all possible assistance to Mahatma Gandhi in his inquiry and also to send at once "telegrams of protest" to the Viceroy and the Lieutenant Governor against such officers as were obstructing Gandhiji in his enquiry.[116]

From the 19th April, 1917, hundreds of tenants arrived at Motihari in different batches, and the assistants of Mahatma Gandhi commenced recording their statements after previous cross-examination and careful scrutiny. Mahatma Gandhi himself recorded statements of some and went through those which others had recorded. On the same day C.F. Andrews came to Champaran. Ramdayal Sahu, a zamindar and banker of Motihari, managed to secure a house for Mahatma Gandhi and his co-workers. He rendered all possible help to them during their stay in Champaran.

At 7 a.m. on the 21st April,[117] the Magistrate, W.H. Heycock, sent a written message to Mahatma Gandhi that the Lieutenant Governor had ordered the case against him to be withdrawn. The Collector wrote to him that he was "at liberty to conduct the proposed enquiry" and that he "might count on whatever help" he "needed from the officials."[118] "The country had thus", remarks Mahatma Gandhi, "its first direct object—lesson in Civil Disobedience."[119] The recording of statements of the ryots, who were arriving in greater numbers,[120] continued on the 21st April. The same afternoon Rai Krishna Sahai and Sachchidananda Sinha (Bar-at-law) reached there from Patna and had a conversation with Mahatma Gandhi for some time. Hasan Imam (Lawyer) could not come personally, but sent Rs. 1000.[121]

This fearless regard for truth of Mahatma Gandhi "had a great effect on our mental outlook," writes Dr. Rajendra Prasad.[122] "There can be no redress of grievances unless they shed fear."[123] Dr. Rajendra Prasad justly affirms that "since that day the presence or absence of a policeman has not made the slightest difference in our method of work with most of us."[124]

"Indeed the situation in Champaran was," as he tells us, "so delicate and difficult that over-energetic criticism or highly coloured reports might easily damage the cause which I was seeking to espouse."[125] In spite of these precautions, the planters engineered "a poisonous agitation"[126] against him and "left no stone unturned in maligning Brajkishore Babu."[127] He decided to get as much as possible from rich Biharis through Brajkishore Prasad's help, and, by exercising the strictest economy managed the whole enquiry with not more than three thousand rupees.[128] The workers were all taught to live on simple meal taken at regular hours in a common self-managed mess.[129]

Mahatma Gandhi started for Bettiah in the afternoon of the 22nd April, 1917[130] in a third class compartment, being greeted at all the stations on the way, and at 5 p.m. at the Bettiah station. by huge crowds of people with shouts of jai and showers of flowers. From the railway station he went on a carriage to the dharmasala of Hazarimal.

With the help of Brajkishore Prasad, Rajendra Prasad and others at Bettiah also statements began to be recorded from crowds of tenants who voluntarily came there for this purpose. He also wanted not "to irritate the planters but to win them over by gentleness"[131] and so not only met the Planters Association, but also saw a number of the planters, some of whom hated him, some were indifferent and a few treated him with courtesy.[132]

On 22nd April, 1917, several pleaders from Chapra came to Motihari to assist Mahatma Gandhi in this noble work.[133]

The District and Sessions Judge of Saran reported that "Shri Chandradew Narain, Shri Bikramjit Sahay, Shri Subh Narain, Shri Lachman Prasad, Shri Bindeshwari Prasad, Shri Madan Mohan Sahay and Shri Madho Singh, pleaders of Chapra have gone to see Mr. Gandhi and have subscribed to his work.[134] Besides these gentlemen, several others also including Ram Raksha Brahmachari[135] alias Bachcha Upadhyaya of village Uttim Bangra, Police Station Gopalganj, assisted Mahatma Gandhi.

Gandhiji's mission was to eradicate an evil which wrought havoc on the poor tenants. So he made it a point to familiarise himself with the actual conditions prevailing in the rural areas. With Brajkishore Prasad, a member of the educated middle class, in his company, he went to a village Laukaria on 24th April. On the 27th,1917, he with Brajkishore Prasad and some other proceeded to visit certain villages under Belwa factory and on 30th he went to Sathi factory.[136]

This shows that Mahatma Gandhi was assisted in carrying on his enquiry into the relations of the tenants and the planters by a band of young and enthusiastic men of the middle class who were ready to follow him to any extreme. This class character of the participants can be proved by mentioning the names and professions of the participants. "The following are at present with him here: Brajkishore Prasad (Vakil, Darbhanga), Rajendra Prasad (Vakil, Patna High Court), Kripalani (a Professor of G.B.B. College), Ramnavami Prasad (Vakil, Muzaffarpur), Anugrah Narayan Sinha (Vakil, Patna High Court), Dharnidhar (Vakil, Darbhanga) and Shib Nandan Ray (perhaps, Vakil, Chapra). Two persons are helping much and supply the party with a lot of materials, viz.

1. Pir Muhammad who subscribes all the articles to the paper *Pratap* of Cownpore, and who wrote the prescribed pamphlet *Champaran Ke Praja Par Atyachar* (Hindi)

2. Raj Kumar Shukla, a peasant of Setamari, a village near Chainpatia.''[137]

By the help of some lawyers and a few others, in spite of several hindrances, Mahatma Gandhi was successful in his mission. The government ultimately appointed a Commission consisting of representatives of landlords, planters, and the government, and Mahatma Gandhi himself who represented the tenants. The Commission after an inquiry submitted a unanimous report practically accepting the complaints of the tenants as valid, and embodying a compromise reducing the enhancements of rent and refunding part of money which the planters had taken from the tenants. The recommendations of the Commission were later on enacted by which growing of indigo on 3/20th of land or Tinkathia was abolished.[138] Sharahbeshi was reduced by 20 per cent in Turkaulia and 26 per cent in other factories. Tenants' holdings were freed from an obligation to grow indigo and new tenants were at liberty to grow indigo on voluntary basis. Arrangement was made to prevent litigation in respect of the matters covered by the Act.[139]

The prejudiced opinion could not conceal the fact that the Champaran Agrarian Act as well calculated measure, piece of humane and enlightened legislation, which served to alleviate the long standing and acutely felt miseries of a vast body of men and secured a "moral victory of the ryots."[140] A grievous malady was removed.

Mahatma Gandhi's mission there was also marked by the inauguration of welfare work for the uncared for rural folk who had been suffering from grievous social maladies. Two of these were colossal: pathetic ignorance and careless living under unhygienic and insanitary conditions. With his instinctive love for mankind, and with a growing experience of Bihar, Mahatma Gandhi was convinced, as he himself noted, that 'work of a permanent nature was impossible without proper village education.'[141] For this he wanted teachers of the right type. 'My idea was', writes Mahatma Gandhi in his Autobiography, 'never to entrust children to commonplace teachers. Their literary qualification was not so essential as their moral fibre.'[142]

In response to Mahatma Gandhi's 'public appeal' for voluntary teachers "received a ready response".[143] A batch of social workers with previous experience came to Bihar from Bombay, Karnataka, Maharashtra and Gujarat.[144] Schools were started at different places, such as Barharwa, at a distance of twenty miles to the east of Motihari, Bhitharwa in the Nepal Tarai, at Madhuban in the house of Seth Ghanshyam Das, a rich merchant, and so on. Along with volunteers from outside, Babu Dharnidhar of Bihar served in the school at Madhuban by staying there for six months with his wife and children.[145] About 100 boys received education at the Madhuban school. A girls' school was also started where about forty girls studied. Weaving was introduced at the Barharwa school. Thus in his social work also he was helped by the members of the middle class.

Medical relief was started at once under the guidance of Dr. De of the servants of India society,[146] and devoted volunteers inspired the village folk to give up their old apathy and dirty habits. Volunteers also inspired them with examples of self-help and corporate activities.

To conclude, we can say that Gandhiji's Champaran Movement was predominantly a movement of the middle class educated elites. It is true that other groups of the middle class also helped Gandhiji in his mission in Champaran. Rajkumar Shukla, a peasant, went to the Lucknow Congress as a representative of the tenants of Champaran and urged Gandhiji to come to Champaran. The resolution to enquire into the causes of agrarian trouble in that area was proposed by Brajkishore Prasad, a pleader at Darbhanga. Since the date he started from Calcutta to Champaran till the end of his mission, he was assisted by the members of the middle class, persons of prominence, who assisted and helped Gandhiji in his mission, were Rajkumar Shukla, J.B. Kripalani. Shyamnandan Sahay, Ramnavami Prasad, Bindeshwari Prasad Verma, Ramdayalu Singh, Janakdhari Prasad, Gaya Singh, Rajendra Prasad, Dharnidhar Prasad, Gorakh Prasad, Brajkishore Prasad, Mazharul Haque, Anugrah Narain Sinha, Sambhu Saran Verma, Krishna Sahai, Ramdayalu Sahu, Sachchidanand Sinha Hasan Imam and several others. Except Rajkumar Shukla, J.B. Kripalani and Ramdayalu Sahu, all were lawyers. Besides, he was received by a crowd of students, peasants, trading and business community.

Thus we see that leading members of the middle class, who were enlisted in the peaceful army of Gandhiji at that time, zealously worked at Champaran under the guidance of Mahatma Gandhi. Mahatma Gandhi's great appreciation of their work was expressed by him in the following brief statement in a letter written by him to Janakdhari Prasad in 1925: 'I treasure the memory of the faithful co-workers of Champaran. I shall never have and never had a more faithful hand to work with. If I had such a hand throughout India, Swaraj will not be long in coming to India.'[147] This expression of Gandhiji signifies the significance of the role played by the leaders belonging to the middle class of Bihar in the Champaran Movement.

The movement of Mahatma Gandhi in Champaran against the atrocities of Indigo planters was in favour of poor wage earning peasant and middle class farmers who were undergoing rigorous agrarian Tinkathia system. It gave an orientation to the national movement by exposing the policy of exploitation adopted by the planters. Gandhiji did his best for eradicating the ills successfully. But the leaders of Bihar did not draw the attention of Gandhiji towards a parallel world of atrocities practised by the Indian zamindars, landed peasantry and above all big mahajans of Champaran where they were active in putting the poor agrarian labourers in condition of serfdom and slavery.

Notes

1. *Appendix V and Appendix VI of History of the Freedom Movement in Bihar*, Datt, K.K., Vol. I.
2. Sinha, Kamleswari Charan, *Sarbajanik Seva-Kshetra Me Mai Aur Mere Kuch Anmol Sathi* (*Hindi*), pp. 1-2.
3. *Ibid.*
4. Prasad, Rajendra, *Autobiography*, p. 56.
5. *The Beharee*, 1st October, 1909.
6. Datt, K.K., *Op. cit.*, Vol. I, p. 150.
7. *Hindustan Review*, April, 1909, p. 388.
8. *The Beharee*, 7th January, 1910.
9. Majumdar, B.B., and Majumdar, B.P., *Congress and Congressmen*, p. 305. Datta, K.K., *Op. cit.*, Vol. I, pp. 154-55.
10. *Report of the Indian National Congress*, Bankipore, December 26-28, 1912, pp. 3-4.
11. *Ibid.*
12. Datta, K.K., *Op. cit.*, Vol. I, pp. 155-56.
13. *File No. 179 of 1914, Political* (*Special*) *Department.*
14. *File No. 729 of 1917, Bihar Political Department* (*Special*). Datta, K.K., *Op. cit.*, Vol. I, p. 156. Diwakar, R.R. (ed.), *Op. cit.*, p. 652.
15. Datta, K.K., *Op. cit.*, Vol. I, p. 156.
16. *The Beharee*, 25th April, 1912.
17. *Ibid.*, 9 February, 1912.
18. *Ibid.*, 30 June, 1912.
19. *Ibid.*, 25 July, 1912.
20. *Report of the Bihar Provincial Conference*, 19 February, 1912.
21. *The Beharee*, 23 February, 1912.
22. *Ibid.*, 16 February, 1912.
23. H. Lemuzier, Chief Secretary to the Government of Bihar and Orissa to the Government of India, Education Department, 6 November, 1912.
24. *Report of the Patna University Committee*, also called *Nathan Committee.*

25. *Proceedings, Government of Bihar and Orissa, Education Department*, 19 May, 1913, No. 28, pp. 15-16.
26. *The Beharee*, 10 August, 1913.
27. *Report of the Patna University Committee*, p. 10.
28. *Proceedings of the Government of Bihar and Orissa, Education Department*, May, 1914, No. 6, p. 5.
29. *Report of the Patna University Committee*, p. 13.
30. *Ibia.*, pp. 14-15.
31. *Ibid.*, p. 9.
32. *Ibid.*, p. 103.
33. *Ibid.*, p. 104.
34. *Ibid.*, p. 105.
35. *Ibid.*, p. 114.
36. *The first Quinquennial Review on the Progress of Education in Bihar and Orissa* (1912-17), p. 43.
37. *Proceedings of the Imperial Legislative Council*, September 1916, pp. 86-87.
38. *Ibid.*, p. 88.
39. *Ibid.*, pp. 89-98.
40. *Educational Proceedings* (*Government of Bengal*), 1917, No. 35, p. 151.
41. *Ibid.* It unanimously adopted a resolution protesting against the Bill.
42. *Ibid.*, Nos. 36, p. 155.
43. *Ibid.*
44. *Ibid.*, No. 37, p. 157.
45. *Ibid.*, No. 41, p. 167.
46. *Ibid.*
47. *The Leader*, 30 September, 1916.
48. *The Times of India*, quoted in B.P.A.T. 11, p. 15.
49. *The Express*, quoted in B.P.A.T. 11, p. 20.
50. *The Modern Review*, November, 1916.
51. *Ibid.*, pp. 551-560.
52. Majumdar, B.B., and Majumdar, B.P., *Op. cit.*, p. 194.
53. *Ibid.*, pp. 194-195.
54. *The Beharee*, quoted in B.P.A.T. 11, p. 106.

55. Majumdar, B.B. and Majumdar, B.P., *Op. cit.*, p. 196.
56. *Patna University Silver Jubilee Souvenir*, p. 30.
57. *Ibid.*, p. 24.
58. *First Decennial Review (1912-22), Bihar and Orissa*, p. 220.
59. Sarkar, J.N. and Jha, J.C., *History of Patna College*, (1885-1963), Patna, 1963, p. 98.
60. *Speeches and Writings of Mahatma Gandhi* (fourth edition), p. 327.
61. *The Indian Book Year*, 1914, p. 436.
62. *The Express*, 5th January, 1916, *The Beharee*, 12th January, 1916.
63. *Report of the Thirty-first Indian National Congress*, 1916, p. 76.
64. *Ibid.*, p. 83-86.
65. *Bihar and Orissa Police Abstract of Intelligence*, 1917, dated 6-1-17.
66. Appendix VIII of *History of the Freedom Movement in Bihar*, K.K. Datta, Vol. I, p. 532.
67. Datta, K.K., *Op. cit.*, Vol. I, p. 163.
68. *Abstract of Bihar and Orissa Police Intelligence*, 1918, dated 27-4-18.
69. Appendix IX of *History of the Freedom Movement in Bihar*, K.K. Datta, Vol. I, pp. 534-40.
70. *Abstract of Bihar and Orissa Police Intelligence*, 1918, dated 24-4-18.
71. *Ibid.*, dated 3-8-18.
72. Prasad, Rajendra, *Mahatma Gandhi and Bihar*, p. 19. *Atmakatha* of Rajendra Prasad, p. 103.
73. Prasad, Janakdhari, *Kuch Apni Kuch Desh Ki (Hindi)*, p. 33.
74. *Police Reports.*
75. *File No. 1571 of 1917, Part II, Bihar Political (Special) Department.*
76. *Ibid.*
77. *Bihar and Orissa Police Abstract of Intelligence*, dated the 16th February, 1918, Para 174.
78. *Muzaffarpur Records.*
79. *The Bihar Darpan*, 28th July, 1917, *The Pataliputra*, 28th July, 1917.
80. Statement of Bajrang Sahay quoted in *History of the Freedom Movement in Bihar*, K.K. Data, Vol. I, p. 165.

81. *Bihar and Orissa Police Abstract of Intelligence*, dated 7-9-18, Para 999.
82. Quoted in *History of the Freedom Movement in Bihar*, Datta, Vol. I, p. 166.
82a. R.C. Majumdar, *History of Freedom Movement in India*, Vol. III, 2nd ed., 1977, p. 37.
82b. *Ibid.*, p. 71.
83. Diwakar, R.R. (ed.), *Op. cit.*, pp. 654-55.
84. Prasad, Rajendra, *Satyagraha in Champaran* (Second Edition, September, 1949), Foreword X.
85. Sitaramayya, B. Pattabhi, *History of Indian National Congress*, Vol. I, p. 138.
86. Prasad, Rajendra, *Op. cit.*, p. 14.
87. Diwakar, R.R. (ed.), *Op. cit.*, p. 655.
88. Sitaramayya, B. Pattabhi, *Op. cit.*, Vol. I, p. 138.
89. *Ibid.*
90. Those who accompanied Braj Kishore Prasad from Darbhanga were Laxman Prasad, Bhuneshwar Misra, Kamleshwari Charan Sinha and Ram Bahadur Prasad Gupta.
91. Mahatma Gandhi, *Autobiography*, p. 494.
92. *Report of the thirty-first Indian National Congress*, p. 68.
93. *Balak* (Hindi), Vol. IV, No. 5.
94. Mahatma Gandhi, *Autobiography*, p. 498.
95. *Ibid.*
96. *Ibid.*
97. *Ibid.*, p. 501.
98. *Ibid.*, pp. 499-500.
99. *Ibid.*
100. *Ibid.*, p. 501.
101. Prasad, Rajendra, *Mahatma Gandhi and Bihar*, p. 4.
102. *Ibid.*, p. 501.
103. *Ibid.*
104. *Ibid.*
105. *Ibid.*, p. 501.
106. Prasad, Rajendra, *Satyagrah in Champaran*, p. 104.
107. Prasad, Rajendra, *Champaran Mein Mahatma Gandhi*, p. 87.
108. Mahatma Gandhi, *Autobiography*, p. 502.

109. Prasad, Rajendra, *Satyagraha in Champaran*, p. 105.

110. Mahatma Gandhi, *Autobiography*, p. 502.

111. *Ibid.*, p. 503.

112. *Ibid.*, p. 504.

113. Prasad, Rajendra, *Satyagraha in Champaran*, p. 112.

114. Mahatma Gandhi, *Autobiography*, p. 505.

115. *Ibid.*

116. *Bihar and Orissa Police Abstract of Intelligence*, Vol. VI, No. 1, 6th May, 1918.

117. 7 p.m., 20th April, according to Rajendra Prasad's, *Satyagraha in Champaran*, p. 506.

118. Mahatma Gandhi, *Autobiography*, p. 506.

110. *Ibid.*, p. 507.

120. According to Rajendra Prasad's *Satyagraha in Champaran*, p. 121, from Bettiah about 500 persons came.

121. *Bihar and Orissa Police Abstract of Intelligence*, Vol. VI, No. 1.

122. Prasad, Rajendra, *Satyagraha in Champaran*, p. 122.

123. Prasad, Rajendra, *Mahatma Gandhi in Bihar*, p. 11.

124. *Ibid.*

125. Mahatma Gandhi, *Autobiography*, p. 507.

126. *Ibid.*

127. *Ibid.*

128. *Ibid.*, p. 510.

129. *Ibid.*

130. *Letter from Mahatma Gandhi to W.H. Heycock*, 22 April, 1917.

131. *Ibid.*

132. *Ibid.*

133. Prasad, Rajendra, *Champaran Mein Mahatma Gandhi*, p. 119.

134. *Abstract from the Confidential Diary of the Superintendent of Police*, Saran, dated 25 May, 1917.

135. Misra, B.B. (ed.), *Mahatma Gandhi's Movement in Champaran*, p. 578.

136. Prasad, Rajendra, *Mahatma Gandhi and Bihar*, pp. 11-12.

137. *Report of the Commissioner of Trihut to the Government of Bihar*, May, 1917.
138. Sitaramayya, B. Pattabhi, *Op. cit.*, Vol. I, p. 140.
139. Prasad, Rajendra, *Mahatma Gandhi and Bihar*, p. 25.
140. Mahatma Gandhi, *Autobiography*, p. 519.
141. *Ibid.*, p. 513.
142. *Ibid.*
143. *Ibid.*
144. Appendix XII of *History of the Freedom Movement in Bihar*, Vol. I.
145. Prasad, Rajendra, *Satyagraha in Champaran*, p. 197.
146. Mahatma Gandhi, *Autobiography*, p. 515.
147. Prasad, Janakdhari, *Kuch Apni Kuch Desh Ki* (Hindi), p. 89.

3

The Nationalist Movement between 1919 and 1929 and the Middle Class in Bihar

In this Chapter I will review the role of the middle class in the Satyagraha of 1919, the Khilafat and Non-cooperation Movements, the formation of Swarajya Party and its working, organising vehement protest to the Simon Commission and in the constructive programmes, etc. With the arrival of Mahatma Gandhi on the political scene of India there was a marked change in the character of the movement for freedom. Now mass participation increased. But the participation of the masses did not diminish the position of the middle class. The middle class still remained in the vanguard of the movement aiming at the exit of the alien rule.

The Satyagraha of 1919 and the Middle Class in Bihar

The Montagu Mission arrived in India on the 10th November, 1917. It put forward a joint scheme of reforms, which was published on the 18th July, 1918, and was ultimately embodied in the Government of India Act, 1919. But these reforms were not adequate to satisfy India's legitimate national demands. To consider these a special session of the Indian National Congress met at Bombay from the 29th

August to the 1st September, 1918, under the presidentship of Syed Hasan Imam (Bar-at-Law) of Bihar. It was a very largely attended meeting. There were no less than 3,845 delegates from the different parts of India who attended the session. Nineteen delegates from Bihar and Orissa attended it including Chandra Diva (Dip) Narain, Vakil, Madhava Sinha, Vakil, Mahabir Sharan, Zamindar and Rajendra Prasad,[1] who came from the educated and landed middle class. It declared that the people of India were fit to shoulder responsible government and repudiated the assumption to the contrary contained in the Report. It asked for simultaneous constitutional advance both in the provinces and the Centre and disagreed with the formula that the provinces were the domain in which earlier steps should have been taken towards the progressive realisation of responsible government leaving the authority of the Government of India in essential matters indisputable, pending experience in the provinces. It also decided to send a Congress deputation to England to press the views of the Congress before the British Government.[2]

We may note here that Hasan Imam, with his wife and daughter, left Bankipur in the evening of the 25th July, 1919, en-route to England as a member of the deputation on behalf of the Congress and also of that for the All India Home Rule League. He was given a hearty send-off at the Railway Station, and amongst those present were P.R. Das, K.B. Datta, a Barrister of Patna, Rajendra Prasad, S.P. Sen, K.B. Zahiruddin, Wasi Ahmad, Maheshwar Prasad, B.B. Verma, S.N. Sahay, Gangadhar Das, Raghubir Dayal and Murari Prasad,[3] who constituted the educated middle class of Bihar.

To curb the progress of Indian nationalism, the government sought to arm itself with extra-ordinary powers through the Rowlatt Bill and the Anarchical and Revolutionary Crimes Act. As a protest against these, Mahatma Gandhi asked his countrymen to offer non-violent Satyagraha by observing hartal on the 6th April, 1919. The Government launched a reign of repression at Delhi and also at Lahore and Amritsar.[4] While on way to Amritsar, Mahatma Gandhi was arrested at Palwal, a wayside railway station in the Punjab, and was sent to Bombay under police escort. To add to all this came the Jallianwala Bagh Tragedy and the proclamation of martial law in the Punjab by its Lieutenant Governor, Michael O'Dyer.[5]

These measures aiming at a ruthless suppression of Indian nationalism produced a wave of discontent throughout the country and the Indian national movement was transformed into a people's fight for liberty in a true sense under the leadership of Mahatma Gandhi.

At the country's clarion call for national resistance against the repressive policy of an alien government, Bihar's soul was stirred and her leaders, who came from middle class, and people gave an enthusiastic response. The agitation in Bihar against the Rowlatt Bill began towards the end of February, 1919, and in March protest meetings, attended by all classes of people, were held at Patna, Gaya, Monghyr, Murzaffarpur, Chapra and Bhagalpur.[6] *The Searchlight* strongly denounced the Rowlatt Bill and began to exercise much influences in stimulating national feelings. The decision to participate in the hartal on the 6th April, the day of humiliation and prayer, was taken at a meeting held at the Qila Maidan, Patna City on the 4th April under the presidentship of Mazharul Haque, attended by prominent persons of the educated middle class like Rajendra Prasad, Hasan Imam and Purnendu Narayan. At the meeting attention of the audience was drawn to the Delhi incidents of the 30th March and great emphasis was laid on Hindu-Muslim unity. Preparations for the 6th April went apace. Another meeting was held in the evening of the 5th April, 1919, at the residence of Mazharul Haque to settle the programme for the next day. It was attended by many prominent persons,[7] and Purnendu Narayan Sinha was its president. The proceedings commenced with the singing of a national song by Tulsi Singh of Ajvan, P.S. Naubatpur, Patna. Rejendra Prasad requested all to be orderly in the next day's procession and some others also spoke.

On the 6th April, 1919, a huge procession under the leadership of Hasan Imam paraded the streets of Patna. On his personal guarantee to maintain order in the gathering, police was kept out of evidence as much as possible.[8] The processionists assembled at about 5 p.m. in the Qila Maidan, Patna City and the procession in fact passed off very quietly. A meeting was held there under the chairmanship of Hasan Imam. Others who spoke at this meeting were Rajendra Prasad, Mazharul Haque, Chandra Bansi Sahay, Mitter Lal of Mesaurhi, Maulvi Khurshed Hasnain and Purnendu Narayan Sinha. A large number of Patna University students were present at the meeting and participated in other activities of the day. People in large numbers from the mofussils also attended the meeting. There was dissatisfaction among the Sikhs in Patna City due to the Jallianwala Bagh massacre and Guru Charan Singh, a Sikh pleader, actively associated himself with the Satyagraha movement.

A number of policemen and office assistants, components of the middle class, did take part in the 'Humiliation Day' celebrations. At Patna, there was a complete hartal—not a shop was open, not a vehicle was plying in the whole town from noon till evening. In the villages the response was no less splendid and spontaneous. It was not only shopkeepers who observed the hartal, agriculturists too did not work in their fields and plough cattle and draught bullocks were given a holiday. All this was so spontaneous![9] These facts prove that the commercial, industrial and landed middle class played a great role in making the Satyagraha a success in Bihar.

Demonstrations took place and hartals were observed that day also at Muzaffarpur, Champaran, Monghyr, Jharia and Katras. At a meeting held on that date at Muzaffarpur a stirring speech containing reference to the Delhi incidents was read by Nafir Imam, nephew of Hasan Imam, on behalf of the president Mahboob Hasan Khan, chairman of the local municipality and late Member of the Legislative Council. In Champaran, Gorakh Prasad and Raghunath Lal, Pleaders of Motihari, Raj Kumar Shukla and Narayan Tammaji, Headmaster of the Gandhi School at Bhitharwa, were taking leading part.[10] The Satyagraha Day on the 6th April was observed in a peaceful manner. It was reported to the local government by one of their officers on the 13th April, 1919, "It is perfectly true that the Satyagraha observance of the 6th April was a thoroughly well-arranged and orderly affair.…"[11]

The agitation against the Rowlatt Bill began at the close of February, 1919 and in March protest meetings, attended by all classes of people, were held at Chapra.[12] On the 6th April, 1919, in response to the calls of Bihar leaders, demonstrations took place and hartals were observed throughout Saran district. Shops were closed. A mammoth meeting was held to the east of the Rajput School, Chapra on that day (i.e. 6th April, 1919) from 4 p.m. to 7 p.m. in which eight persons delivered spirited lectures. On the morning of the 7th April at about 10 o'clock a procession paraded the Chapra town carrying two black flags and shouting Mahatma Gandhi Ki Jai.[13] The news of Mahatma Oandhi's arrest, received at Patna in the afternoon of the 19th April, produced much excitement in Bihar. A meeting of the citizens of Patna was organised by the men of the middle class in the evening of the 11th April, over which Hasan Imam presided. He explained to the gathering the Satyagraha vow of Mahatma Gandhi and himself took this vow publicly. Mazharul Haque and some others followed suit in the meeting, and a registration centre was opened at the house of Rajendra Prasad for those who intended to accept this vow.[14] The other speakers at the meeting of the 11th April were Rajendra Prasad, Khan Sarfaraz Husain, Parameshwar Lal, Uma Shankar Verma, Pandit Balgovind Malaviya and C.B. Sahai. All counselled Hindu-Muslim unity and passive resistance.

Meetings of the Patna Provincial Association and the Patna Bar Association were held on the 25th and 23rd May respectively, at which resolutions were passed condemning the inhuman oppressions of the Government in the Punjab. Both the predominantly middle class associations protested against the action of the Military authorities in prohibiting lawyers from going to Lahore to defend accused persons before the special tribunal. At a joint meeting of the Bihar Provincial

Congress Committee and the Bihar Provincial Association held at Patna on the 13th of July, 1919, resolution was passed expressing feelings of horror at the cruel sentences passed by the martial law commissions and demanding the immediate recall of Lord Chelmsford. It was also deciced to invite the Congress to hold its next session in Bihar, and there was a suggestion that Mahatma Gandhi or Sankaran Nair should be invited to preside.[15] The Bihar Provincial Congress met at Laheriasarai on the 17th and 18th August, 1919. About one thousand people attended it, and among the delegates were Sachchidananda Sinha, Rajendra Prasad and Krishna Prakash Sen of Ghosi, Gaya. Dwarika Nath of Muzaffarpur, then a member of the Bihar Legislative Council, presided. With several resolutions, one was moved by Mr. Sachchidananda Sinha condemning the Punjab atrocities and demanding recall of Lord Chelmsford.[16] The persons of prominence, who dominated the working of the Bihar Congress, were mostly members of the educated middle class.

Thus we see that the middle class in Bihar played a dominant role in furthering the cause of Indian nationalism by enthusiastically responding to the new urge for freedom. The meetings to educate and prepare the people to make the Satyagraha Day a success were organised and addressed by the men of the middle class, particularly by the educated middle class elites of Bihar.

The Khilafat Movement and the Middle Class in Bihar

Turkey's tragic fate after the World War I fanned the flame of discontent which had already been burning in the minds of the Muslims, including those in India. All those had natural repercussions on Bihar. Under the leadership of the middle class this discontent was transformed into vigorous movement to pressurise the British Government to change her policy towards the Khalifa.

The Khilafat question and Turkey's tragic fate as a result of the war deeply wounded Muslim sentiments in India. In fact, while the Versailles Settlement was affected professedly to serve the cause of democracy and peace, India's national aspirations were not fulfilled. The Indian Muslims started a vigorous agitation to bring pressure upon British Government to change her policy towards Turkey. The success of this movement known as Khilafat Movement, was assured by the large measure of sympathy and support which the Muslims received from Mahatma Gandhi.[17]

The All India Khilafat Conference, meeting at Delhi on the 24th November, 1919 with Mahatma Gandhi as its president, adopted a resolution on non-cooperation with the Government. Mahatma Gandhi observed, "The Mussalmans have adopted a very important resolution. If the peace terms are unfavourable to them, which may God forbid, they will stop all cooperation with the Government. It is an inalienable right of the people thus to withhold cooperation. We are not bound to retain Governmant titles and honours, or to continue in Government service. If Government should betray us in a great cause like the Khilafat. we could not do otherwise than non-cooperation. We are, therefore, entitled to non-cooperate with government in case of betrayal.[18]

A public meeting was held at Patna in the Anjuman Islamia Hall on the 30th November, 1919 to consider the question of participation in the coming peace celebrations. The hall was packed to its utmost capacity; a large number of people had to remain standing outside and hundreds had to go away for want of accommodation. Hasan Imam proposed Maulana Shah Rasheed-ul-Haque Saheb to the chair and Rajendra Prasad seconded it. Rajendra Prasad observed in his speech that participation in the celebration was absolutely impossible.[19]

Several others also spoke and the resolution about non-participation in peace celebration was unanimously carried. Numerous leaflets and posters issued by the Delhi Anti-peace Celebration Publicity Board and the Calcutta Khilafat Committee appeared in the province.[20] At almost all important places people with nationalist sentiment abstained themselves from peace celebrations and the Anti-peace Celebrations agitations were most successful at Ranchi due to the extraordinary influence acquired among the people by Maulana Abul Kalam Azad during his internment there.[21]

The Khilafat movement was making progress and from March, 1920 it got additional impetus due to anti-Turkish agitation which had started in England.[22] All this provoked bitter resentment, which had its natural repercussions on Bihar. The police searched out in Patna City posters on the Khilafat question signed by Fazl-ul-Haque, Abdul Kasim, Hasrat Mohani, Taajuddin and Muhammad Akram Khan.[23] As desired by Maulana Abdul Bari, Maulana Abul Kalam Azad, Maulana Shaukat Ali and some others, a hartal was observed throughout the province on the 19th March, 1920. At Patna, the secretary of the Provincial Khilafat Committee A. Sami, son-in-law of Hasan Imam, took a leading part in organising this hartal.[24] At the invitation of the leaders of the Khilafat Movement in Bihar, including Mazharul Haque, Syed Mahmood and A. Sami, Maulana Shaukat Ali came to this province. Meetings were organised at Patna on the 24th and 25th of April, 1920, in which Maulana Shaukat Ali asked the assembled people to be ready to make whatever sacrifices that would be required to solve the Khilafat question. On this occasion, Maulvi Nurul Hasan, a Vakil of Patna High Court, also made a stirring speech.[25]

Leaving Patna on the 26th April, Maulana Shaukat Ali visited both Monghyr and Gaya. He addressed a meeting at Monghyr on the 27th April on the same lines as at Patna. At Gaya meeting Krishna Prakash Sen Sinha announced that he had returned to the Collector his certificate of honour, granted to him probably in recognition of his services in recruiting during the war.[26]

Mazharul Haque, while addressing a meeting at Chapra on the 5th of May, 1920, emphasized the importance of the Hindu-Muslim unity. Referring to the Khilafat Movement, he described the conduct of the British Government as highly treacherous and pointed out that like a thief it had stolen Mesopotamia for herself and distributed large portions of the Turkish Empire to others. He also advised the people to boycott the British goods.[27]

A conference of some of the leading Muslims of Bihar also attended by two Ulemas outside, Maulana Kadir Azad Sobhani of Kanpur and Maulana Abdul Majid of Mathura was held at Phulwari on the 15th and 16th May, 1920, and it was decided there to continue the movement.[28]

In the month of June, Ghulam Imam of Patna City and some others delivered speeches at two or three places in the province condemning the peace terms and advocating non-cooperation with the government. On the 5th June, A. Sami, Khwaja Abdul Majid aad Syed Mahmood arranged a mass prayer meeting in the Bankipur Maidan to offer prayers for the success of their efforts. Maulvi Etmad Husain, a youth of nineteen and Pesh Imam of Bakarganj mosque, joined the prayer meeting.[29]

Even before the meeting of this special session of the Congress, the Khilafatists had formally inaugurated it from the "Khilafat Day" on the 1st August. At a meeting held at Patna on this date, three resignations of titles and honorary offices were announced. Shah Badruddin Saheb of Phulwari resigned the title of Shama-ul-Ulema, Mr. Nurul Hasan resigned his membership of the Provincial Legislative Council and Shah Sulaiman of Phulwari resigned his honorary magistracy. A barrister of Monghyr, Muhammad Zubair also gave up his lucrative practice at the bar.[30]

To conclude, it can be said that the Khilafat Movement was organised by lawyers and other educated persons who constituted the educated middle class. Hasan Imam, Mazharul Haque, Rajendra Prasad, Maulvi Nurul Hasan, Muhammad Zubair and Krishna Prakash Sen Sinha were all lawyers. Besides, some educated persons of other professions and students also did their best to make the movement a success. Successful hartal throughout the province on the 19th March, 1920, proves that the commercial and industrial middle class also contributed commendably to this movement.

The Non-Cooperation Movement and Constructive Works and the Middle Class in Bihar

On the 20th July, 1920, Mahatma Gandhi announced that he would start Non-Cooperation Movement against the British Government from the 1st of August, 1920. Under the leadership of the middle class, Bihar responded enthusiastically. The Provincial Congress Committee at a meeting held on the 31st July in the Searchlight Office with S.C. Mishra, a High Court Vakil in the chair, passed the following resolutions amongst others:

"That the Committee approved of the principle of non-cooperation as the only effective means in the present circumstances of the country, of securing the redress of national wrongs and of the Khilafat question."

"That a committee be appointed to report on the programme of non-cooperation as enunciated by Mr. Gandhi with particular reference to the conditions of the province comprising of Mazharul Haque, Hasan Imam, Ganesh Datta Singh, Rajendra Prasad and Ajodhya Prasad. The Committee was to report by the 8th August and the meeting of this committee will be held on the 10th."[31]

This composition of this Committee proves that the leadership of the movement was in the hands of the educated middle class.

In response to Gandhi's call on 1st August, 1920, the shops were closed and business suspended at several towns including Chapra.[32]

Much more significant was the decision taken at the 12th session of the Bihar Provincial Conference, which met at

Bhagalpur on the 28th and 29th August under the presidentship of Rajendra Prasad, who, in his address in Hindi, put in a strong plea for Non-Cooperation.[33]

The resolution on Non-Cooperation was moved by Dharnidhar of Darbhanga and strongly supported by Muhammad Zubair of Monghyr, Ghulam Imam of Patna and Gorakh Prasad of Motihari. It was passed by an overwhelming majority and ran as follows:[34]

> "(a) Resolved that this conference approves of the movement of Non-Cooperation inaugurated by Mahatma Gandhi as a perfectly constitutional and effective weapon in the hands of the people."
>
> "(b) This conference further resolves that a committee be formed to formulate a practicable scheme suited to the conditions of the Province to give effect to the principle of non-cooperation."

The resolution of the non-cooperation movement was moved and supported mainly by lawyers and other members of the middle class.

The Committee, which consisted of Rajendra Prasad, Mazharul Haque and Shah Muhammad Zubair, was to report to a special session to be held at Saran. It is also highly significant that the Bihar Provincial Conference was "the first, under the inspiration of that veteran and farsighted custodian of our politics, Brajkishore Prasad, to add the attainment of Swaraj to the redress of the Khilafat and the Punjab wrongs as one of the objects for which Non-Cooperation was going to be adopted as the method."[35]

There was by this time profound awakening in Bihar and a considerable number of delegates (over three hundreds from this province) attended the special session of the Indian National Congress, held in Calcutta from 4th to 9th September, 1920, under the presidentship of Lala Lajpat Rai.

In September, 1920, session of the Congress, the following momentous resolution on non-cooperation moved by Mahatma Gandhi, was carried by 1885 votes against 873, about 180 of the Bihar delegates voting for it:

"In view of the fact that on the Khilafat question both the Indian and Imperial Governments have signally failed in their duty towards the Mussalmans of India."

"And in view of the fact that in the matter of the events of April of 1919 both the said Governments have grossly neglected or failed to protect the innocent people of the Punjab, and punish officers guilty of unsoldierly and barbarous behaviour towards them."

At the special session of the Congress held in Calcutta on the 4th to 9th September, 1920, resolution regarding the Non-Cooperation Movement was passed. The chief ingredients of the Movement were—(a) Surrender of titles and honorary offices and resignation from nominated seats in local bodies; (b) refusal to attend government levies, durbars and other official and semi-official functions held by government officials, or in their honour; (c) gradual withdrawal of children from schools and colleges owned, aided or controlled by government and in place of such schools and colleges, the establishment of national schools and colleges in the various provinces; (d) gradual boycott of British Courts by the lawyers and litigants, and the establishment of private arbitration courts by their aid for the settlement of private disputes; (e) refusal on the part of the military, clerical and labouring classes to offer themselves as recruits for service in Mesopotamia; (f) withdrawal by candidates of their candidature for election to the Reformed Councils, and refusal on the part of voter to vote for any candidate who may, despite the Congress advice, offer himself for election; and (g) boycott of foreign goods.[36]

Bihar set herself promptly to act according to this resolution and there were consequently activities in different directions at various places in this province, even before the annual session of the Congress which met at Nagpur in the month of December of the same year to ratify the decisions of the special session. Maulana Abdul Qadir Azad Sobhani of Kanpur halted at Arrah on his way back from Calcutta and delivered two speeches advocating non-cooperation and made a touching appeal to the audience to work for it.[37] Already on the 8th September, 1920, Swami Bidyanand, the leader of Kisan Sabha movement in north Bihar, which had been inaugurated a few months back, delivered a speech strongly denouncing government policy. Ghulum Imam made a speech at Arrah on the 17th September, 1920, charging the British Government with betrayal of Muslim interests.[38] There were soon announcements in the local papers that persons like Mazharul Haque, Rajendra Prasad, Gorakh Prasad of Motihari, Brajkishore Prasad and Dharnidhar of Darbhanga, Muhammad Shafi of Muzaffarpur and some others had withdrawn their candidature in the forthcoming council election.[39] Mazharul Haque announced withdrawal of his candidature in the following letter addressed by him to the Editor of *The Searchlight* and published in its issue of the 19th September, 1920.

The district of Saran took a leading part in the non-cooperation movement launched by the Indian National Congress. Mazharul Haque addressed the following letter to the Editor of *The Searchlight,* withdrawing his candidature from the Council election:

"It is the duty of every Congressman to obey the mandates of the Congress. The Congress has remarkably adopted a policy of non-cooperation with the government in all its aspects.

I as a Musalman can never co-operate with a government which is bent upon destroying Islam. As an Indian I cannot work with a government whose hands are stained with the blood of my countrymen of the Punjab. As long as their grievances remain unremedied, co-operation is simply out of question." He further wrote:

"Through the column of your esteemed paper I beg to thank numerous friends who were working with me to make my election a success. Now my advice to all the voters of the province is that they should refuse to give their votes to such men who intend to flout the resolutions of the Congress and co-operate with a cruel and irreligious government."[40]

On the 29th September, 1920, a letter of Brajkishore Prasad was published in *The Searchlight* which shows that several gentlemen, such as, Rajendra Prasad, Vakil, Gorakh Prasad, Vakil, Chandradeva Narayan, Bankey Bihari Lal, Braj Kishore Prasad, all Vakils, had withdrawn their candidatures from the ensuing elections to the Reformed Council from various constituencies in the province.[41]

On the 6th December, 1920, Mahatma Gandhi paid a visit to Chapra town, the headquarter of Saran. A mammoth meeting was held in the evening on the Collegiate School grounds. Prominent persons of Saran were present. Gandhiji was pleased to note that Zakaria Hashmi and Bindeshwari Prasad had given up their practice of the bar and he congratulated them for it. He observed, "I want Ramraj. But side by side I do not like that the zamindars should tyrannise the peasants. If the zamindars tyrannise them they had a right to resort to non-cooperation with them. At the present we have to non-cooperate with the government and hence we should not think over non-cooperation against each other."[42]

Rajendra Prasad addressed a letter to the Vice-Chancellor of Patna University resigning his membership of the Patna University Senate and Syndicate and various other University bodies and committees.[43] Rajendra Prasad also resigned his membership from the governing body of the Bihar National College (B.N. College, Patna).[44]

Jagat Narain, a laboratory assistant of the Patna College, resigned from his post on the 3rd December, 1920.[45]

Two students, Saiyid Mahmud Sher of Patna Law College and Abdul Bari Muhammad Saqi of the Bihar National

College, left the respective institutions where they had been studying.[46] Abdul Bari "subsequently proved to be one of the firebrands in Bihar."[47] Meetings began to be held by the leaders of Bihar frequently in the Patna and other districts of Bihar. The Bihar Provincial Congress Committee met on the 5th October and appointed a sub-committee consisting of Mazharul Haque, Rajendra Prasad, Brajkishore Prasad of Darbhanga and Muhammad Shafi of Muzaffarpur to give effect to the Congress instructions about non-cooperation. Sachchidananda Sinha, who presided over the meeting, now resigned from the presidentship of the Provincial Congress Committee,[48] as he was not in agreement with the changed policy of the Congress. There were changes in the personnel of the executive also of the Provincial Khilafat Committee. A. Sami resigned from its secretaryship and his place was taken by Hakim Abdul Hai of Bankipur with Abdul Bari and Ghulam Imam as Joint Secretaries and Hasan Imam Arzu of Phulwari and Mahmud Sher of Patna City as Assistant Secretaries.[49] The prominent leaders of the Provincial Khilafat Committee like Mazharul Haque, Ghulam Imam, Hasan Arzu, Abdul Bari and some others delivered highly inspiring speeches by organizing mass gatherings at different places, at Gaya on the 8th October, at Daltonganj on the 10th October, at Hilsa in the Patna district on the 29th October, at Khusrupur in Patna district on 3rd November, at Barh on 4th November, at Arrah on 6th November and at Bakhtiyarpur on 9th November.[50] About the middle of November, anti-liquor movement began at Dumraon in the district of Shahabad, where public meetings were held on the 13th November advocating abstinence from drink. The movement soon spread to other parts, and by January 1921 "it was in full swing in most of the districts throughout the province.[51]

During these few months, under the leadership and guidance of the middle class Bihar had given ample evidence of her fearless response to the new programme for the national fight. Mahatma Gandhi's visit to this province early in December 1920, though short and flying, gave additional impetus to it and had the effect of "rousing the whole province."[52] Subscriptions were collected at all the meetings addressed by Mahatma Gandhi. Over Rs. 7,000 were paid in cash. The women "gave away their ornaments including pearl and diamond bangles and rings."[53] Mahatma Gandhi was accompanied by Maulana Shaukat Ali and Maulana Abul Kalam Azad, and in course of his tour in the province he delivered highly inspiring speeches at several places.[54] Maulana Shaukat Ali and Mazharul Haque also spoke at most of these meetings. From Monghyr, Mahatma Gandhi went to Maqsudpur Mohalla and met there Sajjada Nashin Umar Saheb. One result of Mahatma Gandhi's visit to Bhagalpur was "the inauguration in that district and in the Santhal Parganas of the anti-liquor movement."[55]

At the Muzaffarpur, Mahatma Gandhi addressed a big gathering in the Tilak Maidan. A song, Firangi Sangit, composed by Manoranjan Sinha of Chapra was sung at this meeting.[56] The prominent national leaders of Muzaffarpur, Maulana Shafi Daudi, Vindheshwari Prasad Verma, Maulvi Nazir Ahmad and Janakdhari Prasad, had already begun to tour the district for propagation of the new national programme; and in the beginning of the October 1920, they had convened the first meeting for this purpose at Bhagwanpur in the compound of the local M.E. School.[57] They returned to Muzaffarpur via Biddupur, Desari, Mahnar and Mahuwa. At Biddupur they received much encouragement from Thakur Bimla Prasad. After the Tilak Maidan meeting at Muzaffarpur, referred to above, they divided themselves into two batches. One batch proceeded to Sitamarhi where Nawab Singh and his son Thakur Ramnandan Singh joined them. Meetings were addressed by them in almost every thana of the Sitamarhi sub-division.[58] The other batch went to Katra, Minapur, Paru, Baruraj, Sahebganj and Sakra. Some of these workers addressed meetings in the Sonepur fair, which is held every year during autumn.

It was under Mahatma Gandhi's influence during his short tour in Bihar in December 1920, that in the beginning of 1921 some national schools were started here and some existing schools were nationalised by repudiation of affiliation to University and refusal to accept grants-in-aid from government.[59] In June 1922 there were 41 high schools spread all over the province, teaching 4,500 students, and there were about 600 primary and middle schools teaching 17,000 students.[60]

Mahatma Gandhi was decisively in favour of the establishment of a National College in Bihar. The local leaders of the new movement were at first somewhat vacillating in this respect due to uncertainty of funds for their maintenance as the "senior leaders had all parted company on the question of non-cooperation."[61] But Mahatma Gandhi gave them the much needed impetus by also placing at their disposal for this purpose seven or eight thousand rupees then collected by him in Bihar.[62] Then "with the object of providing instruction to the students who are withdrawing from government and government-controlled institutions and with a view to provide education on sound lines to the youngmen of the province to prepare them for service to the country, as also to give them instructions of a practical nature to enable them to earn their livelihood,[63] the Bihar National College was started on the 5th January, 1921."[64] Its formal inauguration was to be made shortly by Mahatma Gandhi.

The Duke of Connaught reached Patna in the morning of the 6th February, accompanied by Kasturbai and Muhammad Ali,[65] and performed that day the opening ceremony of the National College (already started) and of the Bihar Vidyapith. The Bihar Vidyapith was "to co-ordinate the activities of all the national institutious that were springing up in the province and to control and guide them'.'[66]

Mazharul Haque became Chancellor and Brajkishore Prasad, Vice-Chancellor of the Vidyapith and Rajendra Prasad became Principal of the National College, resigning from their respective posts. Badri Nath Varma of the Department of English, Bihar National College, Jagannath Prasad of the Department of Sanskrit, Patna College, Prem Sunder Bose of the Department of Philosophy, T.N.J. College, Bhagalpur joined it as professors. Jagat Narain Lal, Ramcharitra Singh and Abdul Bari were also among its teaching staff.[67]

The National College started with a few students. "Soon afterwards", wrote Rajendra Prasad in 1931, "some of best students of the University, most of whom were scholarship holders and prizemen, came out of the Government College and marched in a body to the National College where they were welcome by us. Some of them stuck to us and are still doing national work. Others, however, worked for a year or more, then went back and some of them are holding responsible posts in Government service today."[68]

The new spirit of awakening had by this time penetrated into the ranks of the students, who began to play gradually an important role in India's battle for liberty till it was finally won. The various sacrifices aad martyrdom of our unsophisticated, ardent and inspired youths for the achievement of our country's freedom will ever remain written in letters of gold on the pages of its history. By the end of the year 1920 several students of the colleges and schools, including no less than 110 students[69] of the Bihar School of Engineering, left their respective institutions. Foundation of a national school was laid at Hajipur during Mahatma Gandhi's tour in Bihar. A national school was started at Nawadah in the Gaya district and another national school, at first supported by the Khilafat fund, was established at the Bakarganj mohalla of Bankipur, J.B. Kripalani performing its opening ceremony.[70] Students who had left schools and colleges with a batch from the Bihar School of Engineering were accommodated in the Sadaqat Ashram near Digha in the Patna district under the charge of Mazharul Haque, who, like an inspired hero, marched to that site with his youthful comrades by leaving his magnificent building called the 'Sikandar Manzil' on the Fraser Road and discarding all luxuries of life determined to give the rest of his life to Swaraj work.[71]

In Tirhut Division, the Chapra Collegiate School developed into a national school and there was considerable unrest in the Greer Bhumihar Brahman Collegiate School at Muzaffarpur.[72] After Mahatma Gandhi's visit to Muzaffarpur, about thirty students (according to Government report) left the Greer Bhumihar Brahman Collegiate there.[73] There were then some cases of non-cooperation in schools in the mofussil areas of the Tirhut Division. Among others, the headmaster of the Bagaha M.E. School in Champaran took a prominent part in the movement, while one teacher and 34 boys left the Hajipur High School. The Northbrook School (Zila School), Darbhanga and the Watson School at Madhubani were also affected to some extent.[74] In Bhagalpur about forty students (according to Government report) withdrew themselves from the T.N.J. College.[75]

The students of Bihar had for some years an organisation of their own, called Behari Students' Conference, which functioned as a very important institution till 1920-21.

Rev. C.F. Andrews presided over the 15th Session of the Behari Students' Conference held at Daltonganj on the 10th October, 1920. The issue of *The Searchlight*, dated the 10th October contained an appeal to the students by R.K.L. Nandkeolyar, a Patna Barrister, to adopt non-cooperation. At the Daltonganj session of the Conference a resolution was passed requesting the Central Association and the District Association to take the following pledge from the students : "I solemnly declare that I will not use any cloth or clothes unless I am satisfied that it is Swadeshi."[76]

A special session of the conference was to be held at Patna in November. This special session, attended by 157 delegates, actually met at Patna on the 9th January, 1921. Mazharul Haque, Rajendra Prasad and the other leaders were present at its meeting and some of them addressed it. Gajadhar Prasad, B.L., presided. The Bihari Students' Conference in its special session called upon students of Bihar and Orissa, of and above 16 years of age, to withdraw immediately and unconditionally from Government aided or controlled institutions and appealed to the guardians of those below 16 to withdraw their wards from the same.

The 35th ordinary session of the Indian National Congress, meeting at Nagpur in December 1920, with Shri C. Vijayaraghavachariar as its president, ratified the Calcutta Session's resolution on non-cooperation. Two prominent leaders, C.R. Das and Lala Lajpat Rai, had now accepted it. In fact, the former moved the resolution and the latter seconded it.[77]

A large number of Bihar delegates attended the Nagpur session of the Congress and they returned imbued with a new spirit which found expression in varied activities consistent with the changed programme and principles adopted there. Volunteers began to be recruited in different parts.[78] Temperance and anti-liquor campaigns were pushed on, the gospel of swadeshi was preached among the masses with great zeal and vigorous efforts were made for the formation of local Panchayats and Seva Samities.

In fact, the student community in Bihar was intoxicated with the spirit of new patriotism and hundreds of them deserted schools and colleges at Patna, Muzaffarpur, Bhagalpur and Monghyr to join the national movement. Among the Bihari students then reading in Calcutta, Bajrang Sahay had withdrawn himself from the Law College in September 1920, that is, shortly after the meeting of the special session of the Congress in Calcutta. Rajendra Prasad, the principal guide of the non-cooperation movement in Bihar thus reviewed its progress in schools and colleges till the middle of March, 1921 :

"The following professors and teachers have resigned their posts and have either joined national educational institutions or taken to national work—Badrinath Varma, M.A., Professor of B.N. College; Jaleshwar Prasad, M.A., Professor of B.N. College; Jagat Narayan, B.Sc., Demonstrator, Patna

College; Pande Jagannath Prasad, M.A., Professor, Patna College; N.R. Malkani, M.A., Professor, G.B.B. College; Prem Sunder Bose, M.A., Professor, T.N.J. College; Jagdish Sharma, I.Sc., Teacher, Biharsharif; Bindeshwar Prasad, Teacher, High English School, Hajipur; Bulaki Sahu, B.A., Headmaster, H E. School, Hajipur; Dwarka Prasad, B.A., Sub-Inspector of Schools; Jainandan Jha, Teacher, Hajipur High School; Jwala Prasad Sinha, Benares Hindu University; Janki Prasad Varma, Teacher, High English School, Sitamarhi; Nazir Ahmad, B.A., B.T., Teacher, Zila School, Chapra; and Phuldeo Sahai Varma, M.Sc., Professor of Chemistry, Benares Hindu University has promised to join the National University at Patna and has resigned his post there but has not yet been relieved. A National College has been established at Patna. The number of students on the rolls is 71."[79]

Approximately "some two hundred students, most of them belonging to college classes and coming from the educated middle class, are devoting their time to village organisation work. The National College in Patna, which was opened sometime in the early part of January 1921, has since been converted into a University and is arranging to hold examination for non-cooperating students. Already about 500 students have registered themselves for various examinations."[80]

In pursuance of a clause in the Resolution on Non-cooperation passed at the Nagpur Congress, a Sub-Committee, called the organisation committee, was organised with the following gentlemen: Mazharul Haque, Deep Narayan Singh, Braj Kishore Prasad, Rajendra Prasad, Dharnidhar Prasad, Maulvi Mohammad Shafi, Krishna Prasad Sen Sinha, Abdul Bari and Ram Binod Singh. In consultation with Mahatma Gandhi the organisation committee appointed some leaders for the movement in their areas. They were—Gorakh Prasad (Champaran), Brajkishore Prasad (Darbhanga), Krishna Prasad Sen Sinha (Gaya), Gajadhar Prasad (Bhagalpur), Bajrang Sahay (Hazaribagh), Maulvi Mohammad Safi (Muzaffarpur),

Maulvi Zakaria Hashmi (Saran) and Muhammad Zubair (Monghyr).

The above organisational arrangements show that organisational leadership remained predominantly in the hands of the educated elites having landed base.

Bihar did not lag behind in boycotting bars. Besides Rajendra Prasad, who had been by now duly recognised as an all-India national leader, there were several other lawyers in different parts of this province who renounced their practice to join the movement for the country's emancipation from the deadening evils of an alien rule.[81]

By the beginning of 1921, non-violent non-cooperation for the country's independence and regeneration had become a confirmed faith with many in Bihar. Rajendra Prasad and the other leaders of the province began to undertake extensive tours and to hold frequent meetings to propagate the message of non-cooperation among the people in general. These were attended by thousands of people.[82] We read in a Government report: "The situation was most serious in the Tirhut Division where Muzaffarpur was the storm centre. Between the 25th January and the 5th February (1921) no less than 56 non-cooperation meetings were held in this district alone."[83]

The movement made rapid progress in the Shahabad district in the early months of 1921. As a result of a meeting held at Piru, a panchayat for the trial of civil and criminal cases was started. Panchayats were established also in villages Jamauli and Deorhia of Rajpur P.S. and at several other villages in the jurisdiction of Barhara, Shahpur, Dumraon and Barhampur thanas. A Swaraj Sabha was formed in the village Darigaon, and national school was started at Koath, P.S. Bikramganj. Teachers and students of different schools had begun to take interest in the movement, viz., Shivpunan Sahay, then a teacher of the Arrah Town High School, Suraj Prasad Tiwari and Ramdeo Tiwari, Pandits of the Sanskrit Tol in Barhara P.S., the teachers of Dehri P.S. and some others.

Bindhya Basini Prasad, after giving up the bar, became the Headmaster of the Arrah National School. In the Shahabad district, as also in some other areas, by the months of February and March 1921, the non-cooperation movement had "reached the phase of intensive organisation." The workers also continued to hold meetings. On the 11th March, a meeting was addressed at Koath by Swami Sahajanand, leader of the Kisan Sabha, Bindhya Basini Prasad and Jaiprakash Lal, a teacher of the B.S. School at Buxar. A police officer visiting Koath in the end of March "found the non-cooperation movement there very strong", as he writes in his own report. On the 20th March, a meeting was held in the Arrah National School and Bindhya Basini Prasad, Arunjay Sahay Varma, Swami Sahajanand and Mahfuz Alam addressed it; and a definite programme was formed for the propaganda work in which the district was divided into four parts according to subdivisions.[84]

There was considerable stir in Monghyr under the leadership of Maulvi Muhammad Zubair, a lawyer of the town. Monghyr observed complete hartal on the occasion of the visit of His Excellency, Lord Sinha, the Governor of Bihar & Orissa. Deep Narayan Singh made regular tours throughout the Bhagalpur district and meetings were frequently held at different places. On the 19th February there was a partial hartal and on the 21st February a complete hartal in Bhagalpur. Purnea district had also begun to experience the influence of the non-cooperation movement. Rajendra Prasad addressed meetings at Purnea on the 13th and 14th February, 1921.[85] Some other workers also helped the spread of the movement there, the ferry-farmers and the pound-keepers of the Kishanganj subdivision completely boycotted the auction settlements.[86] At Gaya there was a police strike on the 9th February. Though the government ascribed it to economic causes, there is no doubt that the non-cooperation movement also influenced it. Its leader Damodar Prasad, a writer head constable, was, as a government report notes, "certainly in communication with the non-cooperationists."[87]

The Chhotanagpur Division also was stirred by the movement from the middle of November, 1920, and from January

1921, the Adivasis of that area, such as Oraons and the Mundas, responded in large numbers to the appeals made to them by a batch of Congress workers. This was due to the influence also of the Tana Bhagat movement, which had started among the Oraons from 1915 as a reform movement laying stress on "increased simplicity and purity of life."[88]

Prominent among the Congress workers, who came from the educated middle class, of that area in those days were Gulab Tiwari (formerly a typist in the Ranchi District Board Office), Usman, Head Maulvi in the Anjuman Islamia Madrasa and a follower of Maulana Abul Kalam Azad, Ram Tahal Brahmachari and Ramchandra Prasad, Swami Biswanand, a famous labour leader of the time, occasionally visited Ranchi and the coalfield areas and delivered inspiring speeches. On the 19th February, a meeting was held at Lohardaga and by this time three other non-cooperation leaders, namely, Imam Ali, Ram Rachhya Sharma and Swami Biswanand had come to Ranchi.[89] On the 16th March there was almost a complete hartal at Ranchi[90] as a protest against settlement of excise shops to some Kalals and Sundis. At Purulia also there was complete hartal on the date fixed for excise settlement.[91] The Tana Bhagats were attending the meetings organised by non-cooperation workers and their leaders were in touch with the non-cooperation leaders.[92] The Deputy Commissioner of Ranchi had informed the Commissioner of Chhotanagpur on the 9th March 1921: "The Tana Bhagat movement continues to give trouble and there is ample evidence that the efforts of agitators to associate it with non-cooperation has given the movement new life."

From about the 7th of March Rajendra Prasad began his touring to places like Dhanbad, Hazaribagh, Daltonganj and Ranchi. At Jharia, Mazharul Haque addressed a meeting in stirring language.[93] Speeches were delivered by Rajendra Prasad and Swami Biswanand at Ranchi on the 21st March and very soon after this earnest efforts were made by some to organise the movement in the Khunti subdivision.[94] Pandit Motilal Nehru paid a hurried visit to the coalfield areas on the

26th March, 1921, and addressed meetings at Dhanbad, Jharia and Chatra.[95]

There was rapid progress in the establishment of panchayats. At Saran, Rajendra Prasad and Mazharul Haque gave personal attention to it. It is stated in a Government report that "Panchayats had been established in a large number of villages in the following districts every day : Saran, Muzaffarpur, Champaran, Darbhanga, Patna, Gaya, Shahabad, Bhagalpur, Hazaribagh, Ranchi and Palamau.[96] In a statement on this subject issued by Rajendra Prasad in *The Searchlight* of the 16th March, 1921, he mentioned that the number of Panchayats would be several thousands. Cases were tried in the panchayat courts. But at some places the people carried their zeal so far as to resort to social boycott to enforce their decisions.[97]

At Giridih, there was a tremendous enthusiasm for Non-cooperation movement, the most prominent worker there being Bajrang Sahay, an inhabitant of Pachamba. The Commissioner of Chhotanagpur wrote to the I.G., Police, Bihar on the 2nd May 1921, "You are perhaps aware that Non-cooperation has probably taken a stronger hold in Giridih than anywhere else in this Division. It is easily accessible to the agitator and there have been a large number of meetings held. It is also quite clear that they have got a very thorough organisation of volunteers and they have started panchayats and have a very fullfledged system of boycott."

At Jamshedpur a mass meeting was organised on the maidan of the G. Town in the evening of the 8th March, 1921. Krishna Ram, K. Bhatta, G. Setti and Teja Singh delivered speeches on Non-cooperation, boycott of foreign goods and swadeshi and for giving up drinks.[98] A batch of Non-cooperation volunteers had come to Chaibasa from outside to prevent the settlement of excise liquor shops and a mass meeting was held there in the evening of the 13th March, 1921. Maulana Osmal Ali, Bibhuti Bhusan Banerjee, an ex-Mukhtear of Ranchi and Ramchandra Sahi also of Ranchi, addressed this meeting and delivered stern speeches against drink and holding liquor leases. Similar meetings were held both in morning and evening on the 14th March. The Deputy Commissioner held an auction at noon on that day, and, as he writes, for "liquor shops not a single bid was obtained."[99]

Santhla Parganas was also influenced by the movement from its very beginning. Several workers for its cause visited different parts of this district from that time. Danshanand, a non-cooperation leader, arrived at Jamtara on the 26th February and exhorted the people to give up drinking. Santhals numbering not less than twenty (according to Movernment report), attended the meeting addressed by him.[100]

There was undoubtedly unique awakening in Bihar during the early months of 1921, and the Government in their anxiety to suppress it resorted to various means of repression. Armed with the authority of the Rainy Circular, the Government officers began to follow repression on a large scale in different ways. On hearing from the Superintendent of Police, Arrah, that Mazharul Haque and Rajendra Prasad were to visit Arrah on the 17th February, 1921, W. Johnston, District Magistrate of Shahabad passed an order on the previous day under section 144 Cr. P. C. preventing them to enter Arrah. There was a wave of repression in the Muzaffarpur, Darbhanga and Champaran districts. E. O. Lee, the Subdivisional Officer of Sitamarhi, passed an astounding order to prohibit or restrict the despatch of any telegram, which was considered "objectionable (by Government) from the violent seditious character of the language applied."[101]

Mahatma Gandhi had already expressed his opinion in an article entitled "Repression in Bihar", reproduced in *The Searchlight* of the 13th March, 1921 from *The Young India* dated the 2nd March, 1921 :

"Bihar is a province in which the most solid work is being done in connection with Non-Cooperation. Its leaders understand the true spirit of non-violence."

The meeting of the All-India Congress Committee, held at Bezwada in the Madras Presidency on the 31st of March and 1st April, 1921, declared[102] the Government's repressive policy to be "totally unwarranted by the situation in the country." This Committee was, however, of opinion that, "apart from the fact that Civil Disobedience is not expressly comprised in the Congress resolution in relation to Non-Cooperation, the country is not yet sufficiently disciplined, organised and ripe for the immediate taking up of Civil Disobedience", advised by way of preparation, "all those upon whom orders may be served voluntarily to conform to them." For purely constructive work it passed a resolution asking the people to concentrate on three items—(1) bringing the All-India Tilak Swaraj fund to one crore of rupees, (2) putting on the Congress register one crore of members, (3) introducing the villages and cities twenty lakhs of charkhas (spinning wheels). All the three items were to be completed by the 30th June next, the respective provinces contributing to each according to the ratio of its population.[103]

Bihar promptly set herself to the task of fulfilling these conditions. On the commencement of the Satyagraha week on the 6th April 1921, Rajendra Prasad observed, "The Satyagraha week has come once again. It was on the 6th April that India recovered her soul. The Congress Committee has laid severe tests and we have to get through it, if we are worth anything. In this province we have to raise 10 lakhs of rupees and to enroll 10 lakhs of members on the Congress register and to set 2 lakhs of Charkhas in good working order. In a province with a population of nearly 3 crores, 10 lakhs of rupees and members ought not to be difficult to get in the sacred satyagraha week. It ought not be difficult to find men to devote themselves to this work."[104]

Patna duly observed the Satyagraha Day.[105] There was almost complete hartal in this city on that day, and Rajendra Prasad then made another stirring appeal to the people.

During the Satygraha week efforts were concentrated on the collection of Tilak Swaraj Fund, and a second hartal was observed in most of the districts. With various handicaps, Bihar collected Rs. 7.5 lakhs for the Tilak Swaraj Fund, enrolled a large number of members,[106] and introduced many charkhas for khadi work. Further, by the end of June, a Congress Organisation was built up here, which "stood the test of the time and government repression."[107] When the All-India Congress Committee, elected under new rules, met in July 1921, Bihar was given a seat in All-India Working Committee.[108]

In fact, the province was marching on the road to Swarajya with remarkable speed, undaunted by the odds of different kinds. The leaders from within and outside continued to supply impetus to it by their inspiring speeches and unceasing activities. At the annual conference of the Anwarul-Ulama, held at Gaya in April 1921, Maulana Abul Kalam Azad delivered a fiery and highly appealing speech, which produced a great impression on the minds of the audience.[109] Lakshmi Narain Misser (an externee in 1919) of Jogia, P.S. Barahpur in the Shahabad district, opened a national school at Gaighat. Another National School was established at Simri, P.S. Buxar in the month of June.

In the Ranchi district, the Non-Cooperation movement spread among the Mundas. Deo Narayan Mehta, an inhabitant of Parsa in the district of Gaya, who had been taking a prominent part in anti-liquor campaign, addressed a meeting at the National School of Daltonganj on 31st May, 1921, in which he strongly criticised government's repressive actions.[110] Bindeshwari Pathak of Palamau district spoke in the same strain before a gathering at Panki in that district on the 9th June, 1921.[111] Mazharul Haque had undertaken an extensive tour in Orissa and the South Chhotanagpur. He delivered a highly impressive speech at Chakradharpur on the 19th June, 1921.[112]

With a view to nationalising the Municipalities and District as well as Local Bodies, the Congress candidates, most of whom came from the middle class, decided now to contest the Municipal elections. Their efforts were remarkably successful in the Municipal election held at Muzaffarpur in the month of April, 1921, where "practically all the votes were in the hands of the Non-Cooperators."[113]

Congress candidates won the Municipal elections at some other places also. For example, at Motihari, four staunch Non-Cooperators, namely, Gorakh Prasad, Debi Lal Sahu, Kedar Nath Sahu and Ramdayal Prasad Sahu, were elected.[114]

The Indian National Congress continued to lay great stress on constructive activities. The All-India Congress Committee, the first to be elected according to the new constitution, meeting at Bombay on the 28th, 29th and 30th July, 1921, passed a resolution for concentrating attention "upon attaining complete boycott of foreign cloth by the 30th September next and on manufacture of Khaddar by stimulating hand-spinning and hand-weaving."

The 31st of July, 1921, witnessed a bonfire of foreign cloth by Mahatma Gandhi at Umar Sobhani's yard at Pearl (Bombay). The 1st of August was the death anniversary of the great patriot Lokamanya Tilak, and the whole country celebrated it with deep inspiration and feeling of reverence. Bihar celebrated the death anniversary of Lokamanya Tilak on the 1st August by organising processions and meetings at all important places. Boycott of foreign cloth was also formally inaugurated here on that day, and some quantity of foreign cloth was burnt after the meetings were over.[115]

On the 16th August, 1921, a meeting of the All-India Congress Working Committee was held in the Sadaqat Ashram at Patna. The members present were Mahatma Gandhi, Pandit Motilal Nehru, Rajendra Prasad, Maulana Muhammad Ali and Seth Jamuna Lal Bajaj. It passed eighteen resolutions. The most important of them was regarding boycott of foreign cloth.

The Bihar Provincial Congress Committee, which was constituted by the middle class, also met at Patna towards the end of August and decided to take certain steps to make boycott of foreign cloth effective by the 30th September next. Steps were taken at different centres for furtherance of anti-liquor movement, training of volunteers of the right type and boycott of foreign cloth. The last item now engaged the greater attention of the workers, and special effort was made in this respect at Bhagalpur, the chief centre of cloth distribution in the province. Lala Lajpat Rai visited this place on the 10th September, 1921, and appealed to the people to carry on boycott work with vigour.[116] Success attended cloth boycott campaigns at other places too, and persons inspired by the feelings of patriotism were making fervent appeals to the common people through their speeches.[117]

To help Bihar in meeting the financial needs for organisational work of Khadi, Mahatma Gandhi secured for the Provincial Committee a substantial grant from the All-India Swarajya Fund and loaned to the Khadi Kutir, which was engaged in the production of Khadi.[118]

Arrest of Ali Brothers and some other leaders caused much excitement throughout the country and hundreds of meetings began to be held where the Karachi resolution was repeated word by word. Mahatma Gandhi intensified the campaign by deciding to take tearing of cloth; and on the 21st September he became a 'half-naked Fakir'. In Bihar, protest meetings were held at all important places. At a cloth boycott meeting, held at Patna City on the 21st September, Syed Mahmood expressed that the Muhammadans of Bihar shared the sentiments of this resolution and were prepared to join the Ali Brothers in prison.[119] On the 30th September, Khaddar processions were taken out and meetings were held at Patna, Muzaffarpur, Bhagalpur and other places. There was public bonfire of bundles of foreign cloth at all these meetings and enthusiastic speeches in support of swadeshi. In a meeting at Dhanbad one of the speakers strongly supported the Karachi resolution and advocated immediate introduction of civil disobedience.[120]

The Bihar Provincial Conference met at Arrah early in October 1921 under the presidentship of Maulvi Muhammad Shafi. Here the resolution of the Karachi Conference was endorsed and a resolution was passed to boycott the visit of the Prince of Wales. Another resolution, moved by Babu Dharnidhar Shroff of Bhagalpur, "recorded the expression of Conference opinion that the Sifton Circular (about the boycott of foreign cloth) made it perfectly clear that the British Government existed in India solely for trade and that its real objective was to so strengthen the foundation of trade helping those engaged in exploiting the country." The next resolution was on the subject of Civil Disobedience. By it a request was made to the Working Committee of the Congress and Mahatma Gandhi "to permit them in Bihar to start Civil Disobedience and to specify the items which might be taken up."[121]

On the occasion a special meeting of persons interested in the Seva Samiti Movement was convened at Arrah on the 3rd October, 1921. A strong Central Committee was formed to make it effective and by the end of November there were about 1500 members of Seva Samities, pledged to do social service in the districts of Tirhut and Patna Divisions, Bhagalpur, Monghyr, Manbhum and Hazaribagh. The Central Committee was composed of Mahendra Prasad of Chapra (President), Badrinath Varma of Patna (Vice-President), Baijnath Prasad Singh, M.L.A. from Muzaffarpur, Jagat Narain Lal of Patna, Maulvi Muhammad Latif Husain of Muzaffarpur and Bhagwan Prasad of Bankipur (all Secretaries), Ganesh Datt Singh, M.L C. (Treasurer), Mathura Prasad of Chapra (Captain), Purnendu Narayan Sinha, M.L.C. and some others (Members).[122]

Rajendra Prasad had to leave the conference on the 2nd October, as he was required to attend a meeting of the leaders convened by Mahatma Gandhi at Bombay on the 4th October, 1921. Copies of this manifesto and of the Delhi Fatwa were circulated in Bihar; and, as in other parts, Bihar indeed was forging ahead in the fight for freedom on the path chalked out by the Indian National Congress. Constructive activities were pushed on with accelerated speed in the teeth of governmental opposition and systematic efforts were made to foster the use of Swadeshi cloths and Charkha. "Forty-eight depots were opened in eleven districts of the province to place cotton and Charkhas within easy reach of the people. In most of the districts the sale of Swadeshi cloth was reported to have increased considerably."[123] Shrimati Sarla Devi visited several districts in the Chhotanagpur Division preaching the cult of Khaddar and Charkha. The local leaders of Bihar spoke for these at meetings held in different parts of the province[124] during October and November, 1921, to propagate the instructions of the leaders.

The sixteenth session of the Behari Students' Conference met at Hazaribagh on the 5th and 6th October, 1921, under the presidentship of Sarla Devi. She made a stirring appeal to the students for dedication to the service of the country and for throwing off the "yoke of foreign domination over the soul." Bajrang Sahay and Ram Narayan Singh of Hazaribagh district delivered inspiring speeches on the occasion. Resolutions were passed at this conference, which were: (1) recommending the boycott of government schools and colleges; (2) that students should devote atleast half-an-hour every working day and two hours every Sunday to the spinning of yarn; (3) prohibiting the student community from taking part in the festivities connected with the visit of His Royal Highness, the Prince of Wales;(4) requiring every student to boycott foreign cloth and use Khaddar only; and (5) commending the action of those students who had offered their services as volunteers for propaganda work.[125]

The All-India Congress Committee met at Delhi on the 5th November, 1921, to authorise every province on its own responsibility to undertake Civil Disobedience including non-payment of taxes in the manner considered most suitable by the respective Provincial Congress Committees, subject to the conditions that every individual civil resister must have fulfilled the part of the N.C.O. programme applicable to him, should know spinning, must have discarded foreign cloth and taken over khaddar, must be a believer in Hindu-Muslim unity, believer in Non-violence as absolutely essential for the redress of the Khilafat and Punjab wrongs and the attainment of Swarajya, and, if a Hindu must by his personal conduct show that he regards untouchability as a blot upon nationalism. In regard to mass civil disobedience, a district or tahsil should be treated as a unit and therein a majority of the population must have adopted full Swadeshi and must be clothed out of hand-spun cloth in that area and must believe in and practise all the other items of N.C.O. No one should expect support out of public funds. It was to the working committee to waive any condition on the application of P.C.C S.[126]

At several places in Bihar the constructive programmes were carried on, e.g., in Dighwara Police Station there were then about seven thousand spinning wheels and five to six thousand looms that were working. The Gandhi Kutir at Malkhachak under the Dighwara Police Station in the district of Saran, was doing very useful work under the direction of Ram Binod Singh.

Madan Gopal Joshi, Professor Bari and Kashinath were deputed by the Bihar Provincial Congress Committee for the swadeshi propaganda in Sonepur fair. They reached Sonepur on the 12th November 1921, accompanied by a dozen of students of Bihar Vidyapith. Posters were affixed on the walls of a large number of buildings at Sonepur. Leaflets were distributed daily, in which the use of swadeshi clothes was advocated. Batches of hawkers were engaged to go round the Mela and sell khaddar. Music procession also used to pass daily through all roads and lanes atleast once a day.[127]

In the matter of arbitration also, the Dighwara thana was doing well. Each village had a Panchayat Committee which decided matters of disputes in that village. Appeal against its decision could be made to a body called Halka Panchayat, consisting of representatives of ten to fifteen surrounding villages. From the Halka Panchayat a case might go up to the final Panchayat Board consisting of five honest and influential men, nominated by the Thanas Congress Committee itself.[128]

The Prince of Wales landed in Bombay on November 17, 1921, at about 10 a.m. In accordance with the resolution of the Working Committee of the Congress, the hartal was observed all over India on that day as a mark of the people's dissatisfaction and disaffection with the system of government. Referring to Patna, a government report states, "In Patna the hartal of the 17th November, 1921, was complete success. There were a large number of meetings at which Delhi Fatwas were repeated. About 400 national volunteers were present in the Sonepur fair on the 17th November, and there was complete hartal there on that day.[129] In Bhagalpur 200 copies of the Fatwa printed in Meerut were distributed and cyclostyled copies were circulated in Gaya. In the month of November, two Sub-Inspectors, four Head Constables and 10 Constables resigned. Ten School-masters, one Sub-Inspector of Schools, one Inspector of Sanskrit Schools and two Clerks also joined the Non-Cooperation. Earlier in this year Ramnandan Singh, a Sub-Inspector of Police had resigned at Hajipur. Subsequently in Purnea a Writer Head Constable, father of Rambinode Singh, "was discovered (by the government) spreading Non-Cooperation ideas and encouraging hostility to government among chaukidars and villages in Palasi Police Station where he was stationed."[130]

At a meeting of the Provincial Congress Committee, held at Patna on the 27th November, 1921, it was thought that either Basantpur thana in the Saran district or Katra in the district of Muzaffarpur would be selected as the place for first experiment in civil disobedience in Bihar, the final selection being reserved for a meeting fixed to be held at Chapra on the 10th December.[131] Arrangements in view of the Prince of Wales' coming visit to Patna on the 22nd and 23rd December were considered. Preparations had been proceeding everywhere for observing a hartal throughout the Province on that day, and at this meeting the leaders decided upon taking all possible precautions to prevent disturbances in that connection.[132]

In fact, when the fixed time came, hartal was observed in a perfectly peaceful manner at all places in the province.[133]

It was as its meeting of the 27th November, 1921, that the Bihar Provincial Congress Committee, following the instructions issued by the Working Committee of the All-India Congress after its meeting at Bombay on the 23rd November, also formed the Bihar National Volunteer Corps (Qaumi Sevak Dal) "out of the members of the Seva Samitis, Khilafat workers and Congress workers from the whole province." A Central Board of control was formed with its headquarters at Muzaffarpur and consisting of the following members of the middle class of Bihar: M. Muhammad Shafi, Deep Narayan Sinha of Bhagalpur, Mazharul Haque, Arunjay Sahay Varma and Narayan Prasad of Chapra.[134] A set of rules was drawn up defining the duties, organisation and uniform of the Sevak Dal. Its "foremost duty was to keep peace in the Province."[135]

Under the leadership of the middle class, the number of Congress volunteers in general was rising rapidly. In the Gaya town only it rose to 1600 by the third week of December 1921, and in the rural areas thousands enlisted themselves as such.[136]

Large scale preparations of the country for further struggle in the cause of freedom could not but aggravate anxiety of the government. Failing to realise the true nature of the inner current of discontent among the people, the government sought to arrest it by force.

In Bihar also, many leaders were arrested, viz., Maulana Khurshed Husnain, Jagat Narain Lal, Krishna Prakash Sen Sinha at Patna; Maulvi Muhammad Shafi, Vindheshwari Prasad Varma, Janakdhari Prasad, Lachmi Narayan Singh, Dhwaja Prasad Sahu, Thakur Ramnandan Singh, Mathura Prasad Singh, Manzoor Husain and Maulvi Wadood in Muzaffarpur; Shah Muhammed Zobair, Shrikrishna Sinha, Dharmanarayan Singh in Monghyr; Ram Narayan Singh at Hazaribagh; Brajen

Dutt, Ram Shankar and Qazi Husain at Gaya and Madhav Singh and Bharat Mishra at Chapra.[137] On the 15th December, the government of Bihar and Orissa obtained sanction of the Government of India for applying the provisions of the Seditious Meetings Act. About 158 volunteers were also arrested at that time and sentenced to various terms of imprisonment. But their places were taken by new recruits.[138] On the 10th December, 1921, the Congress and volunteers offices at various centres were rigorously searched and their registers and other records relating to the Non-Cooperation movement were seized and indiscriminately destroyed.[139] Within a few days the Congress Office at Sonepur was "looted by the police under the supervision of a European Superintendent of Police and all office records, papers and khaddar stock found therein were set on fire, volunteers were assaulted and their flags and vests of khaddar were torn and snatched away."

While steadfastly following the programme of the Non-Cooperation movement, Bihar bore all the rigours of governmental repressions with remarable calmness and patience. "Bihar", as recorded in *The Young India* of 22nd December, 1921, "is a province which has kept most non-violent. It has shown splendid results in most items of Non-Cooperation."

When the Prince of Wales visited Patna on the 22nd and 23rd December, the moderates and loyalists of course greeted him. But at Patna there was then a complete hartal. Every "shop in the city was closed and shuttered; the main thoroughfares were almost empty, no vehicles plied for hire, and no crowd lined on the streets along which the procession passed."[140] As a government account notes, "A fairly complete hartal was observed at Puruila on the 23rd December."[141] Other cities of the province observed hartal in a peaceful manner in strict conformity with the instructions of the Congress.

The thirty-six session of the Indian National Congress was held at Ahmedabad on the 27th and 28th December, 1921. Five hundred and fifty-eight delegates from Bihar attended it, of whom twenty-two were the members of the Subjects Committee which had its sitting on the 24th, 25th, 27th and 28th December. The main resolution moved by Mahatma Gandhi in a memorable speech and passed by the Congress, placed on record the fixed determination of the Congress to continue the programme of non-violent Non-Cooperation with greater vigour hitherto. It affirmed that "Civil Disobedience is the only civilized and effective substitute for an armed rebellion" and so advised all Congress workers and others who believed in peaceful methods, "to organise individual Civil Disobedience and mass Civil Disobedience, when the mass of the people have been sufficiently trained in the method of non-violence." Students of the age of eighteen and above, particularly those studying in the National Institutions and the staff thereof, were asked to become members of the National Volunteer Corps immediately.

After returning from Ahmedabad, a meeting of the Provincial Congress Committee was convened at Patna on the 5th January, 1922 to discuss the future plan of action keeping in view the Ahmedabad resolutions. It was resolved not to introduce Civil Disobedience immediately but to concentrate efforts, for the time being, on the recruitment of volunteers. The following instructions were issued to the District Congress Committees:[142]

(i) The Congress has authorised the Provincial Congress Committees to allow any individual or the masses of particular area to begin civil disobedience on its own responsibility if he or they has/have fulfilled all the conditions mentioned below and can act up to the principle of non-violence. Till all the conditions are fulfilled and the Provincial Congress Committee does not accord its sanction, the Civil Disobedience cannot be begun.

(ii) The conditions whose fulfilment is necessary for Civil Disobedience are as follows:

In order to start Civil Disobedience, the district or tahsil should be regarded as one unit. In that area swadeshi should have been fully popularized and the majority of the inhabitants of that area should have begun the use of hand-woven and hand-spun cloths. They should have faith in the principles of Non-Cooperation and should act up to them, e g., not to attend courts, withdraw boys and girls from schools and colleges, get their cases decided by the panchayats, and suspension of practice by Vakils.

Popular enthusiasm for the cause of nationalism was daily rising high and recruitment of volunteers was being made in large numbers. The Government considered the Muzaffarpur district to be still "the storm centre of Non-Cooperation activity in the province. In the Sitamarhi sub-division alone over 20,000 people were said to have been recruited from other parts of the district."[143] To uphold their prestige and strength, the Government decided to post military and additional police force at selected places. Half a squadron of the cavalry was then "engaged in a route march through the Sitamarhi Sub-division."[144]

On January 29, 1922, the people of Bardoli in the Gujarat of the Bombay Presidency, decided under the presidentship of Vitthalbhai J. Patel to embark on mass Civil Disobedience.[145] The Working Committee met at Surat on 31st January 1922 and gave the green signal to the people of Bardoli to start it. But before the people of Bardoli had actually commenced mass Civil Disobedience, Mahatma Gandhi requested His Excellency, the Viceroy, on the 1st February, 1922, urging him to revise his policy of repression, to set free the non-violent non-cooperating prisoners and to rescue the country "from paralysis of freedom of association and freedom of press." But, on the 6th February, the government rejected the demands of Mahatma Gandhi. He sent a rejoinder on the 7th February cataloging "facts beyond challenge," as "infallible proofs of official lawlessness and barbarism."[146]

On the 5th February, 1922, 21 Constables and one Sub-Inspector were burnt by a violent mob in a police station at

Chauri Chaura.[147] It gave a rude shock to Gandhiji and he decided to stop the programme of mass Civil Disobedience. The Working Committee of the All-India Congress Committee met at Bardoli on the 11th and 12th February, 1922 and passed the resolution suspending the mass Civil Disobedience till peaceful atmosphere was restored.[148] Rajendra Prasad, who was at Bardoli at that time, sent the following message to the people of Bihar:

"In view of the Gorakhpur tragedy (Chauri Chaura) the Working Committee suspends all Civil Disobedience including activities for courting arrest and picketing except by approved persons for bonafide reform purposes. It directs concentration on detailed constructive programme of enrolling one crore members, organising Swadeshi, National Schools, Panchayats and social service, preaching temperance, collecting funds, levying one per cent on income and uplifting depressed classes."[149]

Bihar under the leadership and guidance of the middle class, stood by Mahatma Gandhi as a solid block. The Bardoli resolutions were passed with some modifications. Right of individual civil disobedience of either a defensive or aggressive character, and the right of picketing foreign cloth shops as well as liquor shops with the previous permission of the respective Provincial Congress Committees, could be exercised.[150]

In this tense situation the Government arrested Mahatma Gandhi on the 10th March, 1922. His trial[151] began on the 18th March, 1922, before Mr. C.N. Broomfield, I.C.S., District and Sessions Judge, Ahmedabad and lasted only hundred minutes. Mahatma Gandhi was sentenced to six years' imprisoment. The news of the arrest of Mahatma Gandhi reached Patna in the afternoon of 11th March, 1922. The people of Bihar, though deeply grieved at this incident, received it with equanimity without making any demonstrations. But voices of protest were raised at meetings organised under the leadership of the middle class at different places in

Patna, Gaya, Champaran, Monghyr and Bhagalpur districts and hartal was observed at Dhanbad on the 14th March, 1922.[152] A meeting was held at Patna on the 28th March in which some of the 'moderate' members of the Legislative Council were present. The first resolution moved by a member of the Legislative Council ran as follows : "The meeting of the citizens of Patna representing all shades of opinion records its sense of gratitude to Mahatma Gandhi who stands as an embodiment of our nation's aspirations and sacrifice for the valuable service to the country."[153]

Government followed at this time a mixed policy of conciliation and repression. On the one hand, they made arrests and commenced the collection of cost for additional police deployment in Sitamarhi; and, on the other, in the month of April, Sir Basanta Kumar Mallick, a Judge of the Patna High Court was given the files regarding the cases of the political prisoners for further enquiry, and as a result of his recommendations some prisoners were released.

In the district of Santhal Parganas "there had been going on intensive picketing of liquor shops with a view to boycotting the excise sales."[154] The Congress volunteers were working successfully even in the government estate in the portion of the district called the Damin-e-Koh (skirts of the hills), and established so much influence of their own that when the Subdivisional Officer of Rajmahal proceeded to Borio with an armed force he saw a state of things which he, in his own way, described as "a sort of minor revolution." The Subdivisional Officer prosecuted several persons, especially of the merchant class.[155] In Chhotanagpur, "stringent measures" were adopted by the Government in June against the Tana Bhagats at the Bero Polise Station and some other localities.[156]

In the month of April, the "National Week" was duly observed, there being a hartal on the 13th April. In the same month Syed Mahmood was convicted under section 124A for a speech delivered during the tour of the mother of Ali

Brothers early in February last. Two Assistant Jailors and two Wardens of the Muzaffarpur Jail resigned by way of protest against this conviction.[157] At Bhagalpur, Deep Narayan Singh was elected Chairman of the Municipality and another Non-Cooperator was elected Chairman of the Bhagalpur District Board. Soon after that, as a result of the Municipal elections in Biharsharif (Patna District), the Non-Cooperators obtained full control of the Municipality there.

Two highly significant events of the year 1922 in Bihar were the visit of the Civil Disobedience Enquiry Committee, and the meeting of the All-India National Congress at Gaya. The Committee visited Bihar and spent the 15th and 16th August at Patna. The Committee as a whole considered Civil Disobedience impractical at the moment. The meeting of the 37th Session of the All-India Congress met at Gaya in the month of December under the presidentship of Deshbandhu C.R. Das. Shri Braj Kishore Prasad was chairman of the Reception Committee. The most burning question in the Gaya Congress was that of "Council Entry." Deshbandhu Das was in favour of it and suggested a plan of obstraction from within the Councils. But the Gaya Congress decided against it and Bihar, Orissa, Gujarat, Andhra and Madras remained strongholds of "No Changers".[158] About Civil Disobedience the Gaya Congress passed a resolution calling upon all Congress workers to complete the preparations for offering Civil Disobedience, strengthening and expanding the National Organisation and to take immediate steps for the collection of atleast Rs. 25 lakhs for the Tilak Swarajya Fund and the enrolment of atleast 50,000 volunteers, satisfying the conditions of the Ahmedabad pledge by a date to be fixed by the All-India Congress Committee at Gaya."[159]

Formation and Working of the Swarajya Party and Constructive Works and the Middle Class in Bihar

After the Gaya Congress, Rajendra Prasad became Secretary of All-India Congress Committee and so long as he held this office the Congress Office was located at Patna. Majority of the workers continued to carry on activities according to the decision of the Gaya Congress. During the month of January 1923, Seth Jamunalal Bajaj, the Treasurer of the All-India Congress Committee visited a number of places in the Bhagalpur and Tirhut Divisions and addressed meetings for the collection of funds and spoke also about other constructive works. At Bhagalpur and Sahebganj he received warm welcome for the members of the Marwari community. At Muzaffarpur, some meetings were held under the presidentship of Maulvi Muhammad Shafi.[160]

The Tana Bhagats, who attended the Gaya Congress, were deeply influenced by its proceedings; and, on their return to Ranchi, they held several meetings to draw up a programme for national work.[161] During the national week from the 6th to 13th April, the local leaders made earnest efforts to collect money for the Tilak Swaraj Fund and to enlist more volunteers. On the 13th April they organised two meetings, one at Ranchi proper and the other at Doranda.[162]

According to the instructions of All-India Congress Committee, from the 10th March to the 18th March, the Congress workers made intensive efforts to popularise the cult of khaddar and for enlistment of volunteers, and they organised successful hartals at a number of places. On the 18th March, the Gandhi Day, i.e., on the anniversary of Mahatma Gandhi's conviction, meetings were held at important centres. There was a large and enthusiastic audience in a meeting in Shahabad. At Muzaffarpur, a large number of people (15,000 according to government report) assembled to meet the All-India Congress Deputation consisting of Rajagopalachari, Moazzam Ali and Rajendra Prasad. There was a meeting at Chapra too when the deputation visited that place.[163]

But as Deshbandhu Das and some other prominent leaders like Pandit Motilal Nehru and Vitthalbhai Patel were definitely in favour of Council entry and, on the other hand, there was also a very strong feeling for 'No Change', a schism in the Congress could not be avoided. On the 1st January

1923, the pro-Council group formed the Swarajya Party with Deshbandhu Das as its President and Pandit Motilal Nehru as its Secretary. The Swarajya Party wanted to work within the Congress "having full faith in the creed of the Congress, believing that the Gaya programme is not conducive to the speedy attainment of Swarajya."[164]

Bihar, as it has already been noted, stood mostly for 'No Change' in the Gaya Congress. But here also a Swarajya Party soon came into being. Those who were in sympathy with the Council Entry policy, met at Patna on the 26th February, 1923 and formed a nucleus of this new party. Its office-bearers consisted of Narayan Prasad of Chapra (President), Professor Abdul Bari, National College, Patna (Secretary), Krishna Ballabh Sahay, National College and Harnandan Sahay of Chapra (Assistant Secretaries).[165]

The Bihar branch of the Swarajya Party met again at Gaya on the 9th May and set up a new executive for the work in this province. Arunjay Sahay Varma was elected President and Krishna Ballabh Sahay and Professor Abdul Bari as Secretaries. Chandra Bansi Sahay and Rai Hari Prasad Lal were elected members of the General Council from Bihar. The Executive was authorised to carry on constructive works regarding spread of khaddar, education, temperance and for collection to the Municipalities, District Boards and Councils. The Provincial Congress Committee also met at Patna on the 19th May, 1923, and one of its resolutions was to the effect that no active propaganda against Council Entry should be carried on in Bihar.[166] Another meeting of the Bihar branch of the Swarajya Party was held at Patna on the 2nd June, 1923. Rajendra Prasad simply attended this meeting as a matter of courtesy, but did not address it. It was decided that the Provincial Council of this Party would consist of all members of the Congress Committee who accepted the party creed, and also of elected members.[167] Composition of the office bearers of the Swarajya Party shows the predominance of the middle, especially of the educated middle, class.

The Bihar Provincial Congress Committee which met at Monghyr in April, 1923, under the presidentship of Braj Kishore Prasad, the brave son of Saran, passed the following resolutions regarding elections to the Municipalities and the District Boards under the new Act:

(i) Resolved that all the seats in the Municipalities and District Boards of Bihar be contested at the coming elections on behalf of the committee.

(ii) That it is desirable for the members of the village unions and other Congress Committees to get themselves elected to various Union Boards and Village Panchayats under the Village Administration Act when it comes into force and to carry on village administration under the guidance of the Congress Committee.

(iii) Resolved that to carry out the said resolution and to take all the necessary steps in connection with the said elections and to form rules, a committee of the following gentlemen with power to co-opt be formed:

1. Rajendra Prasad
2. Maulvi Muhammad Shafi
3. Bipin Bihari Verma
4. Tajeshwar Prasad
5. Shrikrishna Sinha, Convenor.[168]

So far as enrolment of volunteers and collection for the Tilak Swaraj Fund were concerned, about 4,000 volunteers were enrolled and 41,000 rupees were collected in Bihar till the month of May, 1923.[169]

In view of the controversy on the question of Council Entry between the two parties, viz., 'No Change' party and the 'Pro-Change' party (or the Swarajya Party), in the Congress, a special session of the Congress was called to meet at Delhi on the 15th to 19th September, 1923 under the presidentship of Maulana Abul Kalam Azan, which resolved, "While reaffirming its adherence to the principle of non-violent Non-Cooperation, it declared that the legislators are at liberty to stand as candidates." This Congress, at the same time, called upon all Congressmen to redouble their efforts to carry out the constructive programme of their great leader, Mahatma Gandhi, by united endeavour to achieve Swarajya at the earliest possible moment, and also resolved to form a committee consisting of Rajendra Prasad and some other prominent leaders to organise an effective campaign of civil disobedience."[170]

In the meantime, an event of outstanding importance, in which Bihar enthusiastically participated, had occurred in Madhya Pradesh (C.P.). It was the heroic Satyagraha at Nagpur to defend the honour of India's National Flag, where the Government had placed a ban on procession with National Flags within the Civil Lines of the City under an order of the 1st May, 1923. Soon it developed as an All India movement. Thousands of people ran to Nagpur from different parts to vindicate national honour. Bihar not only sent contributions towards the fund that was being collected for this purpose, but also hundreds of her sons including Shri Rajendra Prasad, went there as volunteers. Many of them were put under arrest and one of them, Shri Hardeo Narayan Singh, died in the Nagpur jail on a day when Shri Rajendra Prasad was present there.[171] In the third batch of Bihar, volunteers, who started for Nagpur on the 2nd July 1923, was an old man of eighty-six years, named Babu Jhauri Sahu, a resident of Bikram (Patna district) and an opulent businessman. As he could not see with his own eyes, the Secretary, Bihar Provincial Congress Committee tried to dissuade him from proceeding to Nagpur. But he remained firm in his determination.[172] The 18th of July was celebrated in Bihar as the Flag Day.

At this time was started an organisation called the 'Gandhi Seva Sangh' to push forward the constructive activities according to the ideas of Mahatma Gandhi. Shri Rajagopalachari, Sardar Vallabhbhai Patel, Gangadhar Rao

Deshpande, Seth Jamunalal Bajaj, Rajendra Prasad and some others became members of its executive. Its branches were started in Bihar and some other provinces. But no centre was established in Bihar for its work. After a few years, an attempt was made in this direction at village Mairwa in Saran district, but it did not prove fruitful.[173]

From the month of October commenced municipal elections on the basis of the new Act. According to the decision already taken by the Provincial Congress Committee in April last, the Congress candidates, without any distinction between those of 'No Change' majority party and those of the Swarajya Party, fought these elections with considerable enthusiasm and remarkable success. Bihar contributed much in the victory of the Congress in the elections by holding meetings and attracting huge gatherings of audiences at important places like Monghyr and Muzaffarpur.[174] At all centres in Bihar the Congress achieved a fair measure of success. At Patna Rajendra Prasad, who got the largest number of votes, and Shri Anugraha Narayan Sinha were elected Chairman and Vice-Chairman, respectively, of the Municipality. Among the 10 out of 18 Congress candidates contesting here, were also Shri Jagat Narayan Lal, Acharya Badri Nath Varma, Muhammad Khurshed Hasnain. Soon Shri Anugraha Narayan Sinha was elected Chairman of the Gaya District Board. So he had to resign from Vice-Chairmanship of the Patna Municipality, making room for Syed Mahmood. The latter was not a Congressman, but he did good work in the Municipality.

While the Congress candidates were working in the District Boards and Municipalities, the Bihar Government introduced the Audit Bill. To consider this bill and certain other matters relating to the Boards, their representatives held a conference at Patna. Shah Muhammad Zubair inaugurated this conference and, as Shri Mazharul Haque, who was to preside over the meeting, fell ill, Shri Rajendra Prasad presided over it. The Audit Bill was very much criticised.[176]

By the end of November, 1923, much interest was shown in certain quarters in general elections for the Legislative Council and the Legislative Assembly. The Swarajya Party candidates, who belonged generally to the middle class, contested these elections, in which they received no support from the members of the 'No Change' faction of the Party.[177] Eight Swarajists succeeded in capturing eight, out of twelve, seats available in the Legislative Assembly. From the Tirhut Division, Maulvi Muhammad Shafi and Shyama Charan were members of this party. From Patna, Khan Sarfaraz Husain, formerly a member of the Assembly and contesting as a Swarajya Party candidate, was returned after defeating Khan Muhammad Ismail, a pro-government candidate. Ambika Prasad Singh was returned to the Assembly from Patna-cum-Shahabad constituency by signing the Swarajya Party declaration. In the Legislative Council, twelve Swarajists were returned. The Maharaja of Hathwa (Saran) was defeated in his own Zamindari by a Swarajist candidate; Krishna Ballabh Sahay was returned as a Swarajist from Hazaribagh and Rameshwar Lal was also returned as such from the South Santhal Parganas constituency.[178] Jaleshwar Prasad was leader of the Swarajya Party and its members did good work in the Legislature.[179]

Before the close of the year 1923 the different political bodies in Bihar discussed some significant matters. The Bihar Provincial Conference met at Motihari on the 31st October and the 1st November, 1923, under the presidentship of Dharnidhar of Darbhanga. Gorakh Prasad was chairman of the Reception Committee.

Resolutions were passed reaffirming faith in Mahatma Gandhi's non-violent Non-Cooperation and for concentrating on village organisation work in selected localities.[180] This was followed by Khilafat Conference over which M. Saiyid Sulaiman Naqvi presided. Resolutions were passed here condemning communal differences and urging Muhammadans to support the Congress and appealing for subscriptions.

The thirty-eighth annual session of the Congress was held at Cocanada from the 28th to 31st December, 1923, under the presidentship of Maulana Muhammad Ali. It practically reaffirmed the resolution about Council Entry, passed at a special session of the Congress at Delhi. The Swarajists were permitted to enter Council, though the principle and policy of that (triple) boycott remained unaltered. The Congress further appealed to the nation to carry out the programme of constructive work as adopted at Bardoli and prepare for the adoption of civil disobedience.[181]

Mahatma Gandhi received the news of his release on the ground of ill-health at Sassoon Hospital, Poona, on the morning of the 5th February, 1924. On that very date a meeting was held at Patna to celebrate the release of this great leader, "whose incarceration," wrote *The Searchlight*, "was an outrage against humanity."[182]

On the 12th February, 1924, the Bhagalpur District Khilafat Committee held its annual meeting with Maulvi Nurul Hasan of Phulwari as president. Thakur Bhagwat Singh, who had been convicted of sedition in 1922, addressed the audience, particularly drawing their attention to India's sacrifices during World War I, for which she did not get adequate return, and to the cruelties of Dyerism in the Punjab.[183] He spoke again in the same strain on the 19th February.[184]

In the District Board elections held in the spring of 1924, the Swarajists achieved a fair measure of success at different places in the province, there being however comparative setback at Patna due to the strong opposition of the zamindar class.[185]

An attempt was made in 1924 to revive the Behari Students' Conference on its old model. In addressing a preliminary meeting held at Patna in this connection in April 1924, Rajendra Prasad exhorted the audience to develop in their hearts the noble sentiment of patriotism, wearing of khadi and to dedicate to constructive works like spread of swadeshi, removal of untouchability and education of the untouchables at night schools, etc.[186]

Spread of khadi work in Bihar, in 1924, also deserves special notice. Rajendra Prasad engaged himself intensively in constructive works in Bihar, particularly national education and spread of khadi. On the 19th February, 1924, Nilkantha Chatterjee moved a resolution in the Bihar and Orissa Legislative Council to the effect that "in all public schools arrangements be made for teaching boys and girls above the age of ten the art of spinning by Charkha." Krishna Ballabh Sahay, Jimut Bahan Sen and Dwarka Nath strongly supported it alongwith many others, and it was passed.[187] The Congress members elected to the District Boards and Municipalities tried their best to introduce spinning and khaddar in schools under their control. A Khadi Exhibition was organised at Patna in December, 1924 under the guidance of Rajendra Prasad. He made it purely non-political function, and some high government officials participated in it. In the Charkha competitions during this exhibition, two boys of Malkhachawk Gandhi Kutir (Saran) got the first prize. One of them was Satyanarayan Singh. Lady Miller distributed the prizes. In his speech Rajendra Prasad reviewed the progress of Khadi work in Bihar till then.[188] Rajendra Prasad opened the All India Swadeshi exhibition at the Belgaum Congress.

Another incident of the year was that Sir J.C. Bose, who came to address that year's convocation of the Patna University, was also taken to the Bihar Vidyapith by Rajendra Prasad. He delivered there a highly inspiring and instructive speech. It may be recalled that a few years later Sir J.C. Bose made a handsome donation for prohibition work in Bihar under the leadership of Rajendra Prasad. This work was done in the coalfield area at Jharia but could not be carried on further due to some untoward circumstances.[189]

One highly disquieting feature in Indian politics in 1923-24 was the growing tension between the Hindus and the Muslims and the consequent outbreak of communal riots at several places in India. Bihar did not escape the infection of communal frenzy and, in September-October 1924, Hindu-Muslim riots occurred at several places in the province, the most serious one being at Bhagalpur. Rajendra Prasad and some other leaders did best to ease the situation by staying there for a few days.[190]

The severe disappointment of India at the speech of Lord Birkenhead, Secretary of State for India, dated the 10th July 1925, facilitated transfer of authority into the hands of the Swarajya Party, and it was completed[191] at the session of the All India Congress Committee, which met at Patna on the 22nd and 23rd September, 1925. The Swarajya Party was also absolved from the conditions of the Belgaum Pact, and the membership of the Congress was now open to anyone who paid four annas annually or 2,000 yards of self-spun yarn. The Swarajya Party was invested with full authority of the Congress to deal with the political affairs in the country. It was at Patna that the All India Spinners' Association was born. An organisation called the All India Spinners' Association is hereby established with the consent of the All India Congress Committee, as an integral part of the Congress organisation, but with independent existence and powers.[192]

Mahatma Gandhi's Bihar trip this time began with his attending the Bihar Provincial Conference at Purulia for three days in September, 1925. Maulvi Muhammad Zubair was president of this Conference, which met for the first time now in Chhotanagpur, and Nilkanta Chattopadhyaya was Chairman of the Reception Committee. The Hindu Sabha, and on the next day the Khilafat Conference, also met in the same pandal. An industrial exhibition was arranged carefully and one could see there, as Mahatma Gandhi noted, "the undoubted evolution of khaddar."[193]

Shortly before attending the political conference at Purulia Gandhiji visited Jamshedpur. From Purulia he visited Chakradharpur, Chaibasa, Ranchi, Hazaribagh, Patna, Gaya, Bhagalpur, Deoghar, Giridih, Madhupur, Purnea, Kishanganj, Vishanpur, Hajipur and Sonepur. At these places meetings were held to impress upon the people the dignity of social service through the spinning wheel and khaddar and sincere contact with the village folk, which could help them "to know the maker because the selfless service of the poor was the service to God."[194]

The total collection for Deshbandhu Memorial Fund throughout his Bihar tour then amounted to Rs. 50,000. A portion of it was added to the capital of the All India Spinners' Association.[195] The Ali Brothers also visited Bihar at this time for collections to the Khilafat fund.[196]

Mahatma Gandhi's second Bihar tour in this period began from the 11th January 1927. To those who came to receive him at the railway station, he spoke in his one minute speech, "I have come here to do business, to collect money for Charkha and Khadi and to sell khadi. Who knows, this may be my last visit to Bihar! Let me do as much business as I can."[197] Starting from Daltonganj in the Palamau district, he went to Gaya. He crossed the Ganges at Patna and reached Muzaffarpur on the 27th January. In the afternoon he attended a meeting in the Tilak Maidan and addressed there. At night Mahatma started for Motihari with his party consisting of Rajendra Prasad, Mahadev Desai, Kasturbai and Prabhavati (wife of Jai Prakash Narayan).[198] Passing across the rich alluvial tracts of Chapra district, Mahatma Gandhi spent one quiet day at Jiradei, which he considered to be "a place of pilgrimage" as the birth place of Rajendra Prasad.[199] Then moving through some other subdivisions in Chapra district, "studded at every half a mile with emeralds of mango groves and carpeted with green fields smiling with green tuar, wheat, gram and peas",[200] he went again to E st and North to Darbhanga. The largest collection during tour of Bihar was on the 18th January, when Rs. 6,500 were received from Dalsingsarai, Samastipur and Darbhanga. At Begusarai in the Monghyr district arrangement for a meeting to be addressed by Mahatma Gandhi was better than at other places, "the platform being something over six feet supported on four strong pillars, between which men could come and go."[201] During this tour of Bihar, Mahatma Gandhi came in touch with several National Schools which continued to exist despite tremendous odd, the general condition of which was but sad.[202] According to the report of the Bihar Vidyapith for 1926, there was then one college with 32 students, 15 middle and 10 primary schools affiliated to the Vidyapith, as against 9, 16 and 30 respectively a year before. The last day of Mahatma Gandhi's Bihar tour was given to the students and professors of the Vidyapith and to the khadi workers. The Vidyapith was then struggling against various impediments, chiefly of financial stringency. But Rajendra Prasad and some other organisers were doing their best to maintain it by collecting funds from public subscriptions as far as possible. The authorities of the Vidapith also organised a khadi exhibition on the occasion. It was opened by Satish Chandra Das Gupta of Khadi Pratisthan, Calcutta, who delivered a speech[203] emphasising the importance of charkha and khaddar for solution of India's poverty and dependence. He paid eloquent testimony to the work of the khadi centres in Bihar itself, which had been organised mainly by Rajendra Prasad and Ram Binode Singh.

Mahatma Gandhi addressed the convocation of the Bihar Vidyapith in 1927 when Rajendra Prasad, as its Vice-Chancellor, gave away degrees to nine Snatakas. In all the institutions the medium of instruction was Hindi, spinning was compulsory and weaving was also taught in some of them.[204]

By the end of January 1927, Mahatma Gandhi left Bihar. The collections made by him in Bihar this time for Das Memorial Fund amounted to Rs. 40,685. This tour was "remarkable for rousing the masses" in Bihar. Gandhiji, during this tour, was always assisted by leaders who belonged to the middle class.

As already noted, Mahatma Gandhi met the Khadi workers also on the last day of his tour of Bihar. Rajendra Prasad arranged on this occasion a special khadi exhibition in the Sinha Institute. Owing to tremendous rush, the ministers, some barristers and government officials, whom Rajendra Prasad had invited to the function, attended it next day and in one day and a half, over Rs. 2,000 worth of khaddar was sold.[205]

Khadi work began in Bihar from 1921 when the Provincial Committee got a good amount for it from the Swaraj Fund. With the help of Acharya Kripalani, Ram Binode Singh did excellent work in this respect independently by starting a Khaddar Producing Centre at Madhubani. Through the recommendation of Acharya Kripalani and consent of Rajendra Prasad, he got for it a substantial amount as loan from the Khaddar Board.[206] After the formation of the All India Spinners' Association (Akhil Bhartiya Charkha Sangh) and a branch of it in Bihar with Rajendra Prasad as its agent and Lakshmi Narayan, Secretary, Khadi work was reorganised here on new lines, resulting in greater produce and sale of khadi.

As Darbhanga district was famous for khadi production, the office and chief depot of the Bihar Branch of A.I.S.A. was shifted from Patna to Muzaffarpur, and again, for comparative convenience, to Madhubani where gradually the Charkha Sangh constructed its own building.[207]

In the report of the Bihar Branch of the A.I.S.A. for the year ending September 1926, sent by Rajendra Prasad to Mahatma Gandhi, the following information about the progress of khadi work in Bihar since its inception in the year 1924, till its centralisation under the Khadi Board and later under the A.I.S.A., gives an idea of the degree of sincerity and enthusiasm of Bihar Unit of Congress Party and Rajendra Babu.

(*In rupees*)

Period	*April '24 to Sep. '24*	*Oct. '24 to Mar. '25*	*April '25 to Sep. '25*	*Oct. '25 to Mar. '26*	*April '26 to Sep. '26*
Production	21,588	35,273	47,031	51,080	96,273
Sale	17,478	27,784	33,335	51,865	59,687

The statement did not include the figures for production and sale of khaddar by the Gandhi Kutir, whose work till the beginning of 1926 was on a more extensive scale than of the Provincial Khaddar Board, laterly the Bihar Unit of the A.I.S.A.[208] The period from October 1926 to September 1927 opened with large stock of khadi in the stores at different places in Bihar, which reduced the liquid capital in the hands of the workers and necessitated the curtailment of production. But Mahatma Gandhi's tour gave considerable impetus to khadi work.[209] It should be noted that to popularise khadi, exhibitions were held in 1926 at different centres in the province under the guidance of Rajendra Prasad. The first one, to which a reference has already been made, was opened by Satish Chandra Das Gupta of the Khadi Pratisthan, Calcutta, on the grounds of the Bihar Vidyapith. The second one was held in the Bihar Young Men's Institute, Patna, and it was opened by Sadhu Vaswani of Sindh. The third one was organised at Arrah, the fourth at Muzaffarpur by Maulvi Muhammad Shafi and the fifth one at Chapra by Mazharul Haque, the sixth was held at Mairwa (a small village in the district of Saran), the seventh at Gaya on the 11th June 1926, and eighth at Bettiah in July 1926. Khadi exhibitions were arranged at some other places also. Khadi was hawked and sold at these exhibitions and magic lantern lectures were delivered in the evenings illustrating the necessity and importance of the Khadi Movement. These exhibitions were visited by Congressmen, non-Congressites, government officials, zamindars, lawyers, big and small merchants and in some cases even by Europeans.[210] Another exhibition at Motihari was inaugurated. At Jamshedpur the exhibition was opened by a highly placed officer of the Tata and Company, Mr. Temple. There was a good sale of khadi at this exhibition.[211] In August 1926, one exhibition was held at Laheriasarai, Darbhanga, its opening ceremony being performed by Rajendra Prasad, and another exhibition was inaugurated in the same month at Deoghar by Seth Jamunalal Bajaj.[212] The thirteenth Bihar Khadi exhibition was held in Hazaribagh from the 14th to 16 August, 1926, and this too was opened by Rajendra Prasad.[213] At Ranchi, the Khadi exhibition was opened, in the presence of Rajendra Prasad, by S.K. Sahay at 4 p.m. on the 5th October, 1926 in the Ranchi Arya Samaj Hall. Some Tana Bhagats attended it.[214]

Thus, in spite of the formal suspension of the Non-Cooperation Movement, constructive activities were vigorously continued in this province under the guidance of the middle class members who had been the political leaders also.

The Congress met for its 40th annual session at Cownpore from the 26th to 28th December, 1925, under the presidentship of Sarojini Naidu. Part of the resolution passed by the A.I.C.C. at its Patna meeting, held on the 22nd September 1924, was confirmed by it. As regards future policy, it laid down, "The Congress reiterates its faith in Civil Disobedience as the only effective weapon to be used as a last resort to enforce the national claim and vindicate our national honour, but realises that the country is not now ready for it." The main plank of future programme remained Mahatma Gandhi's constructive work.[215]

Meanwhile, the A.I.C.C. meeting at Delhi on the 6th and 7th March, 1926 had passed a resolution for a walk-out from the legislatures. It called upon the members of the Swaraj Party in the Assembly to leave their seats. By another resolution, the A.I.C.C. decided that the ensuing general elections shall be run by and in the name of the Congress on the programme fixed by the Congress. It issued an Election Manifesto in October, 1926, and general elections took place in November. The Swarajya Party was handicapped because some Muslim members left it and some Hindus also joined the other parties. In Bihar, as in other places, vigorous election campaigns were conducted by leaders of the different parties and regrettable communal as well as caste considerations influenced the election propaganda very much.[216]

The general result of the elections in Bihar was that Congress candidates were returned by the electorate in large numbers, both for the Provincial Council and Central Assembly.[217]

The cancer of communalism was still gnawing at. Communal riots broke out at several places, the most fierce being those at Calcutta during the month of April 1926. These had natural repercussions on Bihar where communal tension increased during April and May, resulting in some minor clashes in Shahabad, Monghyr, the Santhal Parganas and on the borders of the districts of Muzaffarpur and Darbhanga.[218] Mazharul Haque, Maulvi Muhammad Shafi, Jagat Narayan Lal, Rajendra Prasad and some others began to tour in the province in this work. As a result of it, the atmosphere in Bihar remained comparatively free from the pernicious effects of communal riots, but excitement continued.[219] The Delhi proposals for joint electorate were considered at a special meeting of the Muslim representatives of Bihar in the Anjuman-e-Islamia Hall at Patna on the 8th May, 1927. Sir Ali Imam, Maulana Safi and prominent Muslims led the opposition to the joint electorate; and, consequently, demand for separate electorate was upheld.[220] Thus we see that members of the middle class were working both for unity and separatism.

The Simon Commission and the Middle Class in Bihar

The exclusion of the Indians from the personnel of a Commission formed to enquire into the working of the Montague Chelmsford Reforms and to make recommendations for the future constitutional status of their country, naturally caused countrywide resentment and evoked "universal condemnation", from organisations representing varied shades of opinion as a negation of the fundamental right of self-determination which is inherent in every nation."[221] On the 16th November, 1927, was announced the Leaders' Manifesto bearing signatures of prominent leaders of all parties, including those of Ali Imam, Sachchidananda Sinha and Ismail Khan from Bihar, who came from the educated middle class. The Manifesto stated: "Unless a Commission on which the British and Indian statesmen are invited to sit on equal terms is set up we cannot conscientiously take any part or share in the work of the Commission as at present constituted."[222]

The Indian National Congress, meeting at its 42nd session at Madras in December 1927, resolved that "the only self-respecting course for India to adopt is to boycott the Commission at every stage and in every form." In his Presidential Address at the Calcutta session of the Indian National Congress, held in December 1928, Pandit Motilal Nehru expressed: "The solemn promises of responsible Government have found fulfilment in that colossal fraud, the Statutory Commission, which is now careering along our streets leaving bleeding heads and broken bones behind."[223]

The country's mandate with regard to the attitude towards the Indian Statutory Commission was followed by Bihar with profound courage, earnestness and fidelity. A Conference attended by men of all parties was held at Patna under the presidentship of Ali Imam and boycott of the Simon Commission was decided upon there.[224]

In the meantime, after the Gaya meeting referred to above, it had been decided by the leaders to hold a session of the Bihar Provincial Conference at Patna. So this Conference met at Patna on the 9th December, 1928, a few days before the arrival of the Simon Commission there.[225] Anugraha Narayan Sinha was its president and Sachchidananda Sinha was Chairman of the Reception Committee. This Conference was largely attended by delegates from all parts of the province and was so timed as to contribute very much to the success of the anti-Simon Commission demonstrations. When this Commission reached Patna on the 12th December, 1928, most of those who came to attend the Conference from different districts, participated in the demonstrations against it. Thus the Patna demonstration against the Simon Commission was a demonstration on behalf of the Province as a whole.[226] About 30,000 people, in their enthusiasm to express their feelings against the unwanted Commission, assembled in the cold morning of the month of December in front of the special platform opposite Hardinge Park. They cried 'Go back Simon' and also showed black flags. Thousands of them had been waiting near the platform even from 3 or 4 o'clock in the morning. The entire demonstration was orderly, there being no untoward incident as in some other parts (Madras, Calcutta, U.P. and Lahore), where even great personalities like Lala Lajpat Rai, Jawaharlal Nehru and Govind Ballabh Pant had received very rough treatment at the hands of the police.[228] Some members of the Commission went to Dumraon for a day as guests of the local Maharaja. A demonstration was organised there against them on the morning of the day of their arrival.[229]

The Commission left Patna on the 19th December for Calcutta, some members of it visiting en route Ranchi and others and Jharia coal-fields.[230] At a meeting of the citizens of Ranchi, held already on the 18th December, 1927 under the presidentship of S.K. Sahay, a resolution had been unanimously passed to boycott the Simon Commission.[231] Some of the Muslims of that city, however, held another meeting on the 23rd December, 1927, and expressed their willingness to co-operate with the Commission.[232] But the local Congress workers under the guidance of Deoki Nandan Lal and P.C. Mitra, and many Tana Bhagats coming from different parts of Chhotanagpur, joined in demonstration against it and showed black flags.[233] On the 27th December, 1928, P.C. Mitra and some others, alongwith about 150 Tana Bhagats, left Ranchi to attend the Calcutta session of the Indian National Congress meeting from 29th December, 1928. The Congress at its session considered the All Parties Committee Report and also passed a resolution outlining future programme of constructive works for Congressmen, in the legislatures and outside.[234]

Constructive Works and the Middle Class in Bihar

To give effect to this resolution, the Bihar Provincial Congress Committee, immediately after the Calcutta Session had been over, addressed all the District Congress Committees, among other matters, on the need of enrolling a large number of Congress members, and strengthening the Congress organisations where these already existed and starting new ones where they did not. This matter was not taken up seriously except by a very few of the District Congress Committees. But after the penal resolution of the A.I.C.C., passed at its Bombay meetings on the 24th and 25th May, 1929, all the districts began to make strenuous efforts to fulfil the quota of membership on the date fixed by the All India Congress Committee (31st August). The result was that Bihar was able to enrol above 80,000 members by that time whereas its quota was for 72,558 members. By the end of 1929 there were 90,525 Congress members in this Province.[235]

The Province of Bihar had its own Provincial Board to control and carry on the activities of the Hindustani Seva Dal, affiliated to the Congress. This Board consisted of Kumar Ganganand Singh, Kumar Kalika Singh, Acharya Badrinath Varma, Mathura Prasad, Bipin Behari Varma, Gyan Saha (Secretary), Jimut Bahan Sen and Abdul Bari, who all came from the educated middle class.[236]

The Board was able to secure the services of Ranendra Nath Roy Chowdhury and Kishori Prasanna Sinha, who were working with single-minded devotion. A Trainers' Training Camp was opened in August, 1929, at the Sadaqat Ashram, Patna. Seventeen volunteers received training here for one month and most of them, afterwards, devoted themselves to training volunteers, in their respective districts. Eleven camps were since then opened at Gogri, Monghyr, Kharagpur and Gorwadih in the district of Monghyr, Bettiah, Myanaten, Nawalpur and Malahi in the districts of Champaran, Sitamarhi in the district of Muzaffarpur, and at Arrah and Patna towns, and 200 volunteers were trained there. Services of the volunteers of the Hindustani Seva Dal were utilised for a session of the Provincial Political Conference at Monghyr in December, 1929.[237]

The Bihar Provincial Congress Committee was composed of the following members during the year 1928-29: Anugrah Narayan Sinha (President), Braj Kishore Prasad, Deep Narayan Sinha and Shah Muhammad Zubair (Vice-Presidents),

Rajendra Prasad and Shrikrishna Sinha (Secretaries), Abdul Bari and Binoda Nand Jha (Assistant Secretaries), and Sarangdhar Sinha (Treasurer).

In addition to the above-mentioned members, the Working Committee was composed of the following: Ram Dayalu Sinha, Badrinath Varma, Syed Mahmood, Bipin Bihari Varma and Krishna Ballabh Sahay.[238]

Composition of the Bihar Provincial Congress Committee shows that it was dominated by men of the educated middle class who came from land-owning families of Bihar.

According to a resolution of the meeting of the Working Committee of the Congress, held in Calcutta on the 3rd January 1929, Mahatma Gandhi prepared a scheme for the boycott of foreign cloth through khadi. Meeting at Delhi on the 17th and 19th February, 1929, the Working Committee adopted this scheme. Mahatma Gandhi arranged a cloth burning demonstration in Calcutta on the 4th March, 1929, for which he was subject to prosecution and fine of one rupee. This fine was paid by someone without his knowledge.

In Bihar, the Sunday programme regarding the boycott of foreign cloth was well observed; meetings were held and foreign cloth was publicly burnt. In well organised districts the volunteers carried on successful propaganda through private discourses, pubic lectures and in some cases by magic lantern lectures. An effective method of propaganda was to secure signatures on forms containing the pledge on the part of the signatories that they would not purchase any foreign cloth thenceforward either for their personal use or for the use of their dependents. To facilitate this work, Rajendra Prasad suggested a scheme that workers in each district should distribute themselves in respective areas and should thus try to visit every home in each area. He personally addressed the workers of four districts, Saran, Champaran, Darbhanga and Bhagalpur. He could not address the workers of the other districts due to some pressing engagements. But practically nothing was done to "carry the message of the boycott among the dealers of foreign cloth."[239]

On the 4th October, 1928, met the twenty-first session of the Bihari Students' Conference at Motihari in the Heycock Academy amidst scenes of great enthusiasm. In the unavoidable absence of Prof. Vaswani, the President-elect, owing to illness, Shri Rajendra Prasad read his Address. He observed in this Address: "Be strong—is my earnest appeal to the nation's youth. Inheritors of an ancient past, possessors, too, of the rich revelations of modern science, you are called to be creators of a mighty future. Behold! the highways of the East are covered with ruins of the past. Behold ! the highways of the West are strewn with ruins of the present—ruins of the world war which has been an inevitable result of a cruel industrialism, an aggressive, unspiritual nationalism. India and Asia and the West ask for men and women of the new spirit—ask for new creators, for them that would build a new brotherly Civilization—a new Divine Humanity."[240]

Proscription of some books, said to be seditious by the Government, and rigorous measures against the Press, were also marked features of the year 1929. In Bihar, *The Search-light*, *The Tarun Shakti* of Chaibasa and *The Mukti* of Purulia, became the special targets of Government attack. The Government of Bihar and Orissa forwarded a copy of this order to all District Officers for proper action. According to it, an additional force was stationed within the jurisdiction of Siwan, Barharia, Basantpur and Maharajgunj police stations in the district of Saran.[241]

Bihar observed the Political Sufferers' Day on the 10th August, 1929. To celebrate it at Patna, a procession, led by Rajendra Prasad, started this day at about 3.30 p.m. It included a large number of students and many of those who had joined it carried National Flags. At the meeting arranged at Gulzarbagh, Abdul Bari proposed Rajendra Prasad to the Chair and it was seconded by Baladev Sahay. With sincere convictions of a noble patriot, Rajendra Prasad delivered a highly impressive speech exhorting the audience to imbibe and develop the spirit of self-sacrifice as an indispensably needed means for the attainment of freedom. He referred to the sufferings of the political prisoners under inhuman tortures in the jails and to the virulence and rigours of the jail rules in India as compared with those of England. "In England", he observed, "conspiracy and sedition could really be counted as crimes as England was a free country. But in India, which was under the yoke of foreign Government, sedition was but duty and religion. It was the duty of every body here to be seditious. By the irony of fate patriotism had come to be branded as crime in India, but in England it was a virtue." He reminded the audience about the sacredness of the National Flag, asking them to be always ready to safeguard its honour whatever might be the risks. After the National Flag had been unfurled, Praful Chandra Ganguly of Bengal, who had that day come from Benaras for this meeting, delivered a short speech. Rajendra Prasad had to leave this meeting before it was over for Patna City, where he was required to address another meeting. Badrinath Varma then took the Chair. A resolution praising the courage and bravery of the Punjab hunger strikers and condemning Government for not conceding to their just demands was moved by Abdul Bari and seconded by Jaichand Vidyalankar. Similar meetings and processions were organised in the other districts of Bihar.[242]

Nationalist India was determined to go ahead, and the new spirit of advance was remarkably strong in Bihar under the leadership of alumni of the middle class. The 28th session of the Bihar Provincial Conference met at Monghyr on the 9th December, 1929. In the absence of the President-elect, Rajendra Prasad, Ram Dayalu Singh read the Hindi translation of the Presidential Address. This Conference passed a resolution advocating Independence, though the elderly persons were in favour of waiting till this point had been decided by the Congress. Sardar Vallabhbhai Patel also attended this Conference. He toured the Province of Bihar exhorting the people to implement the constructive programme of the Congress and to be ready for the inevitable struggle.[243]

The Bihar Youth Conference met at Monghyr on the 12th December, 1929. In the absence of Subhas Chandra Bose, Pandit Prajapati Mishra presided. He spoke with great emphasis on the use of khaddar by young men. This Conference passed several resolutions which expressed in indubitable terms the new urges of the youths of the Province like those in other parts of the country. One of these proclaimed that "India's goal is nothing but independence."[244]

During the month of February, 1930, an attempt was made to start a branch of the Yuvak Sangh in Bihar in which the students of the Nalanda College took prominent part.[245] The Subdivisional Officer of Bihar was asked by his authorities to "keep an eye on the College" regarding this matter.

During the session of the Bihari Students' Conference held at Motihari in 1928, the Bihar Youth League had come into existence. Its organisation and aims were thus described by its Secretary, Gyan Saha (also Secretary, Hindustani Seva Dal) in an appeal issued by him in November, 1928 : "On truth we stand, service is our religion and freedom is to be won. The association should aim at imparting to the members ideas of purity and simplicity, fearlessness, equality, fraternity, dignity of labour and discipline. Any person, male or female, who is above 18 years of age and who believes in the ideal of complete independence of India, who wears khadi, does not observe touchability and is not a member of any communal organisation, is entitled to be a member of the League."[246] He issued another appeal on the 10th April, 1929, exhorting the youths to celebrate the First Youth Day on the 14th April next, and concluded it with the observation, "The salvation of the country rests on the Youth Power." The Patna Youth League celebrated its second anniversary on the 22nd September, 1929.[247] Students' Youth Organisations were formed by University students, components of the educated middle class, under the patronage of leaders coming from the middle class.

Bihar was forging ahead in all respects when the 44th session of the Indian National Congress met at Lahore on the

29th and 31st December, 1929, with Jawaharlal Nehru as its President. It passed the momentous resolution on complete independence, sponsored by Mahatma Gandhi himself, to the following effects :

"This Congress appeals to the nation zealously to prosecute the constructive programme of the Congress and authorises the All India Congress Committee, whenever it deems fit, to launch upon a programme of civil disobedience including non-payment of taxes, whether in selected areas or otherwise, and under such safeguards as it may consider necessary." At midnight the Tricolour, the flag of Indian Independence, was unfurled amidst shouts of 'Inquilab Zindabad', 'Long live Revolution'. Bihar voted solidly for Mahatma Gandhi. Syed Mahmood was appointed one of the Secretaries of the Congress with Prakash.[248]

A study of the period under review shows that the struggle for freedom was being transformed into a mass movement under the leadership and guidance of the middle class of Bihar who imbued the general mass with consciousness and moral faith in the righteousness of their cause, which were supremely important factors for the progress of freedom movement and successful consummation of a creative and constructive revolution. Most of the persons whose names figure in the struggle for dismantling the British sovereignty over India, belonged to the middle class. Persons of eminence, such as, Hasan Imam, Rajendra Prasad, Mazharul Haque, P.N. Sinha, Sachchidanand Sinha, Gorakh Prasad, Dharnidhar Prasad, Janakdhari Prasad, Brajkishore Prasad, Chandradeo Narayan, Madhav Sinha, K.B. Dutta, B.B. Verma, Gajadhar Prasad, Chandra Bansi Sahay, Guru Charan Singh, Raghunath Lal, Krishna Prakash Sen Sinha, Dwarikanath, S.C. Mitra, Shah Muhammad Zubair, Muhammad Shafi, Chandra Dip Narayan, Bankey Bihari Lal, Saiyid Muhammad Sher, Vindeshwari Prasad Verma, Bindheshwari Prasad Singh, P.R. Das, Bindhya Basini Prasad, Deep Narayan Singh, Ali Imam, Bajrang Sahay, Bibhuti Bhushan Banerjee (Mukhta), Anugrah Narayan Sinha and Srikrishna Sinha were lawyers, who dominated the educated elite group of middle class.

There was another set of persons including Abdul Bari, Badrinath Varma, Gyan Saha, Jagnath Prasad, Prem Sunder Bose, J.B. Kripalani, Jaleshwar Prasad, N.R. Malkani, Jwala Prasad Singh, Phuldeo Prasad Verma (all professors), Narayan Tammaji, Jagdish Sharma, Bindeshwar Prasad, Bulaki Sahi, Janki Prasad Verma, Nazir Ahmad, Shivpujan Sahay, Suraj Prasad Tiwari, Ramdeo Tiwari, Jai Prakash Lal, Usman and Jainandan Jha (all teachers), who formed the educated middle class. Besides, there were several others who belonged to the educated middle class as they took University education. Some of them were: Syed Mahmood, Ghulam Imam, Mahmood Saqi, Hakim Abdul Hai, Bhuvneshwar Prasad, Dwarka Prasad, S.N. Sahay, Arunjay Sahay Verma, K.B. Sahay, Binoda Nand Jha, Ram Nirikshan Singh, Qazi Abdul Wadood, Jagat Narain Lal, Manoranjan Sinha, P.C. Mitra and Sarangdhar Singh. Besides, University students, who played a commendable role in the national movement, also belonged to the middle class.

Important persons of the middle class landed interest, who contributed much to the freedom movement, were Mahabir Sharan, Maheshwar Prasad, Tulsi Singh, Raj Kumar Shukla, Khan Sarfaraz Husain, Jadunath Singh, K.B. Zahiruddin, Thakur Bimla Prasad, Nawab Singh, Ram Bindo Singh, Mahendra Prasad, Baijnath Singh, Satyanarain Singh, Dharamnarayan Singh, Ram Narayan Singh, Dharam Narayan Singh, and several others.

The commercial and industrial middle class also played an important role in the struggle against the British Imperial rule. Members of the commercial and industrial middle class contributed too much, particularly in urban areas, in observing successful hartals on different dates. Important persons, coming from the commercial middle class, were Debilal Sahu, Kedarnath Sahu, Ramdayal Sahu and Luxmi Narayan Chaudhary.

Thus we see that during this period members of the middle class played the key role in the national movement and under their guidance and leadership movement for emancipation from the British yoke was progressing. But one disquieting feature of our national movement was the growing tension between the Hindus and the Muslims for which some members of the middle class in Bihar were also responsible.

Notes

1. Datta, K.K., *History of the Freedom Movement in Bihar*, Vol. I, pp. 552-53.
2. Sitaramayya, B. Pattabhi, *History of Indian National Congress*, Vol. I, pp. 153-54.
3. *The Searchlight*, July 27, 1919.
4. Mahatma Gandhi, *Autobiography*, p. 564.
5. *Ibid.*, p. 578.
6. *Bihar and Orissa Police Abstract of Intelligence*, 1919, The Non-Cooperation and Khilafat Movement in Bihar and Orissa.
7. For the names of prominent persons see pp. 292-93 of *History of the Freedom Movement in Bihar*, Vol. I, K.K. Datta.
8. *The Non-Cooperation and Khilafat Movement in Bihar*, p. 2.
9. Prasad, Rajendra, *Mahatma Gandhi and Bihar*, p. 37.
10. Datta, K.K., *op. cit.*, Vol. I, p. 294. *The Searchlight* of 7, 8, and 9 April, 1919.
11. Quoted in K.K. Datta's *History of the Freedom Movement in Bihar*, Vol. I, p. 294.
12. *Bihar and Orissa Police Abstract of Intelligence*, 1919.
13. File No. 57, Paper relating to Freedom Movement, Bihar Record Room.
14. *Government List of Registered Satyagrahis*, Corrected upto 15th April, 1919, p. 295, Vol. I, of K.K. Datta's *History of Freedom Movement in Bihar*.
15. *Police Abstract of Intelligence*, 1919.
16. Datta, K.K., *op. cit.*, Vol. I, p. 296.

17. Majumdar, R.C., *History of Freedom Movement in India*, Vol. III, p. 55.
18. Mahatma Gandhi, *Autobiography*, pp. 590-91.
19. *The Searchlight*, 4th September, 1919.
20. *The Non-Cooperation and Khilafat Movements in Bihar and Orissa*, p. 4.
21. *Ibid.*, p. 5.
22. *Ibid.*
23. *Ibid.*
24. *Ibid.*
25. *Ibid.*, p. 6.
26. *Ibid.*
27. *File No. 94, July 1920, Home Political Departmeni*, National Archives of India, New Delhi.
28. *Non-Cooperation and Khilafat Movements in Bihar and Orissa*, p. 7.
29. *Ibid.*, pp. 7-8.
30. *Ibid.*, p. 8.
31. *The Non-Cooperation and Khilafat Movements in Bihar and Orissa*, p. 8.
32. *The Searchlight*, August 6, 1920.
33. Prasad, Rajendra, *Mahatma Gandhi and Bihar*, p. 40.
34. *The Searchlight*, September 3, 1920.
35. Prasad, Rajendra, *Mahatma Gandhi and Bihar*, p. 41.
36. Sitaramayya, B. Pattabhi, *op. cit.*, Vol. I, pp. 200-203.
37. *The Non-Cooperation and Khilafat Movements in Bihar and Orissa*, p. 11.
38. *Ibid.*
39. *Ibid.*
40. *The Searchlight*, September 19, 1920.
41. *Ibid.*, September 29, 1920.
42. Datta, K.K., *Gandhiji in Bihar*, p. 75, *The Searchlight*, December 10, 1920.
43. *The Searchlight*, December 8, 1920.
44. *Ibid.*
45. *Ibid.*, December 5, 1920.
46. *The Non-Cooperation and Khilafat Movements in Bihar and Orissa*, p. 11.
47. *Ibid.*, p. 12.

48. *Ibid.*
49. *Ibid.*
50. *Ibid.*, pp. 14-15.
51. *Ibid.*, p. 17.
52. Prasad, Rajendra, *Mahatma Gandhi and Bihar*, p. 42.
53. *Young India*, December 20, 1920.
54. *The Non-Cooperation and Khilafal Movements in Bihar and Orissa*, p. 18.
55. *Ibid.*
56. Prasad, Janakdhari, *Autobiography*, Part I, p. 94.
57. *Ibid.*, p. 92.
58. *Ibid.*
59. Prasad, Rajendra, *Mahatma Gandhi and Bihar*, p. 43.
60. *Report of the Bihar Vidyapith and its Affiliated Institutions*, 1921-26, by Badri Nath Verma, p. 2.
61. Prasad, Rajendra, *Mahatma Gandhi and Bihar*, p. 43.
62. *Ibid.*
63. *Report of the Bihar Vidyapith*, etc., p. 4.
64. *A brief sketch of the Non-Cooperation Movement by Rajendra Prasad*, *Young India*, 1919-22.
65. *The Searchlight*, February 9, 1921.
66. *Report of the Bihar Vidyapith*, etc., 1921-26, pp. 4-5.
67. Datta, K.K., *op. cit.*, Vol. I, p. 312.
68. Prasad, Rajendra, *Mahatma Gandhi and Bihar*, p. 43.
69. *Young India*, December 20, 1920.
70. *The Non-Cooperation and Khilafat Movements in Bihar and Orissa*, pp. 19-20.
71. *Young India*, December 20, 1920.
72. *The Non-Cooperation and Khilafat Movements in Bihar and Orissa*, p. 20.
73. *Ibid.*
74. *Ibid.*
75. *Ibid.*
76. *Ibid.*, p. 12.
77. Sitaramayya, B. Pattabhi, *op. cit.*, Vol. I, p. 207.
78. *The Non-Cooperaiion and Khilafat Movements in Bihar and Orissa*, p. 26.
79. Datta, K.K., *op. cit.*, Vol. I, 323-24.
80. *The Searchlight*, March 16, 1921.

81. Datta, K.K., *op. cit.*, Vol. I, p. 326.
82. Prasad, Rajendra, *Atmakatha*, p. 136.
83. *The Non-Cooperation and Khilafat Movements in Bihar and Orissa*, p. 26.
84. Datta, K.K., *op. cit.*, p. 27.
85. *The Non-Cooperation and Khilafat Movements in Bihar and Orissa*, p. 27.
86. *Ibid.*
87. *Idid.*, p. 28.
88. *Man in India*, December 1921, *Census of India*, Vol. VII, Part I, pp. 126-130.
89. *Letter from Mr. Whitty, D.C. of Ranchi to F.F. Lyall, Commissioner of Chotanagpur.* dated February 24, 1921.
90. *Ibid.*, March 19, 1921.
91. *Police Reports.*
92. *Letter from Commissioner, Chotanagpur Division, to the Chief Secretary, Bihar and Orissa*, dated April 15, 1921.
93. *Police Reports.*
94. *Letter from the Commissioner, Chotanagpur Division to Chief Secretary, Bihar and Orissa*, April 15, 1921.
95. *The Non-Cooperation and Khilafat Movements in Bihar and Orissa*, p. 33.
96. *Ibid.*, p. 32.
97. Prasad, Rajendra, *Atmakatha.*
98. *Letter from J.C. Scott, Deputy Commissioner, Chaibasa to F.F. Lyall, Commissioner of Chotanagpur Division, Chaibasa*, February 12, 1921.
99. *Ibid.*, March 14, 1921.
100. *Letter from S.D.O., Jamtara to the Deputy Commissioner, Santhal Parganas*, March 2, 1921.
101. *The Searchlight*, March 20, 1921.
102. Sitaramayya, B. Pattabhi, *op. cit.*, Vol. I, p. 212.
103. Bamford, P.C., *Histories of the Non-Cooperation and Khilafat Movements*, p. 27.
104. *The Searchlight*, April 6, 1921.
105. *Ibid.*, April 8, 1921.
106. *The Non-Cooperation and Khilafat Movements in Bihar and Orissa*, p. 58.
107. Prasad, Rajendra, *Mahatma Gandhi and Bihar*, p. 47.

108. *Ibid.*
109. *The Non-Cooperation and Khilafat Movements in Bihar and Orissa*, p. 42.
110. *Ibid.*, p. 49.
111. *Ibid.*, p. 54.
112. *Ibid.*, p. 53.
113. *Ibid.*, p. 47.
114. *Ibid.*, p. 58.
115. *Ibid.*, p. 59.
116. *The Non-Cooperation and Khilafat Movements in Bihar and Orissa*, p. 62.
117. Datta, K.K., *op. cit.*, Vol. I, p. 383.
118. Prasad, Rajendra, *Mahatma Gandhi and Bihar*, p. 48.
119. *The Non-Cooperation and Khilafat Movements in Bihar and Orissa*, p. 65.
120. *Ibid.*
121. *The Searchlight*, October 7, 1921.
122. *The Non-Cooperation and Khilafat Movements in Bihar and Orissa*, p. 82.
123. *Ibid.*, p. 67.
124. *Ibid.*, pp. 69-78.
125. Datta, K.K., *op. cit.*, Vol. I, pp. 394-395.
126. Sitaramayya, B. Pattabhi, *op. cit.*, Vol. I, pp. 218-219.
127. *The Searchlight*, December 21, 1921.
128. Datta, K.K., *op. cit.*, Vol. I, p. 399.
129. *Speeches of Nirsu Narayan Sinha in Bihar and Orissa Legislative Council*, on January 25, 1922. *The Searchlight*, November 20, 1921.
130. *The Non-Cooperation and Khilafat Movements in Bihar and Orissa*, p. 79.
131. *Ibid.*
132. *Ibid.*, p. 82.
133. *Ibid.*
134. Datta, K.K., *op. cit.*, Vol. I, pp. 401-2.
135. Appendix XV of K.K. Datta's *History of the Freedom Movement in Bihar*, Vol. I.
136. *Young India*, January 12, 1922.

137. *Proceedings of the Bihar and Orissa Legislative Council*, Vol. V, January-February, 1922, p. 8.
138. *Ibid.*
139. *The Non-Cooperation and Khilafat Movements in Bihar and Orissa*, p. 85.
140. *Bihar and Orissa in 1921*, p. 156.
141. *The Non-Cooperation and Khilafat Movements in Bihar and Orissa*, p. 88.
142. Datta, K.K., *op. cit.*, p. 409.
143. *The Non-Cooperation and Khilafat Movements in Bihar and Orissa*, p. 94.
144. *Ibid.*, p. 95.
145. Sitaramayya, B. Pattabhi, *op. cit.*, Vol. I, p. 23.
146. Datta, K.K., *op. cit.*, Vol. I, p. 416.
147. *Near Gorakhpur in U.P.*
148. Sitaramayya, B. Pattabhi, *op. cit.*, Vol. I, pp. 235-36.
149. *The Searchlight*, February 15, 1922.
150. Datta, K.K., *op. cit.*, Vol. I, p. 417.
151. *The Great Trial with an introduction by Mazharul Haque. The Sadaqat Ashram Press*, Patna, 1922.
152. *The Non-Cooperation and Khilafat Movements in Bihar and Orissa*, p. 104.
153. Quoted in History of the *Freedom Movement in Bihar*, by K.K. Datta, Vol. I, p. 421.
154. *The Non-Cooperation and Khilafat Movements in Bihar and Orissa*, p. 104.
155. *Ibid.*, p. 105.
156. *Ibid.*, p. 106.
157. *Ibid.*, p. 107.
158. Sitaramayya, B. Pattabhi, *op. cit.*, Vol. I, pp. 250-51.
159. Datta, K.K., *op. cit.*, Vol. I, pp. 433-34.
160. *The Non-Cooperation and Khilafat Movements in Bihar and Orissa*, p. 120.
161. *Report of the Superintendent of Police*, *Ranchi*, January 2, 1923.
162. *Ibid.*, April 16, 1923.
163. *The Non-Cooperation and the Khilafat Movements in Bihar and Orissa*, p. 123.
164. Datta, K.K. *op. cit.*, Vol. I, p. 446.

165. *The Non-Cooperation and Khilafat Movements in Bihar and Orissa*, p. 122.
166. *Ibid.*, p. 127.
167. Datta, K.K., *op. cit.*, Vol. I, p. 450.
168. *The Searchlight*, April 18 and 23, 1923.
169. *Ibid.*, June 6, 1923.
170. Quoted in *History of the Freedom Movement in Bihar*, Vol. I, p. 447.
171. Prasad, Rajendra, *Atmakatha*, p. 212.
172. *The Searchlight*, July 9, 1923.
173. Prasad, Rajendra, *Atmakatha*, p. 213.
174. *The Non-Cooperation and Khilafat Movements in Bihar and Orissa*, p. 132.
175. Datta, K.K., *op. cit.*, Vol. I, p. 451.
176. Prasad, Rajendra, *Atmakatha*, p. 235-36.
177. *Ibid.*, p. 215.
178. *The Non-Cooperation and Khilafat Movements in Bihar and Orissa*, pp. 132-33.
179. Prasad, Rajendra, *Atmakatha*, p. 215.
180. Datta, K.K., *op. cit.*, Vol. I, p. 453.
181. *Ibid.*, p. 454.
182. *The Searchlight*, February 8, 1924.
183. *The Non-Cooperation and Khilafat Movements in Bihar and Orissa*, p. 137.
184. *Ibid.*, p. 138.
185. *Ibid.*, *Bihar in 1924-25*, p. 3.
186. *The Searchlight*, April 11, 1924.
187. *Proceedings of the Bihar and Orissa Legislative Council*, Vol. IX, January-February, 1924, pp. 293-332.
188. Prasad, Rajendra, *Atmakatha*, pp. 242-43.
189. *Ibid.*, pp. 243-44.
190. *Young India in 1924-26*, Introduction by Rajendra Prasad, XXVIII.
191. *Ibid.*, 1924-26, p. 564.
192. Datta, K.K., *op. cit.*, Vol. I, p. 469.
193. Desai, Mahadev, *Gandhiji in Indian Villages*, p. 232.
194. *Ibid.*, pp. 238-65, 283.
195. *Ibid.*, p. 283.
196. *Bihar and Orissa*, 1925-26, p. 29.
197. *Young India*, 1927-28, p. 83.

198. Prasad, Janakdhari, *Autobiography*, p. 144.
199. *Young India*, 1927-28, p. 53.
200. *Ibid.*
201. *Ibid.*, p. 77.
202. *Report of Bihar Vidyapith and its Affiliated Institutions* (1921-26), p. 9.
203. *Young India*, March 25, 1926.
204. *Ibid.*, 1927-28, pp. 80-81.
205. *Ibid.*, p. 80.
206. Prasad, Rajendra, *Atmakatha*, pp. 264-265.
207. *Ibid.*, p. 226.
208. Datta, K.K., *op. cit.*, Vol. I, p. 489.
209. Appendix XXII of *History of the Freedom Movement in Bihar*, by K.K. Datta, Vol. I.
210. *Young India*, July 1, 1926, pp. 266-67.
211. *Ibid.*, August 19, 1926.
212. Prasad, Rajendra, *Atmakatha*, pp. 266-67.
213. Datta, K.K., *op. cit.*, Vol. I.
214. *Report of the Superintendent of Police*, Ranchi, dated 8.10.1926.
215. Datta, K.K., *op. cit.*, Vol. I, p. 493.
216. Prasad, Rajendra, *Atmakatha*, pp. 258-261.
217. *Annual Report of the All India Congress Committee for the Year 1926*: *Bihar and Orissa in 1927-27*, pp. 1-4.
218. *Bihar and Orissa in 1926-27*, pp. 6-8.
219. *The Indian Quarterly Report*, 1926, Vol. I, p. 16.
220. *Ibid.*, pp. 33-34.
221. *Annual Report of the Congress for the year 1927.*
222. *The Indian Quarterly Register, 1927*, Vol. II, pp. 98-99.
223. *Annual Report of the Congress for the year 1927.*
224. Datta, K.K., *op. cit.*, Vol. II, p. 5.
225. *The Indian Quarterly Register, 1928*, Vol. II, pp. 441-42.
226. Prasad, Rajendra, *Mahatma Gandhi and Bihar*, p. 70.
227. Lala Lajpat Rai died on the 17th November, some days after the assault suffering from its after effects.
228. Pandit Nehru, *Autobiography*, pp. 180-181.
229. *Patna Commissioner's Fortnightly Report*, Dec. 28, 1928.
230. *Bihar and Orissa in 1928-29*, p. 2.
231. *Police Report.*

232. *Ibid.*
233. *Ibid.*
234. *The Indian Quarterly Register, 1928*, Vol. I, p. 513.
235. *Annual Report of the Congress Secretaries for* 1929, *Bihar Provincial Congress Committee's Annual Report*, 1928-29.
236. *Bihar Provincial Congress Committee's Annual Report*, 1928-29.
237. *Ibid.*
238. *Ibid.*
239. *Ibid.*
240. *The Indian Quarterly Register, 1928*, Vol. II, p. 463.
241. Prasad, Rajendra, *Atmakatha*, p. 300.
242. *Police Report*, dated 18.8.30.
243. Datta, K.K., *op. cit.*, Vol. II, p. 42.
244. *The Indian Quarterly Register*, 1929, Vol. II, p. 405.
245. *Bihar and Orissa Police Abstract of Intelligence*, February 15, 1930, Vol. XIV, No. 7.
246. *Police Report.*
247. *The Searchlight*, September 24, 1929.
248. Datta, K.K., *op. cit.*, Vol. II, pp. 45-47.

4

The Civil Disobedience Movement and the Middle Class in Bihar : 1930-1934

In this Chapter an attempt has been made to review the role of the middle class in the celebrations of "Independence Day", the Salt Satyagraha, the activities for the boycott of foreign cloth and boycott of intoxicants and non-payment of Chaukidari tax, anti-untouchability campaign, observing successful hartals and other national and constructive programmes. In the period under study we find that the participation of the masses in the struggle for freedom increased. They joined the movement with greater zeal and vigour. But it was the middle class that generated this enthusiastic spirit among the masses. Besides, the leadership still remained in the hands of the members of the middle class.

The Indian National Congress organised the Civil Disobedience Movement in pursuance of the resolution passed at its Lahore session in December 1929. By another resolution the attainment of Purna Swarajya (complete independence) was declared to be the chief objective of the Congress. It was also laid down that this resolution was to be adopted in public meetings throughout the country on the 26th January 1930 and that day was declared as 'Independenee Day'.[1]

In pursuance of the resolution of the Lahore session of the Indian National Congress, on the 20th January 1930, Rajendra Prasad, Shrikrishna, J.B. Sen, Ram Narain Singh and Mathura Prasad, who came from the middle class, issued on behalf of the Bihar Provincial Congress Committee a joint communique indicating the procedure of the celebration of "Independence Day" on the 26th January 1930. The communique ran as follows :

"(1) The National Flag should be hoisted at 8 in the morning at the place where the meeting is to be held. In the evening the flag should be taken down only after the meeting is over.

(2) After the flag is hoisted in the morning, the people should busy themselves with either of the following activities and should not waste a minute of their time :

   (a) As many as possible, houses should be visited and Congress resolution be explained to the people and members be enrolled for the year 1930.

   (b) Hawking of khaddar.

   (c) Charkha spinning.

   (d) Enrolment of volunteers. They should be habitual weavers of khadi and should have signed the Congress pledge.

   (e) Work for the uplift of untouchables, e.g., taking them into the temples, allowing them free use of wells, etc.

   (f) Prohibition.

(3) To hold a meeting exactly at 5 in the evening. Therein a prominent Congress worker should read out to the people assembled, the statement issued by the President of the Congress, slowly and distinctly, and the sense of the meeting should be taken by show of hands, as to how many of them are willing

to support the declaration. No speech be delivered in the meeting."[2]

Under the guidance and leadership of the middle class, the province of Bihar also celebrated the 'Independence Day' with great enthusiasm. For example, at Chapra at 8 a.m. Syed Mahmood, a member of the middle class, President of Saran Congress Committee and the General Secretary of the Indian National Congress, hoisted the National Flag with great enthusiasm on the Ram Lila Mathia ground. In the afternoon, according to the programme, a mass meeting was held at the same place which represented all sections of people. About five to six thousand people participated in celebrating the function. The 'Independence Declaration' was read out and the National Flag was then taken down.[3] 'Independence Day' was celebrated in the whole of Bihar in the same manner and flags were hoisted in most cases by men of the middle class.

According to the mandate of the Lahore Congress, members of the Legislature could not continue as members of the All India Congress Committee or other elective committee and so members of the All India Congress Committee, who had acted contrary to the Congress mandate, were called upon to resign from the All India Congress Committee. In Bihar, by the middle of January 1930, Mahendra Prasad, Maulvi Shah Muhammad Zubair, Anugrah Narayan Sinha and some others had resigned from the Council of State. Of the ten Congress representatives in the Legislative Assembly, only two, Sidheshwar Prasad Singh and Narayan Prasad Singh, resigned till then. The following persons had resigned from the Bihar and Orissa Legislative Council: Deep Narayan Singh, Krishna Ballabh Sahay, Shrikrishna Sinha, Ram Dayalu Singh, Satya Narayan Sinha, Rajendra Mishra, Siddeshwar Prasad, Ram Charitra Singh, Rameshwar Narayan Agarwala, Lingaraj Mishra, Nirshu Narayan Sinha, Pandit Godavari Mishra, Thakur Ram Nandan Singh, Abdul Bari, Guru Sahay Lal, Haribans Sahay, Kailash Behari Lal, Mahanta Ishwar Giri, Kumar Kalika Singh, Pandit Girindra Mohan Mishra, Shashi

Bhusan Rai, Rameshwar Lal Marwari and Dwarka Nath.[4] Persons who resigned, came from the different groups of the middle class, mainly the educated middle class.

Meeting at Ahmedabad, the Congress Working Committee passed a momentous resolution on the 15th February, 1930, to launch Civil Disobedience for attainment of the goal of independence and authorised Mahatma Gandhi and others, who upheld non-violence as an article of faith, to start it as and when they decide. Mahatma Gandhi thought of embarking on it as a Satyagraha by breaking monopoly on salt, a commodity which concerned all from the highest to the lowest and tax on which cost a poor man five annas a year or nearly his three days' income. As Bihar is an inland area having no sea coast and here people manufacture salt only on a small scale as a by-product while preparing saltpetre out of earth at some localities. Rajendra Prasad sought Mahatma Gandhi's permission to start Satyagraha in Bihar by non-payment of the 'Chowkidari tax'[5] which every household in a village had to pay for the maintenance of the village Chaukidars. But Mahatmaji advised him "not to attempt it, at any rate to begin with, as the Government would come down with a heavy hand and it was possible the people might not be able to stand the pressure that would follow non-payment of the Chowkidar tax."[6]

Mahatma Gandhi decided to start the Satyagraha by breaking the salt laws after marching to Dandi, a village on the sea coast, about two hundred miles from the Sabarmati Ashram. On the 12th March, 1930, at 6.30 a.m. he started on a historic march to Dandi with seventy-eight volunteers hailing from different Provinces, including Bihar, and reached there on 5th April.[7] But, according to Pattabhi Sitaramayya, Mahatma Gandhi had left the Ashram with only seventy-five volunteers.[8]

The All India Congress Committee met at Ahmedabad on March 21, 1930. It endorsed the resolution of the Working Committee and also expressed the hope that "the whole country will respond to the action taken by Gandhi" and authorise "the Provincial Congress Committee to organise and undertake such Civil Disobedience as to them may seem proper and in the manner that may appear to them to be most suitable."[9]

There was already abounding enthusiasm and preparedness in the country for a non-violent Satyagraha to affect national deliverance. In Bihar the zeal of patriotism was remarkable. Independence Day was celebrated here with great solemnity.[10] Congress members were being enrolled in large numbers[11] and the leaders of the Province were fully responsive to the demands of the new situation. The Bihar Provincial Congress Committee also met at Sadaqat Ashram, Patna, under the presidentship of Rajendra Prasad on the 30th March 1930, to devise ways and means for the implementation of the resolution passed in the meeting of the Congress Committee at Ahmedabad on March 21, 1930. It was unanimously decided that as soon as Mahatma Gandhi was arrested or if he issued any signal to start Civil Disobedience movement, the Provincial Congress would at once respond to it and the movement be started. It is rather significant that the two districts that were given priority over others for starting the movement were Saran and Champaran in the whole of the Province of Bihar. It was also proposed to enrol atleast fifty thousand volunteers in the province. Sixty-one members of the Provincial Congress Committee, who came from the middle class, signed the volunteers' pledge.[12]

On the next day (31st March, 1930) of this momentous meeting, Saran was the first district in Bihar which was visited by the President of the Indian National Congress, Pandit Jawaharlal Nehru and his illustrious wife, Kamla Nehru. Jawaharlal Nehru's tour in the Saran, Champaran and Muzaffarpur Districts from the 31st March to the 3rd of April was a source of great inspiration to the people. By the first week of April over 5,000 Congress volunteers had been enrolled here and there, their numbers were gradually swelling.[13] *The Searchlight* of the 9th April reported : "The thrill of a new hope, the surge of a new aspiration, the pursuit of a noble ideal and romance of a new sacrifice surcharge the atmosphere."[14]

After Mr. Nehru, Jaleshwar Prasad informed about the decision of the Provincial Congress Committee that the districts of Saran and Champaran have been selected in this province to lead the Civil Disobedience campaign which would be started by disobeying the Salt Law. Besides, the people of these districts might also resort to non-payment of Chaukidari tax when the time demanded. He warned the government that if it did not come to its sense in time they might undertake new forms of civil disobedience, i.e., breaking of railway laws, etc. He further asked the people to travel without ticket, for it were the railways which were responsible for discrimination in freight rates so as to facilitate the import of finished goods into India and export of raw materials outside India.[15]

The next speaker was 'Bihar Bhushan' (then called), Rajendra Prasad "without whom the meeting could not have been kept in control." He asked the people to concentrate in the first instance in breaking salt law but if time required they would also take up chaukidari tax. He again asked the people not to be afraid of the law of sedition which was in his opinion a dead letter then. He said that the Congress was going to enrol fifty thousand volunteers in Bihar for satyagraha and the district of Saran, which was also his home district, should contribute the largest quota of six thousand volunteers for the purpose.[16]

On 6th April 1930, the first day of the National Week Celebration to commemorate the memory of the Jallianwala Bagh Tragedy, after a night of fasting and prayers, Gandhiji broke the salt law by picking up salt on seashore. Thus, a British law was defied in a non-violent manner. It was a signal for starting the mass movement in the different parts of the country.[17]

The movement spread like wild fire. It set the whole country ablaze. In Saran, three places, viz., Bareja, Goreakothi and Hajipur, were selected for violation of salt law, which commenced on the 6th, 7th and 8th April, respectively. After attending a meeting at Chapra the Satyagraha started from there on the 6th April for the respective centres. The three batches were led respectively by Girish Tewary, Secretary, District Congress Committee and Vice Chairman of Saran District Board, Chandrika Singh, a member of the Saran District Board and of the Provincial Congress Committee, and Bharat Mishra, President of the Satyagraha Committee. The gathering at the station numbered about five thousand. Nineteen volunteers were booked for Bareja, eleven for Gorea-kothi and eleven for Hajipur.[18]

On the 6th April 1930, preparation of salt started at Bareja at 9 p.m. On the same day (i.e. 7th April 1930) by 10 a.m. locally manufactured salt was sold worth Rupees fourteen and three paise only.[19] On the 7th April 1930, Baban Singh, the Naik (leader) of the Bareja camp was arrested.

In the meantime, Pandit Jawaharlal Nehru was arrested. His arrest aroused deep indignation amongst the people of Saran. There was a complete hartal at Dighwara Bazar on the 15th April 1930. The liquor and toddy shops were picketed.[20]

The arrest of Pandit Jawaharlal Nehru further embittered the feelings of the people of Bihar. It also brought about intensification of the satyagraha movement which is evident from the circular letter issued by Rajendra Prasad, President of the Bihar Provincial Congress Committee :

"It is time now that satyagraha against the salt law should be given the form of a mass movement. It is, therefore, left within the discretion of every district to begin and carry on satyagraha. And to make it a mass movement, they are to conduct it in accordance with the following directions :

"(a) Satyagraha should be launched in as many villages as possible.

(b) Due attention should be paid to the refinement of salt as much as possible in order to make it fit for human consumption. In this connection the help of experts must be obtained. Not the violation of the law only but also the eatable salt should be the important consideration.

(c) Whatever quantity of salt is manufactured it should be sold to the poor in the villages at the lowest possible rates, while a little quantity of it may be auctioned in cities to obtain some money for conducting the satyagraha movement.

(d) Whoever has enrolled himself in the satyagraha army should be directed in the first instance to manufacture salt in his own place provided there are facilities for it, and in case of want of such facilities he should be asked to go to the place where they are available.

(e) The general public should be told that they should take up manufacture of salt after having thoroughly understood the salt law and know fully the consequences that are likely to follow its breach.

(f) Wherever necessary the satyagrahis may employ "Noniyas"[21] even on wages, according to their needs; and manufacture salt. But this should be resorted to only where the satyagrahis are unable to manufacture salt themselves.

(g) Pamphlets containing the above directions should be freely distributed in the villages."[22]

The directives of Rajendra Prasad gave further impetus to the people. At Bareja a meeting of the workers was held on the 18th April 1930, and it was decided to start some ten new centres within that circle for the manufacture of salt. So far thirty centres had already started at Goreakothi and six centres at Hajipur.[23] By the 23rd April, there were in Saran district about twelve principal salt manufacturing centres with many villages round each centre also manufacturing salt.[24] The whole district was "convulsed with life and vigour" and organised an effective social boycott against the Police.[25] The leaders, who led the salt satyagraha in this district, belonged to the educated middle class having lands.

In the Champaran district, the first jatha (procession), consisting of thirteen men, started on the 6th April 1930 under the leadership of Bipin Behari Varma, President, Champaran District Congress Committee and Chairman of the local District Board. There was much enthusiam in the town when the first batch of volunteers began their march and Rajendra Prasad gave them a hearty send off. In their march they halted at Ankhia, Semara, Sugauli, Phulwaria, Madhopur, Senwaria, Jokaria and reached Bettiah on the 11th April. In the meeting addressed at Bettiah by Bipin Behari Varma a purse of Rs. 593 was presented to him. Salt law was broken on the 15th April in several thanas of the Champaran district, namely, Jogapatti, Motihari, Dhaka, Sugauli, Govindganj, Raxaul and Bettiah. The leaders working in the different thanas were arrested by the police almost simultaneously and, on the same day, Bipin Behari Varma, Shivadhary Pandey, Ganesh Prasad Sahu, Ramdayalu Prasad Sahu, Ramlal Prasad, Sitaram Shah, Ramavatar Singh, Jamuna Prasad, Ramlochan Sinha, Lal Bahadur Sinha, Vaidyanath Prasad Sinha, Pandit Lakshmi Narayan Jha, Ramsundar Tewari, Ram Deo, Kishun Sinha, Natho Sinha and Shukdeo Prasad were arrested and tried.[26]

But repression failed to check the progress of the Satyagraha, and salt began to be manufactured on a mass scale in numerous villages of that area. By the 19th April it was being manufactured at 550 places engaging 2,000 volunteers.[27] Persons who took part in the Salt Satyagraha, were from the middle class.

The Muzaffarpur district launched the Satyagraha movement from the 7th April under the guidance of Ram Dayalu Singh, ex-M.L.A. and President of the District Congress Committee, Janakdhari Prasad and Thakur Ram Nandan Singh, ex-M.L.C. and President, Subdivisional Congress

Committee. In the Ram Bagh at Sheohar, a big meeting was addressed by Ram Dayalu Singh.[28] The Police posted there lost no time in using their usual means of coercion to disperse the people, who had assembled in large numbers, and arrested the leaders Ram Dayalu Singh, Thakur Ram Nandan Singh, Janakdhari Prasad, Thakur Nawab Singh, Lalit Kumar Singh (Natavar), and some others.[29] Ram Dayalu Singh was sentenced to one and half years' rigorous imprisonment, Thakur Ramnandan Singh to two years' rigorous imprisonment, and the rest being sentenced to six months' imprisonment; and all were sent to Hazaribagh Jail. Four more persons were imprisoned,[30] including Rajendra Nath Rai Chowdhury, Captain of the Muzaffarpur Volunteers, and Ramji Prasad Varma, then a student of the Bihar College of Engineering and a volunteer. The former was sentenced to one year's rigorous imprisonment,[31] and the latter and also another volunteer to two years' rigorous imprisonment each. Mathura Prasad Singh was sentenced to one year's rigorous imprisonment at Muzaffarpur.[32] Persons, who took part in the Salt Satyagraha in this district, were mostly from the middle class. Some of them were lawyers, some were landholders and some were university students.

From the 16th to the 21st April, 1930, the city of Patna witnessed one of the most heroic scenes in the thrilling drama of Bihar's national struggle, marked by brave resolve and unflinching determination on the part of some of her sons, most of whom belonged to the middle class, to carry on Salt Satyagraha in the face of the most naked violence on the part of the police. Patna inaugurated Salt Satyagraha on Wednesday, the 16th of April, 1930. Nakhas Pind, a place about two miles to the east of Mangles Tank in the Patna City, had been selected as the spot for violation of salt laws by the manufacture of salt from salt earth. For reaching this place a procession of Satygrahis under the captainship of Ambika Kant Sinha, Manager of *The Searchlight* and Secretary of the Town Congress Committee, started from the Congress Office with National flags in the hands at about 9 a.m. A European Sergeant or D.S.P. "used his cane strick freely and several volunteers received injuries on their persons, some of them severely.[33] But the processionists did not budge an inch and squatted on the ground.

Meanwhile, another procession of volunteers had been formed under the leadership of Pandit Ram Briksha Sharma Benipuri, editor of the "Yovak", and wanted to proceed ahead. But it was stopped near Gulzarbagh and Pandit Benipuri was arrested. He appointed Master Ram Nath as his successor. But the latter was also arrested. Ambika Kant Sinha, Pandit Ram Briksha Sharma Benipuri and Ram Nath were sentenced to six months' imprisonment each. Ram Nath was released on his father giving a security. While all these were happening in the Mahendru area, Jamuna Prasad Jha heading a procession started from Gulzarbagh. Also two other processions proceeded forward to the east[34] and manufactured salt at Nakhas Pind.

Rajendra Prasad had been touring in other parts of Bihar to see how the Satyagraha was progressing there. At Chapra he received the news of what had happened at Patna and hurriedly came here. On proceeding to the scene at about midnight of the 16th April with Anugrah Narain Sinha, Acharya Kripalani and Mathura Prasad, he saw the volunteers asleep on the road and the police standing at a short distance from them. Early next morning, Rajendra Prasad again went to that place, held a meeting at a short distance from it and addressed it asking the volunteers "to remain firm in the face of assaults and to remain non-violent".[35]

Rajendra Prasad and the other Congress leaders at Patna had decided to send out batches of volunteers three times a day at stated hours informing the District Magistrate accordingly. At about quarter to seven in the morning of Saturday, the 19th April, the first batch of five Shahabad volunteers went to offer Satyagraha opposite Sultanganj thana. Some volunteers were pushed down and thrown aside. All the volunteers were seriously wounded, but three of them "were so seriously wounded that they fell down disabled."[36] Two of the wounded volunteers, joined by three others, formed a second batch and proceeding ahead went near Sultanganj. The police constable obstructed them and snatched away their flags. But while they were walking forward they "were mercilessly belaboured by the police and pushed into the Nalla. Two of the first batch were thoroughly disabled by this time."[37]

One of the police officers made a "savage attack" on Abdul Bari, when he was trying to control the crowd in front of the Patna College.[38] One of the policemen on horseback whispered to Abdul Bari, "You are a Mussalman. How is it that you are in this crowd ?" Abdul Bari replied, "Allah has sent me here for you."[39] Kripalani, while standing near the T.K. Ghose's Academy, opposite Patna College, was also assaulted by the police with lathi.[40] Abdul Bari was hurt by the hoofs of the horses.[41]

On the 20th April, the District Magistrate of Patna issued a public notice to the effect that unless the disturbances in the city ceased he would appoint additional police and the citizens would have to pay the cost for it.[42] Rajendra Prasad asked the people to be ready for non-payment of this tax if it was imposed.[43] Government did not approve of this idea of the District Magistrate as they wanted to carry moderate opinion with Government.[44]

Police atrocities, caused considerable excitement among the people, who had assembled on the roads and among others. But under instructions from Rajendra Prasad and other leaders, the former "received blows with courage and determination and there was no attempt at retaliation."[45] But these wounded the sentiments of all classes and, as a result of it, a mammoth meeting of the citizens of Patna was held on 22nd April, 1930, on the Bhanwarpokhar ground under the presidentship of Hasan Imam, a lawyer, to protest against the outrages perpetrated by the police. The conveners of this gathering were Rajendra Prasad, Ali Imam, Sachchidanand Sinha, S.M. Ismail, Mubarak Ali, S.M. Mallick and some others.[46]

This state of public feeling probably had its repercussion on the official mind. So the mounted police were withdrawn; and, on Wednesday, the 23rd April, a procession of volunteers proceeded without obstruction to Nakhas Pind, where salt manufacture continued smoothly.[47] The Salt Satyagraha at Patna was a success. Here also members of the middle class played the dominating role. They organised the Satyagraha and participated in it.

In the Darbhanga district, the first batch of volunteers under the leadership of Satya Narayan Singha started from the Darbhanga town on the 17th April to break the salt law at Pipra.[48]

In the Monghyr district, Congress activities were increasing rapidly under the able leadership of Shrikrishna Sinha, a lawyer and then Secretary of the Provincial Congress Commitee. There, two batches of volunteers started on the 17th April to break salt law, one for the village Gadhpura in Begusarai subdivision and another for the village Chauki in Sadar subdivision, under the guidance of Shrikrishna Sinha and Nand Kumar Sinha respectively.[49]

On the 22nd April one centre for salt manufacture was started at Barahia in the temple of Teja Singh, and salt law was disobeyed here on the 23rd April under the leadership of Shah Muhammad Zubair and Nemdhari Singh. Kumar Kalika Singh also reached here with a batch of volunteers from Deoghar and Monghyr and engaged himself in salt manufacture for several days.[50]

In Bhagalpur, two jathas of eleven volunteers each under the leadership of Mahadev Lal Sharaff and Deep Narayan Agrawal proceeded to village Gouripur in the Bihpur thana to manufacture salt.[51] At a meeting of the Manbhum Congress Committee, held on the 10th April 1930, a District Satyagraha Committee was formed with Nibaran Chandra Das Gupta as its president. Another Committee, consisting mostly of some prominent lawyers, was olso formed to collect funds for the

Satyagraha movement. Salt Satyagraha began in Manbhum in right earnest and contraband salt was being sold in the open market.[52]

In the district of Santhal Parganas too the movement was gathering strength gradually. Shashi Bhushan Roy held meetings at Sarwan, Dakhusia, Sabaijore, Banmangama and Kukraha. Binoda Nanda Jha visited Sabaijore and addressed females there. He visited Kukraha also. In the third week of April, Shashi Bhushan Roy went with a batch of volunteers to Lakhisarai (in the Monghyr district) to manufacture salt and was arrested there. But the movement continued to progress in the Santhal Parganas.[53]

It is evident from the above paragraphs that the Salt Satyagraha in Darbhanga, Monghyr, Bhagalpur, the Manbhum and the Santhal Parganas was organised by the middle class as the organisers and most of the participants too were either educated professionals or university students or land-holders.

The Government so long sought to damage the morale of the Satyagrahis and to break the backbone of the Satyagraha by arresting its leaders at different places. Reviewing the position till the 23rd April, the Bihar Provincial Congress Committee noted in one of its Weekly Reports, "The Government are following the policy of arresting the leaders and organisers only leaving the ordinary volunteers alone."[54]

The Government of India was frightened by the spontaneous manifestations of the national upsurge of the Indian people. The salt satyagraha had aroused the national sentiment of the people throughout India. It appeared as if Mahatma's objective behind the salt satyagraha was going to be realised. Hence, on the 4th May 1930, the Government decided to arrest Mahatma Gandhi who was the chief motivating force behind the entire movement. The arrest of Mahatma Gandhi on May 4, 1930, generated so much anger that hartals were observed throughout the country.[55] In Bihar, there were hartals in district and subdivisional headquarters.

A hartal was organised at Patna on the 6th of May, processions were taken out, and in the evening of that day a large audience assembled in a meeting addressed by Rajendra Prasad in highly inspiring words. At Barh, the Municipality, the Local Board and the Co-operative Bank were closed. Students, including many of the schools, joined in the strikes and demonstrations at all places. On the 8th May, a special meeting for students of all categories was held at Bhanwarpokhar at Patna, at which Abdul Bari presided. At Gaya, the situation was very much similar to that of Patna. Arrah observed a complete hartal. At Muzaffarpur, Monghyr, Champaran, Purulia, Hazaribagh, Dumka, Madhupur and other places, hartals, processions and strikes were successfully organised with active participation of the students.[56] It was noted in a contemporary government report that Chapra was thrown into a state of mild excitement, and almost complete hartal was observed. Several processions were taken out, but as they were orderly, the authorities decided to ignore them. Very few lawyers attended courts and members of the bar led some of the processions and all students of Chapra town with the exception of a few of the Zila School boys, struck.[57] In pursuance of the instruction, picketing of foreign cloth shops started at Chapra town from the 21st May 1930. Before every cloth shop two or three volunteers were posted and customers were requested not to purchase foreign cloths.[58]

Salt manufacture work was to continue[59] till the end of June because on the outbreak of monsoons in Bihar it was not possible to get the kind of earth required for it. Rajendra Prasad, the President of the Bihar Provincial Congress Committee, issued a circular on the 9th May, 1930, directing all subordinate committees to start picketing of foreign cloths and liquor shops from the 16th May. Since then propaganda against the use of foreign cloth and intoxicating drugs and liquors and picketing of shops dealing in them began to be carried on with much success.[60] Within about three weeks, cloth dealers in several district towns and many smaller towns and bazars responded to the appeal of Congress by refusing to place further orders for foreign cloth and stopping sale, packed their stock and got the same sealed by the Congress Committees in their respective areas. The propaganda against intoxicating drugs and liquor was carried on so vigorously that at several places it was almost at a standstill.[61]

In May 1930, a Swadeshi League was formed at Patna of which Ali Imam was the President. Sachchidananda Sinha and K.B. Dutt, Vice-Presidents, Hasan Imam, General Secretary and Baldev Sahay, Joint Secretary[62] (all lawyers).

On the start of the Satyagraha movement, Mahatma Gandhi, in an open letter to the women of India, asked them to help the national cause by participating in the activities for the boycott of foreign cloth and boycott of intoxicants. In Bihar, the women, mostly belonging to the middle class, came out of the purdah and made an enthusiastic response to Mahatma Gandhi's call. At Patna particularly, the success which attended the picketing of foreign cloth was largely due to their efforts. A number of ladies, headed by Mrs. Hasan Imam, went through the streets of Patna urging the shop-keepers not to deal in foreign cloths. Vindyavasini Devi also took a prominent part in this work.[63]

There was considerable progress in boycott propaganda in different parts of Bihar by the first week of June. "Ladies who had never come out of purdah, were then taking part in many places in picketing", notably at Patna.[64] Deoki Prasad Sinha and B.K. Nandkeolear resigned their seats in the Council. On the Government side, the number of police arrests and convictions had also risen daily, the total number of arrests being 508 till then.

A very serious situation had developed at Bihpur in Bhagalpur district. What the magistracy and the police had done so far at other places in Bihar, since the commencement of the 1930 Satyagraha, pales into insignificance before the barbarism at Bihpur. In the afternoon of the 1st June, some of the volunteers, who came mainly from the middle class, engaged in picketing liquor and ganja shops, were asked by one of the European officers, having some constables with him, to go away. On their refusal, they were severely beaten and the National Flag was snatched away from them and burnt. The police then raided and took possession of the Congress Office, the Khadi Depot and Charkha Sangh turning out the inmates of those places.[65]

Terrorism in all its nakedness was rampant at Bihpur and the situation there was terribly deteriorating every day, Rajendra Prasad, accompanied by Abdul Bari, Baladev Sahay, Gyan Saha, Secretary, Bihar Provincial Hindustani Seva Dal, and Murli Manohar Prasad, the famous editor of *The Search-light*, went from Patna for that place and reached Bhagalpur at noon on Sunday, the 8th June. Next day at noon, Rajendra Prasad reached Bihpur with his Patna friends and also with Anant Prasad, M.L.C., Kamaleshwari Sahay, M.L.C., Yakub Arif, who was at one time a member of the Legislative Assembly, Upendranath Mukherjee, President of the Bhagalpur District Congress Committee, and some others of Bhagalpur. There was a meeting in the same orchard where a meeting had held previously, and it was addressed by Rajendra Prasad, Abdul Bari and Arif. The police dealt lathi blows on such respectable persons as Rajendra Prasad, Baladev Sahay, Abdul Bari, Murli Manohar Prasad, Gyan Saha, Ram Bilas Sharma, Motilal Khandelwal, Shyam Sundar Lal and several others. Abdul Bari, Leyakat Husain of Sultanganj and Murlidhar Potdar of Patna, Kantilal Chowdhry and Ramgati Singh of Bihpur received severe injuries due to lathi blows along with many others.[66] Almost all the persons, who received injuries, belonged to the middle class.

Shocked by police repression, four members of the Bihar Council, namely, Anant Prasad, Kamaleshwari Sahay, Shyam Narayan Sinha Sharma and Nawal Kishore Prasad tendered their resignations. Sudhanshu Bhushan Rai, Public Prosecutor of Bhagalpur, resigned in protest against the lathi charge at Bihpur on the innocent gathering in general and on Rajendra Prasad and others in particular, resigned during the week ending July 4, 1930, in acute difference with the local officials over the recent happenings in the district of Bhagalpur holding the action of the magistracy at Bihpur and Sabour quite illegal. Dwarka Nath resigned from the Bihar Legislative Council as a protest against the repressive policy of the Government, in particular the lathi charge on Rajendra Prasad and Abdul Bari at Bihpur. Jogendra Prasad, Advocate, Patna High Court, also resigned from the Bihar Legislative Council for similar reasons.[67] Persons who resigned against the police repression at Bihpur, formed the middle class educated elites of Bihar.

Picketing of foreign cloth and intoxicants had been going on with immense vigour throughout the province and preparations were being made at several places for non-payment of Chaukidari tax. At village Babura, a stronghold of the nationalists in the Shahabad district, some people had already refused to pay Chaukidar tax. At other places, including important trade centres like Muzaffarpur and Bhagalpur, the foreign cloth dealers were getting their stock of foreign cloth sealed with the Congress seal. Bhagalpur was then the largest centre of cloth trade after Calcutta and Kanpur. Caste panchayats at various places banned intoxicants, and in some areas, persons dealing in intoxicants were socially boycotted by the people.[68]

The Government had also begun sending columns of military police to the villages to threaten the rural folk and the police sometimes used physical violence. Till the end of June, the districts of Bhagalpur, Santhal Parganas and Manbhum were subject to such violent police actions. But this intimidation could not stop picketing, carried on mainly by the members of the middle class. As soon as some volunteers were arrested, fresh batches came in their places, and female picketers had also appeared on the scene.[69]

The Government applied such measures almost everywhere. In Bihar, strong action was taken against the Congress Bulletin in Hindi, called the 'Bihar Satyagraha Samachar'. On the 13th or 14th June, 1930, the police raided the office of the

Provincial Congress Committee at Patna in connection with the Bihar Satyagraha Samachar.[70] But the Bihar Satyagraha Samachar still continued to appear and the Government could not locate the place of its publication.[71] Under this campaign several other periodicals and pamphlets were seized by Government during the year 1930. A few books, also, containing revolutionary matters, were banned.

Early in the month of January, 1932, action was taken by Government against the Saraswati Press and the Desh Sewak Press at Arrah. For printing a pamphlet, entitled 'Vijayi Bharat' (composed by Paras Nath Dwivedi and published by Gopilal Gupta) in December 1931, the Desh Sewak Press was asked by the Magistrate of Shahabad to give security of rupees one thousand, on or before the 5th February 1932, against publishing such instigating books or materials.[72]

To stop picketing, Government was also prosecuting the leaders and many other national workers, most of whom came from the middle class. Among the prominent persons arrested during the week ending 13th June, 1930, were Ram Charitra Singh and Purna Chandra Mitra, Gyan Saha, Gauri Shankar Sharan Singh, a prominent Zamindar and President of the Gaya District Congress Committee, Devilal Sahu, a banker and zamindar of Motihari and a great helper of the Congress movement, and Kumar Birendra Singh, a zamindar of Gaya. Five prominent workers of Patna City, Pandit Jamuna Jha, Rambhajan Prasad Gupta, Ghuran Singh, Pandit Jagdish Narayan Pandey and Sardar Ishwari Singh were also arrested during the week. Shah Muhammad Umair of Gaya, Jainath Pati, a Mukhtar of Nawada and Bindhyachal Prasad of Shahabad were also arrested. During the week ending 27th June, 1930, there were more arrests (690 persons) than in any previous week, prominent among the arrestees were Vindheshwari Prasad Varma, President, Muzaffarpur District Congress Committee, Jaleshwar Prasad, Advocate, and leader of the Swaraj Party in the Second Reformed Council, Jagat Narayan Lal, Sardar of Patna Rural District Satyagraha Committee, Motilal Kejeriwal, President, Santhal Parganas

District Congress Committee, Ram Bahadur Gupta, Zamindar, Hriday Narayan Chowdhary, Vakil, Kamaleshwari Charan Sinha, an old national worker of Darbhanga, Suraj Prasad Mahajan, President, Gaya District Congress Committee, Mukutdhari Prasad Varma, Vakil and Vice-Chairman, Gaya Municipality and Chandra Shekhar Singh, Zamindar and Vakil of Shahabad district. For the first time in the province of Bihar, two ladies werc also arrested during this week for political offence. They were Saraswati Devi and Sadhana Devi. The former was President of the Hazaribagh District Congress Committee and the latter daughter of a professor of Physics working in the district of Santhal Parganas.[73]

On 30th June, 1930, Pandit Motilal Nehru and Syed Mahmood were arrested as Acting President and Secretary of the Congress Working Committee, which was declared unlawful. The news of these arrests produced a thrill in the province of Bihar and hartals were observed at all important centres. One striking feature of the hartal at Patna this time was the closing of many Muhammadan shops, the owners of which had not joined the previous hartals. It may be noted here that Maulana Abul Kalam Azad's recent visit to Patna had produced a good effect, from national point of view, on the Muslims of Patna. Many youths among them started an organisation under the Presidentship of Abdul Bari with the object of popularising the idea of independence in their community.[74]

The arrest of Rajendra Prasaad had caused a stir throughout the Province[75] and shocked the feelings of even some moderate thinkers. The movement, therefore, got much impetus. Deep Narayan Singh of Bhagalpur, whom Rajendra Prasad had selected as his successor, accepted the leadership and began touring the province immediately. He visited Arrah and Buxar on the 27th July, 1930, on his way to Bombay.[76]

Hasan Imam addressed several meetings at Patna and Bihta during the week ending 18th July. By the 15th of August, Hasan Imam, Baldev Sahay, Advocate, and Professor

Abdul Bari toured the districts of Champaran and Muzaffarpur. Abdul Bari also visited Pakur in the district of Santhal Parganas.

Women, mostly from the middle class families of Bihar, who had been already feeling the impulse of a new life, now came forward courageously in the "world's broad field" to share the shock of struggle and the joy of victories in the battle of national liberation. In the week ending the 10th of July 1930, a lady worker in Giridih subdivision was arrested and sent to jail. She was Mira Devi, daughter of S.B. Bhattacharya, a Professor of St. Columbus' College at Hazaribagh, and the third lady to be arrested in the province of Bihar. In collaboration with Mrs. Sami (Mr. Hasan Imam's daughter). Mrs. C.C. Das and some other Bihari ladies, she organised a procession of ladies at Patna on the 15th July to inaugurate an intensive campaign of boycott of British goods. During the week ending 25th July, 1930, Patna witnessed two demonstrations of ladis, in one of which nearly 3,000 ladies took part. Mrs. Hasan Imam, Mrs. Sami, Mrs. C.C. Das and Miss Gauri Das were the most active and in the forefront. Through their influence Mrs. Shah Muhammad Zubair of Monghyr came out of purdah as a public worker. She addressed a meeting at Monghyr on the 25th July, 1930, and formed a committee to look after the boycott propaganda. Mrs. Hasan Imam, Mrs. Sami, Mrs. C.C. Das, Miss Gauri Das and Vindhyavasini Devi, wife of Babu Ambika Charan, Mining Engineer, were soon summoned to court under section 30 of the Police Act and section 143 of the I.P.C. Murli Manohar Prasad, editor of *The Searchlight*, Sarangdhar Singh, Advocate, Patna High Court and Secretary of the Town Congress Committee, Patna, and Phulan Prasad Varma, Advocate, Patna High Court, were also summoned under section 32 of the Police Act. This created a great sensation and there were several big meetings and processions at Patna.[78]

The widespread arrests of leaders failed to check the progress of the movement. In fact, fresh batches of volunteers recruited from different sections of the people, including a large number of the rural folk, kept it alive with vigour, and all its items were carried on zealously under the able leadership and guidance of the middle class. The workers, most of whom belonged to the middle class, were now devoting much attention to promote boycott of British goods in addition to the boycott of British cloth and to intensify the movement for non-payment of chaukidari tax. The Bihar Provincial Congress Committee thus reviewed the progress of the movement for non-payment of chaukidari tax has definitely begun in the Province. "Champaran leads where Sugauli, Govindganj, Dhaka, Jogapatti and Majhaulia—the five thanas ars affected. In Sugauli thana, five villages of the Phulwaria beat have stopped paying the chaukidari tax as a result of which moveable goods of some villagers were seized and put to auction. Thare were no bidders of the locality and the properties were sold only to Chaukidars of other beats. Twelve villages of the Sugauli Union Board also will stop payment shortly. In Majhauli thana, a village of Amwa centre has also stopped payment of chaukidari tax. Two villagers have been assaulted and taken into the police custody. Twenty-two villagers of the Madhupur Lulhi centre in this thana have shown their preparedness to enter the list very soon. In Dhaka thana, 46 villages are fully organised to launch the non-payment of chaukidari tax movement and in a few days it will find itself in the thick of the fight."[79] All the villagers of Guthani Thana and the residents of twenty villages of Garkha thana stopped payment of chaukidari tax."[80]

"The total figure of the arrested persons in the whole of Bihar province since the very beginning of the Civil Disobedience Movement rose to 12,194 upto the end of 1930, out of this Saran alone contributed 1,286."[81]

The Government of Bihar, in a communique, announced that they have decided to post a force of 50 additional police in certain villages within the Darauli police station in Saran district for a period of one year (i.e., the whole of 1931) to maintain order in the locality and their expenses were to be borne by the villagers of Darauli police station.[82] The said act of the government was condemned by the Editor of *The Searchlight* in its issue dated 8th January, 1931. Special military force consisting of nearly 600 Gurkha soldiers and 30 mounted policemen was posted at Maharajganj (Saran) to collect the chaukidari tax. They closed the Ashram at Maharajganj and removed the National Flags which were flying on private houses. The militarymen paraded the streets of Maharajganj and neighbouring villages to create a feeling of terror among the masses. However, the people were determined not to pay the taxes.[83]

The movement for the boycott of foreign cloth was making good progress due largely to the zealous participation and able leadership and guidance of the members of the middle class. The cloth merchants offered to set up a Boycott Committee consisting of an equal number of representatives of the Congress and the merchants with an independent President to be chosen by them. On the constructive side, the 'Swadeshi Week' was observed at Ranchi in which two days were specially devoted to Charkha and Takli competitions. One day was reserved for the males and another for the females. The aboriginals, both males and females, enthusiastically participated in these competitions. Such competitions were held at other places too, such as, at Deoghar, Sasaram and Patna City. One Khadi Board was established at Deoghar to organise production of Khadi there and a Mahila Sabha, with about 100 ladies as its members, was also formed at this place.[84]

According to the Report of the Provincial Congress Committee for the week ending 7th November, 1930, village panchayats were being organised in large numbers throughout Bihar under the guidance of the middle class.

The Congress Working Committee meeting at Bombay from July to the 1st August, 1930, passed a resolution congratulating the people of Bihar "on the inauguration of the campaign of non-payment of the chaukidari tax" and expressed the hope that "they will continue vigorously to pursue the programme, whatever the repression they have to face and the sacrifices they have to make."[85] Confiscation of property and goods of all kinds including plough, cattle, corns, cooking utensils, grains, etc., for non-payment of chaukidari tax, and belabouring of persons, became common features of official repression in different areas.[86]

At some places the Congress Offices were burnt and the Congress volunteers arrested while trying to organise picketing of cloth shops and liquor and ganja shops in the Sonepur fair and at other places.[87] Meetings and processions to organize picketing were held by the leaders coming from the middle class. On the 12th November, the police opened fire on a crowd at Jamalpur, as a result of which four persons were killed, 4 seriously injured and some others also got severe injuries. The trouble seems to have arisen on the picketing of liquor shops.[88] For non-payment of chaukidari tax, punitive police were posted at five places in Bihar by the third week of November. These were Bihar (Monghyr district), Bihpur (Bhagalpur district), Bareja, Kateya and Bhore (Saran district).[89]

On the 29th October, a serious clash occurred between the police and the Santhals at Rajaun Hat. The same night five people, all Santhals, were arrested at about 2 p.m. Next morning they were sentenced to various terms of imprisonment ranging from 5 to 18 months.[90] When the Santhals attempted to meet on the 6th November, the Superintendent of Police, with military and other constables charged the Santhals with lathis. Highly enraged at this, the Santhals began to throw stones and brickbats which caused injuries to some among the police. Thereupon, about 200 military police were brought to the scene and 57 persons were arrested.[91]

Rajendra Prasad was released from the Hazaribagh jail on the 14th December, 1930, on the expiry of his full term of six months and reached Patna the same evening. Again there was accelerated speed of the moveme ι n all respects, notwithstanding the increasing firing at several places. By the end of December, the total number of persons arrested in Bihar for this movement rose to 12,194.[92]

Government counter-propaganda to win over the hearts of the people resulted adversely and added to popular discontent, and the Aman Sabhas were not only ridiculed but there were occasionally loud protests against these. Government decided to hold the Provincial Aman Sabha at Gaya on the 31st January and 1st February, 1931. But when the President of the Provincial Aman Sabha reached the Gaya railway station on the 31st January, a large number of people showed him black flags and greeted him with shouts like "go back", "we do not want traitors", etc. The city of Gaya observed hartal as a protest against its meeting. A mass meeting of the citizens of Gaya under the leadership of the members of the middle class protested against the holding of the Provincial Aman Sabha.[93]

But the move of the British Government did not at once mean a real change of policy on their part, nor could it check the flow of Indian Nationalism.[94]

The Congress Working Committee, at its meeting of the 21st January, had passed a resolution advising the "country to carry on the struggle with unabated vigour along the lines already laid down". According to its instruction, the people celebrated the anniversary of the Independence Day with much gusto on the 26th January. Mass meetings were held all over the country in which the people confirmed the resolution of Independence and passed an identical resolution, described as "Resolution of Remembrance."[95]

At Patna, the National flag was hoisted at 8 a.m. on the 26th January at Bhanwar Pokhar Park by a member of the educated middle class Anugraha Narayan Sinha. Prominent among others present on this occasion were Rajendra Prasad, Braj Kishore Prasad, Abdul Bari, Shambhu Saran Varma, Phulan Prasad Varma, Sarangdhar Singh, Mrs. C.C. Das, Miss Gouri Das, and Mrs. Nawal Kishore Prasad.[96] Unfortunately at Begusarai in Monghyr district there was a clash between the police and the people following the arrest of the leaders in the Independence Day procession.[97]

When the whole of Bihar was plunged in the Civil Disobedience Movement at the call of the national leaders belonging to the middle class throughout 1930 and the early months of 1931, political situation was taking a different turn at Delhi. Mahatma Gandhi met Lord Irwin and after parleying for a few days an agreement was signed between them, known as the "Delhi Pact" on the 5th March, 1931. According to this agreement the Civil Disobedience Movement was to be "effectively discontinued" and certain reciprocal steps were to be taken by the Government of India and the Provincial Government, including the declaration of amnesty for persons convicted in connection with the Civil Disobedience, withdrawal of ordinances, restoration of confiscated, forfeited or attached properties except in certain circumstances, and administrative concessions to make salt in certain areas. As regards constitutional questions, there was to be scope for further discussion of the scheme outlined at the Round Table Conference.[98]

In the meantime, Bhagat Singh, Rajguru and Sukdeo were hanged in Lahore jail in the night of 23rd March, 1931. This produced intense indignation throughout India. There was a hartal at Patna on the 26th March, and a meeting was organised by the leaders belonging to the middle class, in which Srikrishna Sinha and Jagat Narayan Lal made rather 'fiery speeches' as the Commissioner of Patna reported to the Government. The Patna District Board passed a resolution condemning it and protest meetings were held at many places in Bihar. Kusum Kumari Devi, wife of Ramayan Prasad, Secretary, Shahabad District Congress Committee, also delivered a speech on this occasion in which she is reported to have said, "Why are you lagging behind? Why don't you come forward to sacrifice yourselves like Bismil, Bhagat and Khudi Ram? The time is coming now. The wave of Bhagat Singh's cremation is still going on in the country. Come up and join the movement."[99] The Saran District Board also passed a resolution on the 11th April, 1931, condemning the execution of Bhagat Singh.[100]

The 45th Session of the Indian National Congress met at Karachi in the last week of March 1931, with Sardar Vallabhbhai Patel as its president. This session passed a condolence resolution on the death of Pandit Motilal Nehru, Maulana Muhammad Ali, Maulana Mazharul Haque of Saran, Shah Muhammad Zubair, and the execution of Bhagat Singh and his comrades. This Congress passed the following resolution on Gandhi-Irwin Agreement:

"The Congress having considered the provisional settlement between the working committee and the government of India, endorsed it, and desires to make it clear that the Congress goal of 'Purna Swaraj' remains intact..." This session further passed the resolution on peaceful picketing, "This Congress notes with gratification the great success that has so far attended to boycott of foreign cloth and the sales of intoxicating drugs and drinks, and calls upon the Congress organisation not to relax their efforts in the matter of peaceful picketing, provided that the picketing shall be in strict accord with the terms of the settlement in this behalf between the Government and the Congress."[101]

Bihar celebrated the 'National Week' from 6th April 1931 and passed the condolence resolution on the death of Bhagat Singh, Ganesh Shankar, Jitendra Nath, Mahmud Ali, Motilal Nehru and other unknown patriots of Jallianwalla Bagh incident.[102]

Release of several Congress leaders and volunteers after the Delhi Pact had given an impetus to constructive works, including village sangathan and peaceful picketing of intoxicating drugs and liquors as well as foreign cloth on the lines approved by the Congress. Rajenda Prasad, a popular and forceful leader belonging to the educated middle class, toured several districts of the province with a view to encouraging constructive works, and much success was achieved in this respect.[103] The visits of Rajendra Prasad to the Shahabad area in the months of August and September, 1931, were followed by "increased activity on the part of the Congress workers in regard to picketing of foreign cloth shops,"[104] and greater efforts for Sangathan and formation of Panchayats. A khadi exhibition was opened by Rajendra Prasad at Arrah on the 30th August and he also addressed a meeting held there on the next day. Meetings were organised by the Congress people in these months also at other places in Shahabad, viz., at Jagdishpur in the sadar subdivision and at Buxar, Dumraon and Berhampur in the Buxar subdivision.[105] A Congress thana was established at Rafiganj in Gaya district which was "to decide by arbitration all cases referred to it."[106]

It may be noted here that the 24th session of the Bihari Students' Conference, an organisation of the educated middle class, was held at Arrah on the 17th and 18th October, 1931. Almost all the prominent Congressmen of the district attended the Conference. Twenty-three resolutions were passed, all of which excepting the first two dealt with educational matters. The first called upon every student to serve his country by using Swadeshi cloth, and the second called upon the district and other branch associations to draw a programme of work providing opportunities to the students to come in contact with the villagers for educating them in matters like untouchability, boycott of intoxicating drugs and liquors and foreign cloths and the evil of communalism.[107]

The terms of the Delhi Agreement were not strictly observed by the Bihar Government. Commenting on the actions of Bihar Government, *The Searchlight* observed in its issue of 8th April, 1931, that the Bihar Government continued to move on their own avis in the age-old manner oblivious of the rapid march of events. As many as 74 prisoners continued to enjoy hospitality of the Government in the Patna Camp Jail made up as follows: Monghyr 26, Chapra 21, Hazaribagh 16, Arrah 16, Champaran 1, Balasore 2, Patna 1, Dumka 1. There were a fair number of district jails also and, in addition to it, in almost every district properties attached or confiscated remained in the possession of the Government, though applications after applications had been made for their return. Punitive police too continued to be posted thereby providing a recurring cause for annoyance, though they had the sense to stop collection of costs. It is absurd to suggest that a whole month is not long enough for the very efficient agents of the Government to get through the scheme examined...."

The Delhi Settlement seemed to have broken down since for weeks there were charges and counter charges on both sides (the Government and the Congress). Mahatma Gandhi started for London on the 29th August to attend the Round Table Conference. Immediately after his return to India on 28th December 1931, Mahatma Gandhi was apprised of the tense political situation. Regarding the main problems of constitutional progress of India, the Round Table Conference did not make any further progress.[108]

There was no favourable response from the Government. Rather they arrested Mahatma Gandhi in the small hours of the morning of 4th January, 1932. Sardar Vallabhbhai Patel was arrested on the same day and detained along with Mahatma Gandhi in the Yaravda Central Jail.[109] Also on the same day the Working Committee, all Congress Committees and branches of the Hindustani Seva Dal were declared unlawful and section 144 was served on persons at many places.[110]

On the 2nd January, 1932, the Government passed an ordinance that all kinds of correspondence of the Congress workers shall be intercepted and detained by the District Magistrate concerned.[111] Various detailed arrangements were made to ensure speedy action.[112]

Rajendra Prasad reached Patna with Mathura Prasad at six in the morning of the 3rd January.[113] Soon he held a meeting on the 3rd January. Soon he held a meeting of the Bihar Provincial Congress Committee. Soon after this, at about 2.30 p.m., the Police Superintendent of Patna reached the spot with some armed constables, surrounded the Sadaqat Ashram, declared the Ashram unlawful (4th January, 1932), seized the building which contained a library and its properties and unfurled the Union Jack in place of the National Flag. They arrested there Rajendra Prasad, Braj Kishore Prasad, Mathura Prasad, Jagat Narain Lal, Krishna Ballabh Sahay and Prajapati Mishra.[114]

As a protest against what the police did at Patna on the 4th Ianuary, a meeting was held at Mangles Tank in which the chief speaker was Rameshwar Gupta and hartal was observed in the city.[115] On the 17th January two processions were taken out at Patna City and a meeting was held at Mangles Tank. Most of the processionists were arrested and the meeting was dispersed by lathi charge.[116] At Gaya, Mrs. Chaudhury, wife of a medical practitioner, was arrested for attempting to hold meetings.[117] The city of Monghyr observed hartal on the 5th January. Namdhari Singh, Tejeshwar, Dharma Narayan, Ram Prasad, Shrikrishna Sinha and others were arrested.[118] It is clear from the above-mentioned names that they belonged to the middle class, mainly the educated middle class.

Issue of 144, promulgation of Ordinances, mass arrests of Congress leaders with promptness, lathi charges, outflowing of Congress organisations, seizure of Congress premises and properties, imposition of heavy fines, confiscation of private properties, banning hartals and gagging of the press and firing were measures of extreme severity and ruthlessness. But these could not dampen the spirit of those for whom patriotism had become an ideal to be pursued by whatever sacrifices were needed for it. At many places demonstrations were organised by the Congress workers, most of whom constituted the bulk of the middle class, on fixed days, viz.

(1) Gandhi Day on the 4th of every month since January,

(2) Independence Day on the 26th January,

(3) Peshawar Day on the 29th January,
(4) Pandit Motilal Nehru's Anniversary Day on 6th February,
(5) National Flag Day on the last Sunday of every month,
(6) Dandi March Day on 12th March and
(7) National Week from the 6th to the 13th April.[119]

Independence Day was celebrated at various places on the 26th January, 1932, and persons participating in processions or attending meetings were lathi charged. The situation at Motihari on that day (26th January, 1932) was marked by wonderful bravery and patience on the part of the people under the leadership of the middle class. But on the Independence Day in 1932 the people of the Champaran district assembled in thousands and squatted on the open space in the compound. The Police made profuse use of lathis to disperse them, but they did not move. The police then opened fire, but to no effect. The people remained there for the whole night and returned to their village homes next morning only after staying long enough to demonstrate that they did not disperse because of the police firing.[120]

The police resorted to firing also at other places besides Motihari. At Rosera in the Darbhanga District, on the 10th of February 1932, they opened fire on a large number of people who had assembled for a demonstration. Some people fell victim of police firing at Begusarai and Tarapur in the Monghyr district. The incident at Tarapur took place on the 15th February 1932, when a few Congress workers arranged a procession and sought to hoist the National Flag on the Police Station building there. This was in accordance with the instructions of the Acting Congress President, Sardar Sardul Singh Caveeshar, to celebrate the 15th of February as a Flag Satyagraha Day for the whole of India. This programme was observed at a large number of places in Bihar including the town of Monghyr and fourteen thanas or centres in that district. The programme was observed at Patna also, where the National Flag was hoisted in the compound of the Secretariat buildings. Tarapur was specially subjected to official vengeance and ruthlessness because of its being a very important centre of Congress activities and of the Kisan movement.[121] But enquiries of other kinds revealed that the number of the dead were not less than 14 and of the injured not less than 100.[122]

There was police firing again at Sheohar in the Muzaffarpur district on the 28th February, 1932. It is noted in an official account that four persons were shot dead and nine were injured, of whom one subsequently died in hospital.[123]

Demonstrations and gatherings organised to celebrate national programmes were participated by the general mass and the members of the middle class. The chief force behind such demonstrations and gatherings was the leadership of the middle class. It is due to the able leadership of leaders belonging to the middle class that for the people patriotism became an ideal to be pursued at any cost, and it was due to this that even measures of extreme severity and ruthlessness could not damp the spirit of those who participated in demonstrations and gatherings at Motihari, Rosera, Begusarai, Sheohar, Tarapur and other places.[124]

But the spirit of nationalism had so profoundly influenced the minds of the people in general that, still in Bihar the movement showed signs of further progress under the guidance of the middle class, and was frequently referred to in some contemporary Government papers.[125] There were processions at Gaya and Aurangabad on the 24th June, 1932, and at Jehanabad on the 4th July. Prisoners' Day was celebrated at Patna and some other places on the 4th July.

The Congress workers were at this time also picketing Post Offices and Banks. During the second half of July they planned also for the recovery of the Congress Ashrams and offices. At Monghyr the Congress volunteers succeeded in hoisting the National Flag at the Congress office at 5.30 a.m. on the 25th July, while the police guards posted there. Till the 31st July about 60 volunteers were arrested there for this work.[126] The effort to recover the Sadaqat Ashram at Patna was forcibly frustrated by the police, who arrested in this connection, according to a statement of the Patna Commissioner, 280 persons upto the 24th July, and altogether 451 men and 7 women by the 31st July, 1932. All these women came from north Bihar, more from Darbhanga than any other district.[127]

Meanwhile the country had been in a state of suspense due to Mahatma Gandhi's fateful resolve to 'fast unto death' on the question of the British Premier's Communal Award published on the 17th August, 1932, giving separate electorate to the so-called 'depressed classes'.[128]

One remarkable effect of Mahatma Gandhi's fast was to set in motion effectual forces throughout the country for removal of the curse of untouchability. Rajendra Prasad had stated, "The Hindu society is on its trial, and if it has any life in it, it must now respond with great and magnificent act."[129] Untouchability week was observed from 27th September to 3rd October and on 30th September was inaugurated the All India Anti-Untouchability League. Bihar's response in this respect was splendid. Here work for the uplift of the depressed classes, or the Harijans as Mahatma Gandhi called them. had already begun under the guidance of the leaders belonging to the middle class. On the 17th July 1932, a meeting was held in the Model School at Gaya for this purpose. A Mehtar (sweeper) of Gaya addressed this meeting and distributed elaichi and supari (betel-nut) to the audience, most of whom took these.[130] In fact, several meetings were held at Gaya, Nawadah and Aurangabad, attended both by the Caste Hindus and the Depressed Classes, attempts being made by the former to embrace the latter.[131] In the Patna district, such meetings were held at Patna City, Barh, Mokameh, Bakhtiyarpur, Bihar, Dinapur, Bihta, Maner, Khagaul and Bikram.[132] In the Shahabad district, similar meetings were held about the middle of September 1932 at Arrah, Buxar, Bhabhua and Durgawati.[133] Efforts made for the opening of temples to the Depressed Classes were successful at some places, *viz.*, Berhampur temple in Shahabad and at Jamhore in Aurangabad, though there was opposition also here and there from the more orthodox people.[134]

A provincial organisation for anti-untouchability work soon came into existence in Bihar. An Anti-Untouchability Conference was held on the 6th November, 1932, in the Anjuman-e-Islamia Hall, Patna with Radhika Raman Prasad Sinha of Surajpura as its President. Pandit Brij Behari Chaube, an eminent Ayurvedic physician of Bihar and Chairman of the Reception Committee for this function, delivered an appealing speech stressing the need for eradicating the evil of untouchability which was eating up the vitals of the Hindu society.[135]

Besides the Provincial Anti-Untouchability Conference at Patna, at which General Secretary A. V. Thakkar was himself present, there were 6 District Conferences at Chapra, Arrah, Bhagalpur, Monghyr, Jehanabad (Gaya) and Bettiah (Champaran) all of which, excepting the last one, were attended by the Provincial Secretary.[136]

According to the instructions of Rajendra Prasad, then acting President of the Congress, on the 4th January 1933 the anniversary of the Gandhi Incarceration Day, a statement prepared for this occasion was read in meetings held at different places in the midst of lathi charge and arrests. At Gaya, two persons were arrested and convicted at Tikari for taking out a procession. J.B. Kripalani, while returning from Patna after meeting Rajendra Prasad, was arrested at the Patna Junction Railway Station on that day under section 17 (1) of the Criminal Law (Amendment) Act, and sentenced to five or six months' rigorous imprisonment at Patna. Another person arrested was Mathura Prasad.[137]

Again also on the 26th January 1933, numerous persons were arrested at different places and many of them were sent to prison for celebrating the Independence Day. Altogether fourteen persons were on that day arrested at Patna, prominent among whom were Anugrah Narayan Sinha, Rajendra

Prasad's wife and four other ladies. M.S. Aney, the Acting President of the Congress, announced on the 20th February 1933 that the next annual (47th) session of the Congress would meet at Calcutta on the 31st March and 1st April. The Government banned the session and arrested M.S. Aney at the Kharagpur station.[138]

Besides, delegates intending to go to Calcutta session were arrested either on the spot or on their way to Calcutta. In Patna, thirty-five persons were arrested on this ground, one of them being Makutdhari Singh, Secretary of the Provincial Congress Committee.[139] About a dozen of delegates from the district of Monghyr were arrested either on the way or in Calcutta.[140]

Mahatma Gandhi's fast, which continued even after his release, caused much anxiety in Bihar as in other parts of India. Meetings were held at various places in connection with his fast and the anti-untouchability movement. The largest meeting was on the Bankipur Maidan on the 18th May, 1933, attended by about 4000 people. Two political prisoners of the Patna Camp jail observed fast, one from the 8th to the 18th May and the other from the 11th to the 13th of May. At Gaya, the President of the Anti-Untouchability Leogue held a prayer meeting on the 13th May in this connection.[141]

The Congress was in a delicate position. Even the temporary suspension of the Civil Disobedience Movement did not appeal to some prominent leaders. Subhas Chandra Bose[142] and Vithalbhai Patel, both of whom were then in Europe on the ground of health, issued a joint statement to the following effect. "The latest act of Mahatma Gandhi in suspending Civil Disobedience is a confession of failure."[143]

On the 17th June the period of suspension of Civil Disobedience was extended by six weeks more. By this time the earlier vigour of the Civil Disobedience Movement had been waning, and a sort of tiredness had appeared. A reorientation of Congress policy was thought necessary even by those, who were then guiding it and by others in the Congress circles.[144]

To decide the future line of action, an informal Conference of leading Congressmen, then outside the jails, was convened at Poona from the 12th to the 14th July, 1933. About 150 delegates from different provinces attended it. The Congress, under Mahatma Gandhi's advice, ultimately decided to suspend mass civil disobedience but permitted individual civil disobedience and barred secret methods. The President also called upon all Congressmen unable to offer the civil disobedience to carry on constructive activities of the Congress.[145]

From July onwards, many in Bihar had started individual civil disobedience under the guidance of the men of the middle class, and had courted arrest. Not only in the cities but also in the interior places, for example, at Sherghati, Aurangabad, Nawadah, Jehanabad, Poonpoon, Asthawan, and Silao picketing of cloth shops and excise shops continued along with other constructive works.[146]

The year 1934 started with an unprecedented calamity in Bihar. On the 15th January, 1934, an earthquake occurred in the afternoon. It devastated an area of 30,000 square miles, destroyed thousand of human lives, caused terrific damages to lands and buildings, railwys and telegraph lines, etc. Rajendra Prasad was then in Patna Hospital under police custody. He was released on the 17th Janury, 1934. Mahatma Gandhi reached Patna in the evening of the 11th March 1934. After moving from place to place in the affected areas and comforting the distressed people, Mahatma Gandhi accompanied by Rajendra Prasad, Mathura Prasad, Miss Loster, Mira Behn, Miss Agatha Harrison, Prabhawati Devi (wife of Jaiprakash Narayan), Bhagwati Devi (sister of Rajendra Prasad), Kishun Devi, Pyarelal, Prithvi Raj and Deva Raj (his Secretaries) went to Chapra and addressed there a mammoth meeting of more than 30,000 people on the 27th March, 1934.[147] This time also Gandhiji was accompanied by important leaders of Bihar who belonged to the middle class.

From Chapra, Mahatma Gandhi went to Muzaffarpur by train in the afternoon of the 28th March 1934. There was tremendous rush of the people at every station. From the doorway of his compartment he spoke to a vast crowd on the platform of the Sonepur railway station :

"I know what this part of Bihar has gone through. The sufferings of the people have drawn the attention and sympathy of the whole world. In spite of liberal response to the Viceregal appeal and that of Babu Rajendra Prasad, it will be impossible to make good the tremendous losses suffered by north Bihar. But even if they were made good, it would be a very poor result of nature's recent terrible warning, if nothing more substantial were to come out of it. The donors of the two funds and numerous other societies have perhaps satisfied their conscience by sending in their donations. Will the recipients be satisfied by merely receiving their share of the timely gift ? What is your reaction to the divine wrath ? If you and I do not learn the moral lesson which the calamity teaches us, then that neglect will be worse than the calamity itself."[148]

Mahatma Gandhi's visit to Bihar in 1934 was significant not only from the humanitarian point of view and social reform, but also from the political point of view. The Working Committee of the Congress had its sitting at Patna from the 18th to 20th May, 1934. It made recommendations with regard to suspension of civil resistance and the adoption of the conciliatory programmes which were accepted by the All India Congress Committee. The Working Committee, in view of the decision of the All India Congress Committee, suspended civil resistance, called upon all the Congressmen all over the country to obey this direction and the civil resistance movement was suspended on the 20th May 1934.[149] Thus ended the civil disobedience movement, the third and the last to be led by Mahatma Gandhi in person.[150] It also passed a resolution asking all Congressmen to re-organise all Congress Committees for the purpose of carrying on normal Congress activities, and in another resolution it called upon Congress organizations to enroll members and complete the elections to various committees before August 31, 1934. In this connection the Working Committee appointed prominent Congress leaders in different provinces, with powers on its behalf, for re-organising Congress Committees in their respective areas, Bihar being placed under Rajendra Prasad.[151]

The month of May 1934 also saw the birth of the Socialist Party in India. It held its first All India Conference at Patna on the 17th May 1934, under the presidentship of Acharya Narendra Deva, and breached off as a separate party known as the Congress-Socialist Party within the fold of Congress.[152] Jaiprakash Narayan was elected as the Organising Secretary, whose duty was to go round the country and organise provincial groups where there was not and then place the whole thing before the general body for the formation of an All India Congress-Socialist Party at the time of the next session of the Indian National Congress.[153]

In the meantime, the British Government lifted the ban on Congress and the Government of Bihar and Orissa issued a Notification on the 9th June. 1934 (No. 31017/C) cancelling their Notification (No. 78/C) dated the 4th January 1932, which had declared, "Associations and combinations formed in pursuance of Civil Disobedience to be unlawful association."[154] On the same day the Chief Secretary to the Government of Bihar & Orissa (D.O. No. 3020/41) directed all the District Officers, "...the local government have also decided to release the Congress Ashrams which are still in possession of government.....Ashrams and other buildings in your district, which have not already been relinquished, should now be handed over to their owners."[155]

Thus we see that the Civil Disobedience Movement was started and carried on till its suspension under the leadership and guidance of the leaders belonging to the middle class, particularly the members of the educated middle class who had strong socio-economic base reinforcing their political importance. From the beginning to the end of the Civil Disobedience Movement lawyers, professors, doctors, educationists, university students and others belonging to the educated middle class dominated the scene of the struggle for independence as is evident from the facts and figures enumerated above.

In this period the number of participants belonging to the commercial and industrial middle class also increased. Besides, the members of the commercial middle class played a great role in making the movement a success by getting their stocks of foreign cloth and other goods sealed by the Congress Committees. Contribution of the commercial and industrial middle class is also proved by the successful hartals in urban centres. Participation of the persons of the middle class landed interest also increased in this period. Thus we see that in this period group of the middle class, other than the educated middle class, became more active and participative and in small urban and rural centres even leadership was shared by them.

Another notable feature of the movement during the period under review was that women, most of whom came from the middle class families of Bihar, came forward courageously and enthusiastically to share with men the struggles and joys in the country's struggle for independence.

To conclude, it may be said that the middle class in Bihar played a commendable role by participating, leading and guiding the irresistible struggle for freedom from alien domination. Zeal and enthusiasm which we find among the masses during this period were, to a great extent, due to the ability of the leaders belonging to the middle class to generate into them enthusiastic spirit of nationalism.

Notes

1. *The Civil Disobedence Movement, printed by the Manager, Government of India Press*, New Delhi, 1956, p. 1.
2. *The Searchlight*, January 20, 1930.
3. *Ibid.*, January 29, 1930.
4. *Ibid.*, January 22, 1930.
5. Appendix II of the *History of the Freedom Movement in Bihar*, Vol. II.
6. Prasad, Rajendra, *Mahatma Gradhi and Bihar*, p. 83.
7. Majumdar, R.C., *History of the Freedom Movement in India*, Vol. III, p. 338.
8. Sitaramayya, B. Pattabhi, *History of the Indian National Congress*, Vol. I, p. 383.
9. Majumdar, R.C., *Op. cit.*, Vol. III, p. 335.
10. *The Searchlight*, February 18, 1930.
11. *Ibid.*, February 14, 1930.
12. *Ibid.*, April 2, 1930.
13. Datta, K.K., *Op.cit.*, Vol. 2, p. 67.
14. *The Searchlight*, April 9, 1930,
15. *Ibid.*, April 6, 1930.
16. *Ibid.*
17. Majumdar, R.C., *Op.cit.*, Vol. III, p. 339.
18. *The Searchlight*, April 9, 1930.
19. *Ibid.*
20. *Extract from the Report of the Superintendent of Police, Saran*, Letter No. 621, dated April 24, 1930.
21. *Noniya* is a caste who manufactures salt.
22. *The Searchlight*, April 18, 1930.
23. *Ibid.*, April 25, 1930.
24. *Ibid.*, April 27, 1930.
25. *Ibid.*, April 9 and 11, 1930.
26. *Ibid.*, April 16, 1930.
27. *Ibid.*, April 21, 1930.
28. Prasad, Janakdhari, *Kuch Apni Kuch Desh Ki* (Hindi), p. 119.
29. *Ibid.*
30. *Weekly Report of the Provincial Congress Committee.*

31. *Young India*, May 15, 1930.
32. *Ibid.*
33. *The Searchlight*, April 18, 1930.
34. *Ibid.*
35. *Ibid.*
36. *Ibid.*, April 20, 1930.
37. *Ibid.*, April 21, 1930.
38. *Young India*, May 15, 1930.
39. Prasad, Rajendra, *Mahatma Gandhi and Bihar*, p. 88.
40. *The Searchlight*, April 21, 1930.
41. *Ibid*,
42. *Letter from the Chief Secretary to the Commissioner of Patna*, April 22, 1930.
43. *Young India*, May 13, 1930.
44. *The Searchlight*, April 24, 1930 and *Weekly Report of the Provincial Congress Committee.*
45. *The Searchlight*, April 25, 1930.
46. Datta, K.K., *Op. cit.*, Vol. II, p. 78.
47. *Young India*, May 15, 1930.
48. *Weekly Report of the Provincial Congress Committee.*
49. *Shrikrishna Abhinandan Granth* (Hindi), p. 49.
50. *Ibid.*, p. 50.
51. *Weekly Report of the Bihar Provincial Congress Committee* and *Young India*, May 1930.
52. *Letter from the Deputy Commissioner, Manbhum, to the Commissioner, Chotanagpur*, April 14, 1930.
53. Datta, K.K., *Op.cit.*, Vol. II, p. 84.
54. *Report of the Bihar Provincial Congress Commitee, Young India*, May 1930.
55. Majumdar, R.C., *Op. cit.*, Vol. III, p. 343.
56. *Patna Commissioner's Records.*
57. Datta, K.K., *Op. cit.*, Vol. II, p. 90.
58. *Extract from the Weekly Confidential Diary of the Superintendent of Police, Saran* (Letter No. 126) for the period ending May 31, 1930.
59. *Patna Commissioner's Records. Police Records.*
60. *Ibid.*

61. *Report of the Bihar Provincial Congress Committee for the week ending May 29, 1930.*
62. (a) *Patna Commissienor's Records.*
    (b) *Young India*, April 10, 1930.
63. *Patna Commissioner's Records.*
64. *Bihar Provincial Congress Committee Reports for the week ending May 25 and June 6, 1930.*
65. *Bihar Satyagraha*, 1930 by Arjun Prasad Singh. *A Few Pages of My Diary* by Ramgati Singh.
66. Prasad, Rajendra, *Mahatma Gandhi and Bihar*, pp. 93-94.
67. Datta, K.K.. *Op. cit.*, Vol. II. p. 98.
68. *Patna Commissioner's Reports for the week ending May 26, 1930.*
69. *Letter from the Dy. Commissioner, Manbhum to the Commissioner of Excise and Salt*, June 7, 1930.
70. Appendix IV of the K.K. Datta's *History of the Freedom Movement in Bihar*, Vol. II.
71. *Patna Commissioner's fortnightly report for the period ending June 27, 1930.*
72. Datta, K.K., *Op. cit.*, Vol. II, p. 105.
73. *Ibid.*, pp. 105-7.
74. *Report of the Provincial Congress Committee for the week ending July 4, 1930.*
75. Datta, K.K., *Op. cit.*, Vol. II, p. 111.
76. *Patna Commissioner's fortnightly report*, August 13, 1930.
77. Datta, K.K., *Op. cit.*, Vol. II, p. 113.
78. *Patna Commissioner's fortnightly report*, August 13, 1930.
79. Datta, K.K., *Op. cit.*, Vol. II, p. 125.
80. *Ibid.*, p. 117.
81. *The Searchlight*, January 1, 1931.
82. *Ibid.*, January 7, 1931.
83. *Ibid.*
84. Datta, K.K., *Op. cit.*, Vol. II, p. 135.
85. *Ibid.*, p. 126.
86. *Report of the Bihar Provincial Congress Committee for the week ending October 17, 1930.*
87. *Ibid.*, November 9, 1930.
88. *The Searchlight*, Nov. 14, 1930.
89. *Ibid.*, November 21, 1930
90. *Ibid.*, November 12, 1930.

91. *Ibid.*
92. *Ibid.*, January 1, 1931. *The Young India*, January 8, 1931.
93. *Ibid.*, February 3, 1931.
94. *A letter dated January 31, 1931, from the Inspector General of Police, Bihar and Orissa to the Superintendent of Police, Champaran and others.*
95. Appendix V of the *History of Freedom Movement in Bihar* by K.K. Datta, Vol. II.
96. *The Searchlight*, January 27, 1931.
97. *The Annual Indian Register*, 1931, Vol. , p. 23. *Young India*, Feb. 5, 1931.
98. Sitaramayya, B. Pattabhi, *Op. cit.*, Vol. I, pp. 437-442.
99. *Report of Speeches of released political prisoners in Shahabad.*
100. Datta, K.K. *Op. cit.*, Vol. I, p. 160.
101. Sitaramayya, B. Pattabhi, *Op. cit.*, Vol. I, pp. 459-461.
102. *File No. 25/1931. Extract from the Confidential Diary of the Superintendent of Police, Saran*, week ending April 1931, Bihar Political (Special) Department, Patna.
103. Prasad, Rajendra, *Atmakatha*, p. 358.
104. *Fortnightly report of the Patna Commissioner for the period ending September 27, 1931.*
105. *Ibid.*, September 13, 1931.
106. *Ibid.*, October 13, 1931.
107. *Weekly Report of the Superintendent of Police, Shahabad, October 23, 1931.*
108. Majumdar, R.C., *Op. cit.*, Vol. III, pp. 396-397.
109. Quoted in *Mahatma* by Tendulkar, Vol. *III*, p. 191.
110. Datta, K.K,, *Op. cit.*, Vol. II, p. 176.
111. *Ibid.*, Appendix IX.
112. *Letter from the Magistrate of Patna to the Commissioner, January 7, 1932.*
113. Quoted in *History of Freedom Movement in Bihar by K.K. Datta*, Vol. II, p. 178. *From unpublished Diary of Shri Mathura Prasad for 1932.*
114. Datta, K.K , *Op. cit.*, Vol. II, p. 178.
115. *Letter from Magistrate of Patna to Patna Commissioner, January 7, 1932.*
116. *Fortnightly Report of the Patna Commissioner for the fortnight ending January 18, 1932.*
117. *Ibid.*, January 27, 1932.

118. *Ibid.*
119. Datta, K.K., *Op. cit.*, Vol. II, pp. 182-83.
120. Prasad, Rajendra, *Mahatma Gandhi and Bihar*, p. 97.
121. Datta, K.K., *Op. cit.*, Vol. II, pp. 184-86.
122. *Ibid.*, Appendix XI.
123. *Bihar & Orissa in 1931-32*, p. 14.
124. Datta, K.K., *Op. cit.*, Vol. II, p. 188.
125. *Fortnightly Reports of the Patna Commissioner for the months of June and July, 1932.*
126. *Shrikrishna Abhinandan Grantha* (Hindi).
127. *Fortnightly Report of the Patna Commissioner for the period ending July 27 and Aug. 13, 1932.*
128. Datta, K.K., *Op. cit.*, Vol. II, p. 191.
129. *Ibid.*, p. 193.
130. *Fortnightly Report of Patna Commissioner for the period ending July 27, 1932.*
131. *Ibid.*
132. *Ibid.*
133. *Ibid.*
134. *Ibid.*
135. Datta, K.K., *Op. cit.*, Vol. II, pp. 195-96.
136. *Fortnightly Report of the Patna Commissioner for the period ending November 13, 1932.*
137. Prasad, Rajendra, *Atmakatha*, p. 380.
138. Datta, K.K., Vol. II, p. 204.
139. *Fortnightly Report of the Patna Commissioner for the period ending April* 13, 1933.
140. *Shrikrishna Abhinandan Grantha* (Hindi).
141. *Fortnightly Report of the Patna Commissioner for the period ending May 27 and June* 13, 1933.
142. *Letter from the Chief Secretary to Patna Commissioner, June* 27, 1933.
143. Datta, K.K., *Op. cit.*, Vol. II, p. 208.
144. *Ibid.*, p. 209.
145. *Ibid.*, Appendix XIV.
147. *Fortnightly Report of the Patna Commissioner from July to November*, 1933.
147. Datta, K.K., *Op. cit.*, Vol. II, pp. 219-20.
148. *Ibid.*, pp. 219-20.
149. Sitaramayya, B. Pattabhi, *Op. cit.*, Vol. I, p. 572.

150. Majumdar, R.C., *Op. cit.*, Vol. III, p. 483.
151. Datta, K.K., *Op. cit.*, Vol. II, p. 229.
152. Sitaramayya, B. Pattabhi, *Op. cit.*, Vol. I, p. 573; Prasad, Rajendra, *Atmakatha*, p. 403.
153. *File No. 105/1934, Bihar Political (Special) Department.*
154. *Bihar and Orissa Gazette, Extraordinary, dated the 9th January, 1937.*
155. *File No. 79/1943, Bihar Political (Special) Department.*

5

Revolutionary Nationalism and the Middle Class in Bihar (1912-1933)

In this chapter an attempt has been made to discuss the role of the middle class in the revolutionary movement, which aimed at complete freedom of India from alien domination. This extreme form of nationalism appeared first in Bombay with Bal Gangadhar Tilak as its leader. Its influence penetrated into other parts of India including the province of Bihar. The persons who carried on revolutionary or terrorist movement in Bihar, were mostly the members of the educated middle class.

While the Indian National Congress was following a moderate policy for the attainment of self-Government through constitutional means, there was another section of nationalists from the closing years of the 19th century and the early years of the present century, whose aim was complete freedom of the motherland from alien domination and whose ideas were radical and methods revolutionary. The first symptom of this extreme nationalism appeared in Bombay under the leadership of Bal Gangadhar Tilak, whom Valentine Chirol has described as 'one of the most dangerous pioneers of disaffection' and 'truly the father of Indian unrest'.[1] This new party's conviction was that it was impossible to gain any concession by petitions and prayers. This was the first difference between the moderate and progressive parties. Bal Gangadhar Tilak did not believe in the philanthropy of British politics. He said that there was no instance in history of a foreign nation ruling another for the benefit of the other and not for its own profit. The rule of one nation by another was in itself unnatural. He granted the efficiency of the British Government and the excellence of its methods for her own purpose, but these methods and that efficiency did not work for the interest of the people of the country, A good foreign government was less desirable than an inferior native government.[2]

Several other factors. both external as well as internal, intensified national discontent in India particularly from the year 1905, which forms a turning point not only in the history of India but in that of Asia as a whole. The effects of the Russeo-Japanese War of 1904-1905 shattered the vanity of the White Man's superiority and generated new hopes of liberation from it in different parts of this continent. Behind these dreams and visions was the one exculting hope that the days of servitude to the West were over and the days of independence had dawned. Much had gone before to prepare the way for such a dawn of hope. The Japanese victories made it, for the first time, shining and radiant.[3]

Within the country, Curzon's system of 'Thorough' characterised by rigorous administrative control, particularly his ill-conceived measure of the partition of Bengal, had intensely excited national feelings and was largely responsible for the growth of extremism in contemporary Indian politics under the leadership of Bal Gangadhar Tilak, Lala Lajpat Rai and Bipin Chandra Pal (Bal-Lal-Pal). The partition of Bengal shocked public feeling in Bengal and elsewhere and at once evoked strong protests. "We felt that we have been insulted, humiliated and tricked", writes Surendra Nath Banerjee,[4] who, of course, thought of reversing the partition by constitutional means. But the bureaucracy remained obstinate and this fanned the flame of national disaffection. "In the evolution of political progress", remarks Surendra Nath Banerjee significanty, "bad rulers are often a blessing in disguise. They help to stir a community into life, a result that years of agitation would perhaps have failed to achieve."[5] Indian nationalism of the post-1905 years was profoundly influenced by religious idealism with Aurobindo as its prophet and with its cult of and worship of Mother India, of which the remarkable song 'Bande Matram' taken from Bankim Chandra's Anandamath, became the sacred mantra. "The new nationalism which Bande Matram reveals", says Bipin Chandra Pal, "is not a mere civic or economic or political idealism. It is a religion."[6] Besides, insecurity among the educated middle class people also aggravated the extremist politics. The educated middle class people did not get enough jobs, although they were capable and competent.

In spite of the growing differences between the two wings of the Congress, the moderates and the extremists, this idealism of Aurobindo was a dynamic force in Indian national life in those days. The paper entitled 'Bande Matram', which he edited, served as its effective organ.[7]

The influence of revolutionary activities penetrated into Bihar also to some extent. The bomb explosion at Muzaffarpur in 1908 by Khudiram is a striking incident in this perspective. Even before the Swadeshi Movement, Indranath Nandy and a few others of the Revolutionary Party, came to Bihar and preached their cult in its different villages with the help of magic lanterns.[8] They formed acquaintance with Punit Lal agent of K.S.K. Lahiri & Co. of Calcutta and leader from old dismembered revolutionary party of Bihar. Bhupendranath Dutta became his guest when he, along with some others, came to Patna to establish a 'Bhavani Mandir'. They received sympathy in their work from some pleaders, teachers and students of Patna.[9]

One of the eminent indologists, Kashi Prasad Jayaswal, was considered by Government to be a dangerous revolutionary since his return to India for his assoclation with his compeers in England. His appointment as a lecturer in Calcutta University was refused by the Government of India in 1913 and caused much sensation. Government came to take a moderate view about him in the next year when he began to practise at Patna and decided to remove the bar. The District Magistrate and the Superintendent of Police, Patna were still advised to 'keep them thoroughly acquainted with his doings and connections.'[10]

Ranchi became one of the important centres of revolutionary activities under the guidance of Ganesh Chandra Ghosh.[11] A section of a battalion consisting of Kanaujiya Brahmans and stationed at Ranchi had sympathy for their party.[12]

In 1913, Sachindra Nath Sanyal[13] started at Patna a branch of the Anusilan Samiti, which he had formed at Benares. He got recruits from the college students here, and one of the successive organisers of this branch was Bankim Chandra Mitra, who joined the Bihar National College in 1919[14] after having passed the matriculation from the T.K. Ghosh Academy, Patna. Another co-worker of Bankim Chandra Mitra was Akhil Chandra Das Gupta, also a student of the Bihar National College. While still at the college, he instilled love of the country into the mind of a Behari student named Raghubir Singh[15] of T.K. Ghosh Academy, who was enthusiastically associated with the distribution of liberty leaflets in September, 1915. Raghubir was sent to Allahabad to tamper with the troops and was arrested in that connection.

Bankim Chandra Mitra's arrest in 1915 and conviction in the Benares case, did not, as a contemporary government report noted, damp the ardour of his disciples, though all high officers of the Government were anxious, as is noted in a correspondence of one of them dated the 11th December 1916, to get rid of the undesirables from the Bihar National College. Another Government report of 1916 mentioned, "Many important discoveries were made showing that a secret gang still existed in Patna, whose members were mostly of Bihar National College and T.K. Ghosh Academy students with one or two from Patna College." Some other members of the revolutionary party at that time among the students of the

Bihar National College were Sudhir Kumar Sinha, Prafulla Kumar Biswas (joined B.N. College in 1916 and left it the same year), Shyam Nath Jha, Deo Kumar Sinha (brother of Sudhir Kumar Sinha). Even a lecturer of the Bihar National College, Nripendra Nath Basu, M.Sc., a man of high character, was watched by Government as a suspicious person and his removal was thought of. But the police satisfied themselves about him and, at last, realised their mistake. Some members of the Dacca Anusilan Samiti worked at Bhagalpur, chief among them being Rewati Nag, obtained some recruits.[16]

Deoghar in the district of Santhal Parganas was another centre of activities of the Revolutionary Party in Bihar. Rajnarain Basu, who had settled there, was the grandfather of Aurobindo Ghosh and Barindra Ghosh. Barindra Ghosh received his early education at Deoghar and was a member of a society there called the 'Golden League', which sought to work for boycott and the Swadeshi movement. It is mentioned in the report of the Sedition Commiitee of 1918, "A printer of the Jugantar was a Bengali from Patna; and members of the revolutionary party have visited and worked on a farm near Deoghar. During the trial of the Alipore conspirators, it appeared that a house at Deoghar, known as Sil's lodge, had been hired and used for the preparation of bombs and training of associates.[17]

Some from Dumka in the Santhal Parganas were implicated in what is known as the Rodda Arms Case, concerning theft of Mauser Pistols from Rodda and Co.,[18] a firm of Gun Makers in Calcutta. One of them was Prabhu Dayal Himat Singhka, who observed, "Messrs. Rodda and Co. was a firm belonging to Europeans dealing in firearms and ammunitions for sale in Calcutta. In August 1914 a big consignment of about 50,000 cartridges[19] and 50 Mauser Pistols from Germany arrived in Calcutta. The whole consignment was taken delivery of from the customs and, instead of being delivered to Rodda & Co., it was removed in collusion with an employee of that Company who was with us, to private destinations. In that business of removal a number of youngmen were concerned and were later on arrested including Bipin Behari Ganguly, Bhujang Banerji, Hari Das, myself and others."

Gyanendra Nath Mitra, a Doctor of Bankipur, Manoranjan Guha Thakurata, a mica-mine owner at Giridih, Saryu Prasad, Barrister, Chapra, Hemendra Nath Ghose of Karmatar in the Santhal Parganas. were considered to be prominent agitators in Bihar by the Police.[20] Their movements were to be reported by wire to the Superintendent of Police of the districts they visited to the C.I.D., Bihar and Orissa.

There were then several others also, though not of the revolutionary group, whom the Government regarded as 'political suspects'. A document entitled 'Establishment' was found in Bihar in 1917. It contained guidance for one selected to start an establishment at a new place. He should set up house with a college or school student and the organisation is then to be spread through the boys and through them throughout the division and down to the village.[21]

In 1919 was found in Bihar leaflet of the title 'Message Salvation', which was posted in Calcutta and addressed to one Shamsul Zoha, a Mukhtar of Arrah. This man took a prominent part in political activities and was one of those who signed the satyagraha pledge in Arrah. This leaflct exhorted the Muslims of India to strive for freedom through revolution.[22]

To arrest the activities of the revolutionaries, on the 20th June 1914, H. McPherson, officiating Chief Secretary to the Government of Bihar & Orissa, issued a circular to each of the Commissioners of the Divisions forwarding along with it a typed copy of Chapter VIII of the Manual issued by the Special Branch of the Criminal Investigation Department which described the procedure to be followed by the District Magistrates and Superintendents of Police when persons whom Government considered to be 'dangerous agitators', visited a district, and also 'to prevent if possible the delivery of seditious speeches and failing that to secure that a full record shall be available of the nature of any speech delivered.''[23]

Swami Satya Deva visited different places in Bihar. He was warned, according to this circular, when he was lecturing at Hajipur. At Arrah, he delivered several lectures advocating political freedom and reorientation of the country's educational system for proper mental development. Government, in their own prospective, considered his speeches to be bordering closely to sedition, and ordered that the District Magistrates should make special arrangements to keep a watch on his movements to obtain full and accurate reports of what he says, and Government officer should have nothing to do with his meetings or lecture.[24] It may be noted here that Swami Satya Deva worked at Champaran in 1918 and delivered learned speeches at several places.[25]

The Sedition Committee (1918) reported, "The province of Bihar & Orissa has been slightly affected by the revolutionary movement."[26] The Government authorlties and their staff have exercised, what this Committee mentioned as vigilance, in various ways, with the utmost rigour to prevent in its opinion, graver mischief."[27]

From the side of Government, repressive measures in different forms were let loose in quick succession for the suppression of Indian nationalist activities in all parts of India.[28] These were, Regulation 111 of 1818, Regulation of Meetings Ordinance (11th May 1907), the Seditions Meeting Act of 1st November 1907, the Explosive Substance Act and the Newspaper (Incitement of Offence) Act of 8th June 1908, the Criminal (Amendment) Act of March 1913, the Defence of India Act of March 1915, under which rules were made authorising the arrest and internment of dangerous persons.[29]

The Intelligence Department was very active in watching the movements of those on whom they had the slightest suspicion. The teachers and the students of colleges and schools were special objects of government vigilance. In 1912, the Government drew up the following set of rules laying down the procedure that should be followed in respect of the control to be maintained over suspects when they become members of

Government or Government-aided schools or colleges.[30a] Teachers were removed on suspicion by be Government. The Commissioner of Tirhut Division suggested removal of Professor Bijoy Kumar Roy of G.B.B. College, Muzaffarpur as he was a suspect and was the most unsafe person to retain.[30b]

The British Government in India, eager to maintain its own hold here unimpaired, sought to curb the forces, which originated out of a desire for the emancipation of the country from foreign yoke, and made unsparing use of the various instruments of authority. On the 30th September, 1918, a youngman who gave his name as Ram Prasad Lal was arrested at Monghyr. The police considered him to be a revolutionary emissary from Muzaffarpur and a member of the revolutionary party named 'Kampta' (? Kamta) Prasad.[31] According to instructions from Government, the Superintendent of Police, Hazaribagh arrested on the 13th December 1918 under the Defence of India Rules, Ram Binode Singh, son of a police employee named Jai Kishan Singh of Muzaffarpur and a student of St. Columbas' Col-ege at Hazaribagh. He was originally recruited to the revolutionary party at Muzaffarpur and became an active member of it at Bhagalpur, where also he had been provisionally a student in the T.N.J. College. Krishna Ballabh Sahay and Bajrang Sahay, an advocate of Patna were also then students of the St. Columbas' College. They sympathised with Ram Binode Singh, who was followed by both of them when he was taken to the Hazaribagh Central Jail. There was a hartal among the students on the day of Ram Binode Singh's arrest.[32] The immediate effect of this incident was to aggravate the resentment of K.B. Sahay and Bajrang Sahay against the British Government.[33] It may be mentioned here that the C.I.D. Sub-Inspector, Baidyanath Banerji, accorded good treatment to Ram Binode Singh.[34] The police considered Ram Binode Singh to be identical with 'Jotin' from whom letters dealing with Bihar affairs had been intercepted in Bengal.[35] He was interned and the police thought of sending him to foreign domicile at Sambalpur.[36] Several arrests were made at Bhagalpur under section 12A of the Defence of India Act on the 22nd December, 1918. According to his own statement before the police and the Magistrate, he had been agent of the Bolpur Conspiracy Party in Bengal and was deputed to Bhagalpur to distribute 'Swadhin Bharat' leaflets and to carry on the work of the party. Rabindranath Tagore protested against his arrest and he was shifted to Bengal.

On the 25th November 1918, the Bengal Intelligence Branch and the Calcutta Special Branch raided a house at 12, Beniapokhar Lane and arrested Basant Kumar Baksi, Nishikant Pyne, Krishna Chandra Sutradhar, Bibhangsu Basu, Jayant Kumar Sarkar and Naresh Chandra Ghosh. Of these, the first was, as the police report noted, an important absconder who has been untraced since 1916 and was believed to have been wandering about in Bihar; the fourth was the Bhagalpur absconder; fifth as found by the police to be Brajendra Lal Banerjee who had been recruited at Muzaffarpur and was working from sometime in the telegraph office at Bankipore as a Postal Signaller.[37] Hari Prasanna Rai Chaudhri and Praful Mukherjee of Monghyr were arrested and expelled for their complicity in revolutionary activities at Monghyr. Sri Rash Bihari Lal of Bhagalpur area was also interned but was subsequently released on security.[38]

It is well known that some Indian patriots of the radical group, finding the situation too hot for themselves, went abroad and were engaged there in their own way in fighting the battle for liberty. Tarak Nath Das (Dr.), one of the leaders of the extreme section who had gone out of India, was advised by his elder brother from Muzaffarpur for taking necessary action in this connection.[39] Their activities, particularly of those belonging to the Ghadar Party, increased during the World War I and they had a plan to push forward their work with German help.[40]

In fact, widespread repression on the part of the Government was not very much responsible for reappearance of Revolutionary Nationalism in India on the suspension of the Non-Cooperation Movement. Exasperated youths, stirred to the very depths of their hearts by feelings of patriotism, resorted to revolutionary methods with the conviction that they would emancipate their motherland from foreign yoke through these.[41]

In Bihar, there was a reoccurrence of Revolutionary activities during the post-1924 years. The Provincial Government took whatever steps they thought necessary on their part against these, more particularly to prevent these from spreading among the impressionable youths in the educational institutions. Three copies of the Revolutionary (an organ of the Revolutionary Party of India), Vol. I, No. 1 of 1st January 1925 were traced by the special branch police at the Patna College. V.H. Jackson, Principal of this College, held that the person who addressed these was evidently ignorant of the Patna College affairs as thes were addressed to monitors and there were no monitors at this college. E.L.L. Hammond, Chief Secretary to the Government of Bihar and Orissa, then issued a circular to the District Magistrates on the 11th February 1925 saying, "I am desired to inform you that a seditious publication in English, entitled 'The Revolutionary', an organ of the Revolutionary Party of India, issue No 1, Vol. I, is now being surreptitiously circulated, not only among the public but also to Colleges and schools where it is calculated to give rise to dissatisfaction. I am to request that you will warn the educational authorities in your district confidentially of the efforts being made to disseminate the same. The publication in question has been proscribed under section 99A of the Criminal Procedure and all copies wherever found may therefore be forfeited to His Majesty." The District Magistrates at once communicated necessary orders to the Principals of Colleges, Headmasters of High Schools and Subdivisional Inspectors of Schools to prevent the circulation of this publication and to seize and forward to them any copies of it found anywhere.[42]

As another step to check the dissemination of Revolutionary doctrine, the Bihar Government sought in 1926 to control effectively all such organisations suspected by them to be in sympathy with these.[43]

Bhagalpur, as during the earlier period of Revolutionary activities, was an important centre of these now too. On the 19th January, 1927, Sachin Bakshi, who was touring in Bihar for about a year, was arrested at Bhagalpur on the charge of being a leader of Revolutionary movement.[44] Then followed the discovery by Government of what was called the Deoghar Conspiracy Case. On the 18th October, 1927, the two persons, suspected to be revolutionory conspirators, had gone to Deoghar in the district of Santhal Parganas, and that arms and ammunition might be found with them. One C.I.D. Officer, who was at once sent to Deoghar, traced that one of the persons, Jiban Kanai Pal, was staying in a boarding house there. With a search warrant, obtained from the local S.D.O. on the 19th October, the boarding house was raided by the police on the 20th October when Birendra Nath Bhattacharya handed over to the S.D.O. two Mauser pistols and a bag containing 82 Mauser cartridges. With Birendra stayed his brother Surendra Nath and one Tajesh Chandra Ghosh. A quantity of revolutionary literature was found with them and a list of names in cypher.[45] The literature included Aurobindo's Essay on Gita, early life of De Valera and Banglar Biplabbad. Further searches were made and 20 persons in all were arrested. Of them, nine were Bengali Brahmins, five Bengali Kayasthas, one a Bengali Kshatriya, one a Bengali Vaidya, one a Bengali weaver, one a Bengali potter, one a Bengali Sadgop, and one was a Punjabi. Most of them were aged between 20 and 27; some were 30 or 32 and one about 44 years old. A case under section 121A I.P.C. was instituted against them. Three of them were charged also under section 19 (b) of Arms Act.[46]

The trial of the case opened at Deoghar before a Special Magistrate on the 31st January, 1928. On the 1st March all the 20 persons were committed to the sessions. The sessions trial commenced on the 3rd April and ended on the 19th July, when twelve of them were convicted and sentenced to long term rigorous imprisonment and eight were acquitted.

Ten of those convicts made an appeal to the Patna High Court, which was heard from the 2nd to the 11th January, 1929, and the conviction of all but one was upheld.[47]

A similar incident took place at Maulania in the Champaran district on the 7th June, 1929, and two more, one again in Champaran and the other in the Darbhanga district in the month of May, 1930. All these were regarded by the Government as 'political dacoities' in which believers in the 'terrorist' methods took the leading part. As regards the Maulania case, it was stated in a police report of 1929, "Two political suspects of Bettiah, Phanindra Nath Ghosh and Manmohan Banerjee, who had been absent from their homes on that night and were arrested and one of them confessed having arranged the dacoity in order to obtain funds for the revolutionary party. Of the 11 men alleged to have taken part in the outrage one is accused in the Lahore Conspiracy Case, two were made approvers, five are still absconding and the remaining three were sentenced to ten years' rigorous imprisonment under section 396 I.P.C. An appeal has been referred to the High Court."[48] Jogendra Shukul, one of the most prominent leaders of the Revolutionary movement in Bihar, whom the police then considered to be the principal absconder in the Maulania dacoity of Champaran in 1929. As is mentioned in a police report for 1930, "Jogendra Shukul and his companions were taken by surprise and were overcome after a severe struggle." Jogendra Shukul and some others involved in the two cases of 1929-30 referred to above were tried next year in what is known as the Tirhut Conspiracy Case. All of them except two, were convicted. Jogendra Shukul was sentenced to ten years' rigorous imprisonment and the sentences of others (Kedar Manvi Shukul, Baswan Singh, Ramparikshan Singh, Ram Binode Singh) varied from five to ten years' rigorous imprisonment. Jogendra Shukul was still to be tried in connection with the Maulania case.[49]

Year after year in the period under review in this chapter, books, leaflets and pamphlets, considered objectionable from the point of view of the Government, were proscribed by them. Thus in 1930, fifty-three leaflets and pamphlets were proscribed in Bihar.[50]

The bomb explosion in the Assembly Hall had its repercussions in almost all parts of India. At Patna, copies of a leaflet, containing picture of Bhagat Singh and Batukeshwar Dutt and the authorship of which was ascribed to Professor Gyan Saha, were sold at one anna each. Several posters were posted up during the night of the 17th August, 1929, on some places including the gates of Chhajjubagh and the Post Office bearing the words : "Every nation has a right to revolt against tyranny and oppression."[51]

Gyan Saha was considered by the Government to be a revolutionary of extreme views who favoured terrorism with a view to gaining complete independence. He was intimately connected with Manindra Narayan Roy, leader of the Patna Revolutionary Party, and with Jaichand Vidyalankar, another Professor of the Bihar National College and leader of the Punjab section of the Hindusthan Republican Association. M.N. Roy, then a leading member of the new violence, suspected confidential discussion with Gyan Saha. In the month of August, 1929, M.N. Roy delivered magic lantern lectures in Patna illustrating the poverty of India as compared with her wealth in the past and the cruelties of the servants of the English East India Company. For those he was arrested on 7th August, but was released on bail by the High Court.[52]

In the meanwhile, the Punjab Police had convicted and brought for trial a number of persons including Bhagat Singh and Batukeshwar Dutt, who, it was alleged, had organised a countrywide terrorist conspiracy. This came to be known as the Lahore Conspiracy Case which attracted considerable attention in India. As a protest against bad treatment given to the accused the undertrial prisoners of the Lahore Conspiracy Case went on hunger strike. Many political prisoners at other places went on sympathetic hunger strike. Bhagat Singh and Batukeshwar Dutt continued hunger strike for thirteen weeks. On the 13th September, Jitendra Nath Das died on the 64th day of his hunger strike. His death was a great shock to the country. "No event for many years past had touched the people as much as all over the country vast demonstrations were held."[53]

When the dead body of Jitendra Nath Das passed through Gaya towards Howrah, about two thousand people, according to a Government report, assembled at the railway station and there was a sympathetic demonstration there.[54] There were demonstrations in almost every important city of Bihar. On the 24th September, a procession was taken at Patna as a mark of sympathy for the deceased patriot.[55] The Government appointed a committee to consider the question of treatment of political prisoners and as a result of its deliberations some new rules were issued creating three classes of political prisoners. But these did not bring any improvement in their conditions in the jails.

Revolutionary nationalism, described by some as 'terrorism', with its faith in methods of violence for securing freedom, which had its recrudescence in the post-Non-Co-operation years, was increasingly active during the period under review as Governmental repression became more and more ruthless.

In Bihar too, as in the Punjab and U.P., there were youthful nationalists fired with revolutionary zeal for freedom of the country. Many of them were from 1930 members of Hindustan Socialist Republic Associations, or Army. In fact, the revolutionary activities were inter-Provincial in scope and extent. In the month of March 1931, Budhan Rai Varma of Dehri in Sasaram was a revolutionary. A branch of Hindustan Socialist Republic Army was working secretly with Chapra as one of their centres. With a view to collecting some money, Ramdeni Singh, a prominent leader of this branch who had escaped from jail in 1930 along with five others, made an attempt to loot the railway mail bag containing money at Hajipur on the 15th June 1931. The station master, who was carrying the bag to the train, was fatally shot by one of them. About two months later, Ramdeni Singh was arrested. One of his partymen turned to be an approver. He was sentenced to death, and his another companion, Triloki Singh, to ten years' rigorous imprisonment. In the same year some of the revolutionists, according to a Government report, attacked a 'math' at Phulwaria in the Chapra district and the leg of one of its inmates was blown off by a bomb. For this, ten men were accused on a charge of conspiracy.[56]

Patna City was an important centre of secret activities on the part of the members of the Hindustan Socialist Republican Army, and some of them were arrested here. On the 28th June, 1931, there was a bomb incident at Patna. On information received from the U.P., C.I.D., some police officers of Patna were lying in wait near Bhikna Pahari to arrest two well-known revolutionaries, Shri Hazari Lal, wanted in connection with the Delhi Conspiracy Case, and Prakash alias Surajnath Chaube, who was suspected to have been involved in a recent bomb case at Lucknow.[57] When these two suspects were coming to the spot from the west on bicycles at about 8.45 p.m., the police party sought to overpower and arrest them. Surajnath Chaube was knocked down and at once captured. His companion evaded a lathi blow, aimed by the Police Inspector, jumped from the bicycle, threw it on the Inspector and attempted to run towards the east. Chased by the police party, he dropped a bomb on the ground, which injured the fugitive himself, a Police Sub-Inspector and a Head Constable. The Police Sub-Inspector succumbed to the injuries in the hospital an hour later. Both Hazari and Chaube were each found in possession of another bomb, Welby 45 revolver, an automatic pistol and a quantity of ammunition. Two other persons of Patna City were also immediately arrested for 'harbouring the offenders'.[58] Hazari Lal was in this case sentenced to fourteen years' transportation and Chaube to 10 years' rigorous imprisonment.

Three country bombs were thrown in two liquor shops in Arrah town in the night of 22nd July, 1931.[59] A very sensational case took place in Patna City on the 31st July,

1931, due to explosion of a bomb in a room in the house of Rai Mahendra, a youth of 15 or so, causing severe injuries to Ram Babu, one of their co-workers who was handling it. The police arrested and complained against eleven persons on charges of conspiracy to wage war against the King, murder and preparation of explosives, in what is known as the Patna Conspiracy Case. They were Suraj Nath Chaube, Kanhai Lal Misser, Shyam Krishna Agarwal, Rai Mahendra, Ram Singh alias Shyamdeo Narayan, Ganga Prasad Mali, Channeshwar Pandey, Tunu Gope alias Lachmi Gope and Mahabir Misser and two others who became later on approvers.[60]

On the 3rd October, 1931. the houses of Chottan Prasad Singh and Jadu Singh at Amhara, Patna district, were searched by the A.S.P., Dinapur, and the S.I. of Police, Maner. The police reported to have discovered there a live bomb, and took into custody Bhagawati Singh and Sudama Singh, sons of Jadu Singh. In the month of December of this year there was a bomb explosion in the compound of the District Magistrate of Bhagalpur.[61] Shortly after this the police discovered in Shahganj Mosque (Patna) two earthen pots, one containing three large bombs and the other several smaller ones. They found also a box containing explosives.[62]

Early in January 1932, a senior police officer arrested M.N. Rai in his house along with two others, who were revolutionary suspects in the eyes of the police. The police discovered evidence of revolutionary activities at some other places too. Thus in May 1933, red leaflets issued by the Hindustan Socialist Republican, Patna Branch, were found by them posted in the Bar Library and the Judge's Court at Gaya and also thrown into some private houses there.[64] They also suspected that manufacture of bombs had been started in a village called Chamarbigha in the Jehanabad subdivision of Gaya district.[65] On the 9th November, 1932, Phanindra Nath Ghose, approver in the Lahore Conspiracy Case, who had opened a shop at Bettiah, was stabbed there and died a week later. Baikunth Shukul and Chandrama Singh, both of whom were absconding, were suspected. They evaded capture for some time, though the police announced handsome rewards for capturing them. One night while returning from Dighwara, Baikunth Shukul was ambushed at Sonepur by a police party and was overpowered by them after a hard struggle. He was sentenced to death and hanged in the Gaya Jail on 14th April 1934. His co-accused, Chandrama Singh, was acquitted in the murder trial. Both of them belonged to Yogendra Shukul's organisation. Rambinode Singh was convicted for harbouring persons whom the Government considered to be undesirable. Yogendra Shukul, Basawan Singh and Rambinode Singh were taken to Bhagalpur Jail. Yogendra Shukul was kept there in fetters for about two years, and he along with two or three others remained on hunger strike for eighteen days as a protest against the harsh treatment meted out to them in the jail. Basawan Singh was sent to Gaya and Ramparikshan Singh to Cuttack.[66]

In the year 1933, took place another sensational case in connection with the revolutionary activities known as the Gaya Conspiracy Case. The police got the clue to the detection of what they called a conspiracy on the arrest of a Bengal revolutionary Prabhat Chakravarty in Calcutta early in January of this year. He had in his possession some documents and a list of names and addresses mostly in ciphers. One of these was of Umanath Sharma, who had agreed to be used as 'Bhagat Manth's post box'. Bhagat and Sahadeo had for some years been staying in Bageswari Prasad's house at Gaya. On this information, the Gaya police conducted a search in the Pahari Kothi on the 16th January and discovered there one revolver, one old pistol and some ammunition. Continuing their investigations the police searched on the 20th January the house of Mithilesh of Aurangabad subdivision and found there 12 cartridges, formulae, which in the opinion of Chief Inspector of Explosives were for bomb preparation, and some proscribed books. On the 30th January there was a Mail robbery near the Gaya city in which two U.P. youths were arrested. They were living with Biswanath Sahay. Eventually eighteen persons,[67] of whom three belonged to U.P. and the rest to Bihar, were charged with conspiracy and sixteen were convicted and sentenced to imprisonment for terms ranging from one to seven years. Then as under-trial prisoners in the Gaya jail some of them went on hunger strike[68] from the month of June, 1933. Bijay Kumar Das Gupta was on hunger strike from the 17th September,[69] and two more, Kedar Nath Malaviya and Ganesh Prasad from the 5th October. All these three broke their fast chiefly owing to the persuasion of Bhagwati Saran Singh, M.L.C., a non-official visitor of the jails.[70]

Basawan Singh started a hunger strike in the Gaya jail on the 9th August, 1932, as a protest against imposition of fetters, for not being placed in the 'B' class and demanding certain improvements in diet and clothing. Kedar Mani Shukul also started hunger strike there from 7th September next on similar grounds. One of the accused, Biswanath, threw a shoe at the approver but missed him. Biswanath was brought back to dock and handcuffed.

Bombs and explosives were found by the police during this year also at some other places in Bihar. In the month of March, they arrested several members of the revolutionary party at Dhanbad on the charge of supplying explosives to the revolutionaries in Bengal. Three of the accused were sentenced to seven years' rigorous imprisonment each. In the month of August, 1933, Shiva Prasad was arrested while loitering near the Gulzarbagh railway station. The police alleged to have found two bombs with him. Later they searched his house in Patna City and reported to have discovered there some materials for preparing bombs.[71] In the same month there was a bomb explosion in a house opposite the Sadar Hospital at Ranchi. A Bengali youth named Malay Krishna and two other occupants of the house were arrested by the police.[72]

At Begusarai in the Monghyr district the son of a shopkeeper received a fatal injury from a bomb explosion.[73] From Monghyr, which had an old tradition of gun manufacture, arms were procured by revolutionary organisations in Bihar and Bengal and, in 1933, five mistries were convicted there for trading in such weapons. In the month of December, 1933, Chandrika Singh attempted to assassinate a special branch officer at Madhubani for which he was sentenced to transportation for life.

Thus we see that throughout the period under study the revolutionary movement was held in saluting position mainly by lawyers, college teachers and students and the members of other educated professions. The Anusilan Samities, the Revolutionary Party, Hindustan Socialist Republic Association or Army got recruits mainly from the college students and other members of the educated middle class. A few from the commercial and industrial middle class also joined the revolutionary movement. There were some members of the middle class landed interest who also took part in the revolutionary movement.

Notes

1. Valentine Chirol, *Indian Unrest*, pp. 40-41.
2. Tilak's Address to the students in College Square, Calcutta on January 4, 1906.
3. Andrews, C.F., *The Renaissance in India*, pp. 4-6.
4. Banerjee, Surendra Nath, *A Nation in Making*, p. 187.
5. *Ibid.*, pp. 63-64.
6. Pal, Bipin Chandra, *Swadeshi and Swaraj*, p. 291.
7. Mitra, Shishir Kumar, *Sri Aurobindo and Indian Freedom*, pp. 24-74.
8. Datta, Bhupendra Nath, *Dvitya Svadhinatar Sangram* (Bengali), p. 63.
9. *Ibid.*
10. Datta, K.K., *op. cit.*, Vol. I, p. 118.
11. Datta, Bhupendra Nath, *op. cit.*, p. 64.

12. *Ibid.*
13. Subsequently convicted in Benares Conspiracy Case and transported for life.
14. Subsequently convicted in Benares Conspiracy Case and sentenced to three years' rigorous imprisonment.
15. *Sedition Committee Report*, 1918, Para 118.
16. Originally started at Dacca by Shri Pulin Bihari Das for physical and moral culture.
17. *Sedition Committee Report*, 1918, Para 116.
18. *Ibid.*, Para 65.
19. 46,000 according to the *Sedition Committee Report*.
20. *Bihar and Orissa Police Abstract of Intelligence*, April to December 1912, Para 296 and *Supplement to Bihar and Orissa Police Abstract of Intelligence*, March 27, 1915.
21. *Sedition Committee Report*, Para 93.
22. Appendix III of the *History of the Freedom Movement in Bihar*, Vol. I.
23. Letter No. 130-34C, dated Ranchi, June 20, 1914, to the Commissioner of Bhagalpur.
24. Letter from Hon'ble H. LeMesurier, Chief Secretary, Bihar and Orissa to Mr. H.J. McIntosh, Commissioner of the Bhagalpur Division, Ranchi, September 18, 1914.
25. Letter from the Chief Secretary, Bihar and Orissa to the Commissioner of Tirhut, February 28, 1918.
26. *Sedition Committee Report*, Para 119.
27. *Ibid.*
28. The papers like the *Yugantar*, the *Sandhya* and the *Bande Matram* ceased to exist after this.
29. *Sedition Committee Report (1918)*, Para 67.
30. (a) Letter from H.A.F. Lindsay, Officiating Under Secretary to the Government of Bengal, Political Department, 5th February 1912, to the Inspector-General of Police, Bengal.
    (b) File No. 86 of 1915, Muzaffarpur.
31. *Bihar and Orissa Police Abstract of Intelligence*, July 1919, No. 27, Para 972.
32. Bajrang Sahay, *My Reminiscences of the Freedom Movement in Bihar (manuscript)*.
33. *Ibid.*
34. *Ibid.*

35. *Bihar and Orissa Police Abstract of Intelligence*, January 1919, Vol. VIII, No. 1, Para 49.
36. *Ibid.*, Pa\ ı 75.
37. *Ibid.*, December 7, 1918, Para 1190.
38. *Ibid.*, August 26, 1919, Para 1537.
39. Appendix IC of the *History of the Freedom Movement in Bihar*, Vol. I.
40. *Report of the Sedition Committee*, Para 144, 145, and 159.
41. Datta, K.K., *op. cit.*, Vol. II, p. 26.
42. *Ibid.*, pp. 26-27.
43. Note in this respect from the Government on Nov. 23, 1926 to P.W. Murphy, District Magistrate, Bhagalpur.
44. He was transported for life in the Kakori Conspiracy Case.
45. Judgement Report on the Deoghar Conspiracy Case.
46. Datta, K.K., *op. cit.*, Vol. II, pp. 29-30.
47. Copy of Judgement in the Deoghar Conspiracy Case, Police Report, *Bihar and Orissa in 1927-28*, p. 60 and *in 1928-29*, p. 60.
48. *Police Reports.*
49. Copy of Judgement in the Tirhut Conspiracy Case, Police Reports.
50. Datta, K.K., *op. cit.*, Vol. II, p. 32.
51. Patna Police Report, August 19, 1929.
52. Fortnightly Reports of the Patna Commissioner for the periods ending August 13 and Aug. 27, 1929.
53. Report of the Congress Secretaıies for 1929.
54. Fortnightly Report of tke Patna Commissioner for the period Sept. 27, 1929.
55. *Ibid.*
56. *The Searchlight.*
57. Letter from the Magistrate of Patna to the Chief Secretary, Bihar and Orissa, July 2, 1931.
58. *Terrorism in India*, 1917-1936.
59. Fortnightly Report of the Patna Commissioner for the period ending July 27, 1931.
60. *The Searchlight*, December 25, 1931.
61. *Ibid.*
62. *Ibid.*, December 22, 1931.
63. Fortnightly Report of the Patna Commissioner for the period ending January 7, 1932.

64. *Ibid.*, May 13, 1932.
65. *Ibid.*, July 13, 1932.
66. Datta, K.K., *op. cit.*, Vol. II, p. 252-53.
67. Fortnightly Report of the Patna Commissioner for the period ending June 13, 1933.
68. *Ibid.*, September 27, 1933.
69. *Ibid.*, October 13, 1933.
70. *Ibid.*, July 27, 1933.
71. *The Searchlight*, October 27, 1933.
72. *Ibid.*, August 13, 1933.
73. *Bihar and Orissa in 1932-33, XII.*

6

The Middle Class and the Nationalist Movement between 1935 and 1941 in Bihar

In this chapther an attempt has been made to review the role of the middle class of Bihar in the constructive programmes, the celebration of the Golden Jubilee of the Indian National Congress, the Independence Day and other national occasions like holding of political conferences, elections to the Provincial Législature and formation of organizations of youths and students, the programme of propaganda against Government's War Policy, holding of session of the Ramgarh Congress, the Satyagraha Camp at Sonepur and the Individual Civil Disobedience Movement.

After having witnessed large-scale demonstrations, strikes and boycotts under the leadership of the middle class consequent upon the declaration of Civil Disobedience Movement in the early thirties of the twentieth century, there dawned a period of comparative lull in the Indian politics from 1945 onwards since Mahatma Gandhi withdrew the said Movement. Besides, the Congress Party under the leadership of the middle class also became engaged in making necessary preparations for contesting the elections which were to be held under the provisions of the Oovernment of India Act, 1935, both at the

Centre as well as in the Provinces.[1] Moreover, the Congress workers, most of whom belonged to the middle class, were also engaged, during this period, in carrying out the constructive programmes as laid down by Mahatma Gandhi. The establishment of All India Village Industry Association was a part of this constructive programme of the Mahatma.[2]

Many provincial workers beloging to the middle class joined Mahatma Gandhi's All India Village Industries Association (A.I.V.I.A.) and All India Spinners Association and began work at several centres. Night schools, village libraries, free dispensaries, flour mills (started at Bihta in Patna district in July 1935)[3] and shops where opened here and there for the benefit of the rural people. In the month of September 1935, the village industries Association in Aurangabad subdivision induced a zamindar of the middle class to give them ten bighas of land for opening a free dispensary, a spinning school and a library.[4] About that time a village improvement society (Gram Sudhar Sabha) was started at Hardi Chapra, a diara village in Dinapur subdivision.[5] At Deoghar in Santhal Parganas, Binoda Nanda Jha, a member of the educated middle class, was taking a keen interest for the revival of some extinct industries and a shop was opened there at Minabazar for the sale of indigenous articles.[6]

In the Muzaffarpur district, persons like Rama Charan Singh, Janakdhari Prasad and Lakshmi Narayan, Secretary, All India Spinners' Association (Charkha Sangh), devoted themselves wholeheartedly to implement the programme of the two Associations mentioned above.[7] In the month of November, 1935, Anugraha Narayan Sinha, Secretary, Bihar Provincial Congress Committee, Gorakh Prasad and Raj Narayan visited Revilganj in Chapra in connection with a plan to open a branch of the Village Industries Association at Gonda. At a meeting that they had with the local Congress workers and other sympathisers to the cause, it was decided to start work in this respect in the villages between Gonda and Seresia under the guidance of Shri Gorakh Prasad.[8]

Some new Congress Ashrams were also started in these days and the old ones were revitalised. At a meeting of the Patna District Congress Committee, held on the 22nd October, 1935, it was decided to open a Congress workers training camp (opened on 5th November) at Bikram near Patna, and Ashrams at Hilsa, Bikram and Patna. A few days before this, Anugraha Narayan Sinha had presided at the opening ceremony of an Ashram at Bakhtiyarpur, which owed its existence very much to the efforts of Shilbhadra Yajee. Many prominent men including Mathura Prasad, Swami Sahajanand, Ambika Kant Sinha, Shah Muhammad Ozair Munemi and Brijnandan Prasad (advocate) were present at this function.[9]

In the month of November next, Anugraha Narayan Sinha, Mathura Prasad, Girish Tiwary and some other Congressmen belonging to the middle class had a meeting in the Sonepur Ashram where all the speakers emphasised on the utility of starting Ashram in the remote villages as a means for preaching the message of the Congress.[10]

The year 1935 was of special significance also for the decision (July-August 1935) of the Congress to celebrate its Golden Jubilee on the 28th December according to a suitable programme drawn up by it in October, 1935. The programme comprised Prabhat Pheries before dawn, flag hoisting and salutation at 8.30 a.m., national service illustrating the constructive work of the Congress, sale of small national flags, processions in the afternoon, public meetings in the evening where the President's message and speeches about Congress were to be read, illumination at night (no fireworks of any kind), sports (wrestling, Indian games and tournaments), mela (khadi exhibition and demonstrations, village industries exhibition and demonstrations, exhibition of other swadeshi articles, kavi sammelan or mushaira on subjects of national interest and importance, music) and Congress propaganda through suitable literature.[11] All the above programmes were carried on under the leadership of the middle class.

The Provincial Congress Committee[12] and District Congress Committees formed Sub-Committees of their own to make necessary arrangements for this solemn occasion. At Patna, in a meeting at the residence of Sachchidanand Sinha, a member of the educated middle class, a general committee of many members was formed with representatives of various shades of political opinion for organising this function.[13] The Bhagalpur District Congress Committee decided to hold an all India Swadeshi Exhibition on this occasion. In fact, the Jubilee was celebrated in a grand manner at all places in Bihar. The City of Patna presented a marvellous artistic decoration and several processions moved round it. At Mokameh the celebrations were very successful. Swami Sahajanand and some other Kisan Sabha leaders, who belonged to the landed middle class, took active part in the celebrations in the neighbourhood of Bihta and Bikram.[14]

Occasions like the Independence Day (26 January), the Gandhi Jayanti Week (24th September to 2nd October), the National Week (6th April to 13th April), the Detenus Day (19th May), the J.P.C. Protest Day (7th February, 1935) and Harijan Day (24th September, 1935) were celebrated under the leadership and guidance of leaders belonging to the middle class.[15]

The different Districts of Bihar vied, as it were, with one another in making elaborate preparations to hold District Political Conferences. The Patna District Political Conference was held in Bihar in November, 1935. The Purnea District Political Conference, held on 9th November, 1935, was presided over by Anugraha Narayan Sinha. Immediately after the Political Conference at Begusarai[16] had closed, a Cane Growers' Conference was held in the same pandal with Anugraha Narayan Sinha in the Chair. Santhal Parganas District Political Conference was held at Rajaun in the Godda Subdivision in the third week of January, 1936, with Srikrishna Sinha as its President.[17] Political Conferences were held under the leadership and guidance of the middle class as evident from the facts enumerated above.

After six years of Governmental ban, the Bihar Political Conference held its 9th Session at Patna on the 15th and 16th

January, 1936, amidst scenes of profound enthusiasm heightened to a great extent by the presence of Rajendra Prasad, the Congress President, belonging to the educated middle class. About 5,000 delegates, including many kisans and Santhals and large number of visitors attended it. Rajendra Prasad also addressed the Conference emphasising on the need of carrying out the constructive programme of the Congress and making a strong appeal of Hindu-Muslim unity.[18]

In the second half of January 1936, Mathura Prasad, Assistant Secretary, Bihar Provincial Congress Committee, forwarded the following circular letter of Rajendra Prasad, President, Bihar Provincial Congress Committee, to all the District Congress Committees as to how to observe 'Independence Day' on the 26th January, 1936. The letter read as follows :

"The 26th of January is approaching and shall be observed in all plaees. At every such meeting the resolution attached herewith should be read out in Hindustani or the local language of the place and pass without any speeches. It is recommended that the National Day be devoted in so far as it is possible to some special constructive effort and a determination be made to develop greater dedication to the cause of Poorna Swaraj. Hartal should not be observed. The 26th of January should be observed with solemnity without coming in conflict with the authorities and there should be no disobedience of orders prohibiting meetings and processions and banning Congress organisation. The following resolution is to be adopted :

"We remind ourselves on this solemn national day that complete independence is our birth right and that we shall use all and only peaceful and legitimate means to achieve it. We shall not rest till we have achieved it. As an essential step in the direction of achieving that end we shall seek to :

(a) Adopt and promote unity of heart among different communities and to establish complete equality of status among all, irrespective of caste, creed or race.

(b) To adopt and promote complete abstinence from intoxicating drinks and drugs.

(c) To promote hand spinning and other village industries and to adopt for personal use khaddar and other products of village industries to the exclusion of their products.

(d) To abolish untouchability.

(e) To serve the starving millions in every way we can.

(f) To engage in all other national and constructive efforts."[19]

On the 17th January, 1936, the Chief Secretary to the Government of Bihar and Orissa asked the District Officers to report to the Government, the speeches delivered in the meetings on the eve of 'Independence Day' celebrations.[20]

The 'Independence Day' was celebrated on the 26th January 1936 throughout the Province of Bihar with great enthusiasm under the overall supervision of the Bihar Provincial Congress Committee, consisting mostly of the members of the middle class. Large number of people assembled in the meeting. No untoward incident, however, occurred on that day.[21]

Though the actual elections were to take place in 1937, preparations for the same had already started one year earlier. The Provincial Congress Party geared up its election machinery along with other political parties and canvassing started by the leaders mainly belonging to the middle class, in different places for their respective candidates.[22]

Jawaharlal Nehru and Govind Ballabh Pant visited Bihar in connection with election propaganda. Their visits very much added to the enthusiasm of the masses.[23] Rajendra Prasad visited those places which the former two could not go on account of lack of time so that the whole province might be covered.

As the time of election drew nearer, all the contesting parties became active. The government was closely watching the activities of the various political parties and, on the 1st July, 1936, issued the following instructions regarding the maintenance of adequate vigilance in the coming election :

"It is particularly important that the officers of Government should refrain from any interference with legitimate electoral activities and should not identify themselves with any party. This does not prevent them from giving their advice to party representatives who ask for it. It will also be necessary for them, in conversation with callers and those when they meet in tour, to counter unwarrantable criticisms and attacks which are made on the existing land tenure and revenue system, when these attacks are of a nature which may give rise to disaffection in the district. The dangers involved in any sudden radical alteration of the existing economic structure should be explained especially to members of those classes who are being enfranchised for the first time, while the benefits which the tenantry derive from the tenancy laws and very real advance in the standard of living and wealth in the last twenty years may well be emphasised."[24]

The latter half of 1936 was spent in brisk canvassing by the different political parties for their respective candidates. The Government, on the other hand, was quite watchful lest these electioneering campaigns should degenerate into some kind of political movement. This see-saw game continued throughout the latter half of the year 1936. Then came the 'Independence Day' celebration of 1937.

On the 26th January 1937, the Independence Day was celebrated in Bihar with great enthusiasm. It is evident from the report of the Deputy Inspector-General of Police, C.I.D., Bihar, dated the 10th February, 1937, that at Siwan, the meeting was held at Sardhanand Bazar between 5 p.m. and 7 p.m. The meeting commenced with the usual national songs sung by Shashi Bhushan Shukul and Jagannath Das Gupta. The national flag was hoisted by Shashi Bhushan Shukul in the absence of Rajendra Prasad, who had gone to Gopalganj. After hoisting the flag Rajendra Prasad arrived and read out the Congress pledge from the *Amrita Bazar Patrika* of the 25th January, 1937. He translated the pledge to the audience in simple Hindi.[25] In the same manner the Independence Day was celebrated at several places of Bihar.

While the whole country was celebrating the Independence Day, the people of Bihar went to polls to elect new members for their Provincial Legislature under the provisions of the Government of India Act, 1935.

The elections to the Legislative Assembly in Bihar took place between the 22nd and 27th of January, 1937. The result of the elections was sweeping victory for the Congress party, which was remarkably disciplined and whose programme genuinely appealed to the people.[26] Out of the total 152 seats of the Assembly, the Congress captured 98; and in the Council, 8 Congress nominees were returned. Thus the Congress commanded an absolute majority in the two houses of the Provincial Legislature taken together.[27] Most of the candidates winning the elections belonged to the middle class.

After certain declarations on the part of the British Government, the Congress Working Committee decided at its meeting held at Wardha on the 8th July, 1937, that Congressmen be permitted to accept office where they may be invited thereto. But it was made clear that office was to be accepted and utilised for the purpose of working in accordance with the lines laid down in the Congress election manifesto and to further, in every possible way, the Congress policy of combating the new Act on the one hand and of prosecuting the constructive programme on the other.[28]

In Bihar, the Governor, Maurice Garnier Hallett, invited Shrikrishna Sinha, leader of the Congress Party in this Province, on the 24th and 25th March 1937, to form such a ministry with himself as the Premier. Shrikrishna Sinha asked the Governor to give him assurances as were required in the light of the Congress resolution noted above, before the formation of the ministry. On the Governor's refusal to comply with this demand, Shrikrishna Sinha rightly expressed inability to undertake the responsibility of forming a ministry.

The Congress at its Faizpur session (December 1936) had passed a resolution calling for a nation-wide hartal or general strike on the 1st of April, 1937, the day on which the new Constitution was to be inaugurated. In response to this, under the leadership and guidance of members of the middle class, hartal was observed throughout Bihar on the 1st of April, meetings were held at different places, many students absented themselves from schools and colleges, and effigies representing the new Constitution were burnt at some places (e.g., at Chandi and Naniganj in the Shahabad district).[30]

Under the leadership of the middle class, National Week was celebrated at various places in Bihar from 6th to the 13th April, 1937. It was marked by sale of khadi, enrolment of Congress volunteers and holding of meetings. At one such meeting, held at Kadamkuan, Patna, on the 13th April with Jagat Narayan Lal as President.[31]

A National Education Conference met at the Sadaqat Ashram, Patna, from the 5th to the 7th May, 1937, at which Rajendra Prasad and some other Congress leaders were present and it was decided to open a number of National Schools both of the middle and secondary standards, under the Bihar Vidyapith. The Working Committee of the Patna Youth League had a meeting on the 22nd May, 1937. Its President, Phulan Prasad Varma, read a paper explaining the role of socialism in national movement and a sub-committee was formed to improve the organisation of the volunteer corps in the town of Patna.[32]

During the fortnight ending 26th May, 1937, the Working Committee of the Bihar Provincial Congress Committee for 1937-38 was reconstituted and consisted mainly of the educated middle class. In view of a resolution of the

Congress for wider mass contacts, this Committee formed a Muslim Mass Contact Sub-Committee. In fact, increasing efforts began to be made by Congress workers in Bihar for enrolment of greater number of Muslim as members of the Congress.[33] The visit of Khan Abdul Ghaffar Khan to Bihar put a new life into the Muslim mass contact movement. He addressed a meeting at the Bankipur Maidan on the 15th July, 1937, another meeting at the Islamia Hall on the 20th July, 1937, a third at Madrasa Mosque at Chawk, Patna City, on the 21st July, 1937, and two meetings at Dinapur. All the meetings were largely attended and many Hindus joined these. He explained in his speeches the creed of the Congress and exhorted the Muslims to join it.[34] On the 26th July he visited Arrah, Piro, Bikramganj and Sasaram and addressed meetings.[35]

In the month of July 1937, the Bihar Provincial Congress Conference met at Masarakh in the district of Saran under the presidentship of Professor Abdul Bari. Several leading Congress workers including Rajendra Prasad participated in it. After the termination of the conference when the leaders arrived at Chapra, they learnt that the Governor of Bihar had invited Shrikrishna Sinha, the leader of the Congress Party to form a Congress Government in Bihar.[36] Shrikrishna Sinha accepted the offer of the Governor and thus the Congress came into power in Bihar.

In Bihar, Congress Ministry came into being on the 20th July, 1937, with Shrikrishna Sinha as the Premier. The other Ministers were Anugraha Narayan Sinha, Syed Mahmood and Jaglal Chaudhury. Ram Dayalu Singh and Abdul Bari became Speaker and Deputy Speaker, respectively. Sultan Ahmad, who had been appointed Advocate-General by the Yunus Ministry, sent his resignation from Simla and Baldeo Sahay was appointed Advocate-General by the Ministry.[37] For the first time, Congress adopted a positive attitude towards administration and agreed to take up the burden of government.[38]

The formation of the Congress Ministry was welcome in almost all quarters.[39] The Political Prisoners' Day was observed on the 24th July, 1937, and the Nation Day the day after. On the latter occasion, two meetings were held, under the leadership of the members of the educated middle class, one at Mangles Tank and the other at Bankipur, the first one being presided over by Anugraha Narain Sinha, the Finance Minister, and the second one by the Premier. The Ministry Day was celebrated[40] throughout the Province on the 1st August, 1937, accompanied by Flag hoisting ceremony, processions and meetings. National Flags were hoisted on a large number of school buildings, including Government Zila Schools and on buildings under the control of the local bodies. The Andamans Prisoners' Day was observed at many places on the 14th August, 1937. A meeting of the Executive Committee of the Bihar Provincial Youth League was held on the 24th August, 1937. Resolutions pressing for the commutation of sentences of the political prisoners, still detained in the Andamans, were passed. The President was authorised to wait on deputation on the Prime Minister to express the views of the meeting.[41]

While contesting the election, the Congress Party had pledged through its election manifesto that political prisoners would be released as soon it came to power. Hence the demand was raised that the Congress Government should honour its pledge. In order to get their release eight political prisoners in the Hazaribagh Jail went on hunger strike from the 26th January, 1938. The Congress Ministries of Bihar and U.P. wanted to release the political prisoners but the Governor-General issued a directive to the Governors under section 126 of the Act, not to accept the advice of the Congress ministers in this regard since it affected his special responsibility regarding the maintenance of peace and tranquillity of the country. Hence, the Governors did not agree to the release of political prisoners. A grave constitutional crisis arose on the question of the release of political prisoners. Hence the Congress Ministry in Bihar resigned in protest on the 15th February, 1938. The Congress held that the interference of the Governor-General was a clear violation of his assurance and amounted to misapplication of section 126 (5) of the Act.[42]

But this political deadlock did not continue for long. An agreement was reached on this question between Mahatma Gandhi and the British Government. Shrikrishna Sinha met the Bihar Governor on the 26th February, 1938, and soon after his interview the following joint communique was issued :

"We have discussed at the earliest possible opportunity the situation arising out of the release of those prisoners who had been classified as political. We have arrived at an agreement in the matter and thus the Hon'ble the Prime Minister and his colleagues have resumed their duties."[43]

As a result of this agreement a large number of political prisoners were released from the jails.[44] The Congress Government of Bihar also resorted to certain measures of social reforms which were not liked by the British Government. One such measure was prohibition. The introduction of prohibition in the district of Saran on 1st April, 1938, was looked with apprehension by the British Government because it might create unemployment amongst the Pasis whose number was considerable.[45]

The Socialist Party was also active in the province of Bihar. It organised a Summer School of Politics at Sonepur, which was inaugurated by Subhas Chandra Bose in May 1938. Again the Socialists held a big meeting at Chapra on the 29th May, 1938, in which strong anti-British speeches were delivered and the people assembled therein were told not to take any part in any future war in which Great Britain was involved.[46]

As regards constructive activities of the Congress during this period, it should be noted that the 5th session of the All India Gandhi Seva Sangh met at Brindaban in the Champaran district from the 3rd to the 8th May, 1939,[47] which resolved,

"The object of the Gandhi Seva Sangh is to serve the people through constructive activities in accordance with Gandhi's principles. As for the fulfilment of that object, it is necessary to participate in political activities also; the Sangh has always permitted its members to take part in politics."[48]

Under the leadership of the persons of the middle class, the Kisan movement gained momentum during these years. It still enjoyed full support of the Congress, and the Socialist members too were actively helping it. As regards the Congress, it passed one resolution at its 49th session held at Lucknow on 12th to 14th April 1936, with Jawaharlal Nehru as its President, emphasising the need for developing closer association between the masses and the Congress organisation, bringing about closer co-operation with other organisations of peasants, workers and others, which aim at the freedom of the Indian people and of making the Congress a 'Joint Front' of all the anti-imperialist forces in the country." To consider and make recommendations, the Congress appointed a committee consisting of Rajendra Prasad, Jairam Das Daulatram and Jai Prakash Narayan, all of whom came from the middle class.[49]

The Kisan Sabha worked so long in alliance with the Congress, and its strength was gradually increasing. In fact, the Kisan Movement had assumed all India character and importance; and Bihar had become now the most important centre of Kisan struggle under the leadership of Swami Sahajanand,[50] belonging to middle class family.

The Kisan Movement began to follow henceforth a separate course as a left wing with vigorous activities. But sometimes its methods were not quite peaceful and the Patna Commissioner reported to Government on the 27th of October, 1937, that the Kisan agitation was becoming dangerous. To check activities which threatened peace, the Government officers took necessary steps. The Ministers still advised conciliation to the Kisans. Thus the Prime Minister, while presiding over the Patna District Conference at Bakhtiyarpur on 4th December 1937, asked the Kisans not to resort to force for possession of the 'bakasht' lands.[51]

Besides, students were also active under the guidance of leaders belonging to the middle class. The All India Students' Day was celebrated in the Bihar Youngmen's Institute on the 20th November with Ram Briksh Benipuri as President. The students were advised to take interest in politics. At a meeting held at the Bihar Youngmen's Institute on the 8th December 1937, a Patna Students' Union was formed with Naqi Imam, a Judge, as President and Biswanath Prasad as General Secretary. A Youth League Conference was held simultaneously with the Bihar Provincial Kisan Conference at Bachwara on the 22nd and 23rd January, 1938. The Socialists were engaged in the formation of Youth Leagues, which sprang up at some places.[52]

At the Conference of the Bihar Provincial Muslim League, held at Patna on the 12th March 1939, a resolution was passed that the Muslim League would start civil disobedience against the Government if the latter introduced the Wardha scheme in the Province, and the Conference requested the Working Committee of the All India Muslim League to sanction the launching of civil disobedience.[53]

Government's war policy caused much resentment in Bihar as in the other parts of India, and voices were raised by leaders of all groups (Congress, Congress Socialist, Forward Bloc and Kisans) belonging to the middle class, against recruitment and support for what was considered to be an 'Imperialist War'. Meetings were held and appeals were issued through leaflets, etc. to advise the people on what should be their duty at this critical moment. For example, one such leaflet entitled 'Piro thana ke Janata aur Karya-kartaon se Appeal,[54] (Appeal to the people and workers of the Piro thana in the Sahabad District), was circulated by the Piro Thana Congress Committee. It was printed at the Bharat Printing Works Ltd., Arrah, and issued over the names of Deo Narayan Sharma, President, and Ganesh Kumar Sinha,

Secretary, Piro Thana Congress Committee. Another leaflet, entitled 'Azadi ki Larayi ke liye taihar raho' (Be ready for the war for independence), was issued to hold a meeting on the 24th September, 1939, in the camping ground at Dehri by Radha Mohan, Secretary, Mazdoor Sangh, Dehri and Bateshwar Singh, Secretary, Thana Kisan Sabha, Dehri.[55]

Subhas Chandra Bose, who had tendered his resignation from the Presidentship of the Congress on the 29th April, 1939 and had announced in Calcutta on the 3rd May next the formation of a new bloc within the Congress to be called the 'Forward Bloc', visited Patna and the neighbouring districts from the 26th to the 28th August, 1939, and addressed meetings regarding the policy of his new bloc and the international situation. Bose visited Arrah on the 28th August and addressed a large gathering on the war crisis and India's duty at that time. Here he was presented addresses of welcome by four local organizations, viz., Students of Arrah Town, Kisan Sabha, Mazdoor Sabha and Youths of Arrah Town.[56]

The Working Committee of the Congress met on the 14th September, 1939, to consider the situation and resolved that :

"Our experience in the past, particularly during the last War, had clearly shown that no trust could be placed in the war statements and war promises of the British Government or the Government of India; and, accordingly, call upon them not merely to elucidate their position vis-a-vis the future of India, but address themselves to an immediate application of the principles so elucidated. The Committee declares that until such a clearing of positions took place, it could not advise the country to extend the fullest measure of co-operation to Government."[57]

On the 16th October, 1939, the Prime Minister, Shrikrishna Sinha, moved the following resolution in the Bihar Legislative Assembly : "This Assembly regrets that the British Government have made India participant in the War between Great Britain and Germany without the consent of the people of India and have further, in complete disregard of Indian opinion, passed laws and adopted measures curtailing the powers and activities of the Provincial Governments."[58]

Rajendra Prasad, President, Indian National Congress, convened another meeting of the Working Committee at Wardha on October 22, 1939. The Committee passed a lengthy resolution calling upon the Congress Ministers to tender their resignations and appealing to the nation to end all internal controversies and to act unitedly in the cause of India's freedom and calling upon all Congress Committees and Congressmen to remain prepared for all developments and eventualities[59] In pursuance of the resolution of the Congress Working Committee, the Bihar Ministry resigned on the 31st October, 1939.[60]

The resignation of Bihar Ministry was welcome by the people of Bihar. Students' meetings were held at Patna which were addressed by student leaders including Zawar Husain, in which the resignation of the Congress Ministry was welcome.[61]

Meeting at Allahabad from the 19th to 23rd November, 1939, the Congress Working Committee declared again that the recognition of India's independence and of the right of her people to frame the constitution through a Constituent Assembly is essential in order to remove that taint of imperialism from Britain's policy and to enable the Congress to consider further co-operation.[62]

In view of the crisis through which India and the world was then passing, and the possibility of India's struggle for freedom being continued in an intenser form, the Working Committee in its meeting at Wardha from the 18th to 22nd December, 1939, decided to celebrate the next Independence Day with a special significance not only as the declaration of India's national will to freedom, but a preparation for that struggle and a pledge to disciplined action. The Working Committee, therefore, called upon all Congressmen to take the following pledge, either in public meetings called for the purpose, or individually in cases of illness or other physical disability.[63]

When the guns were booming on the war fronts, the Province of Bihar was engaged in the celebration of its 'Independence Day'. On the 26th January, 1940, the Independence Day was celebrated with great enthusiasm throughout the Saran district. At Chapra the national flag was hoisted by Mahamaya Prasad Sinha, President, Saran District Congress Committee, in the compound of the Congress Office and the District Board. Mathura Prasad, Secretary, Bihar Provincial Congress Committee, hoisted in the municipality compound. A large number of persons participated and joined in singing the national anthem. In the evening, a public meeting was held under the presidentship of Mahamaya Prasad Sinha. The President read out the Congress pledge.[64] Independence Day was celebrated in other districts with the same enthusiasm.[65]

At Patna, Ram Briksh Benipuri and some others were prosecuted for helping in the organisation of a student procession which had no licence. On the 27th January, 1940, Rajendra Prasad paid a brief visit to Gaya, an address was presented to him by the Gaya Municipality and a public meeting was also held. Money was collected there for the Ramgarh Congress. Shrikrishna Sinha, Anugraha Narayan Sinha and some other provincial leaders were then touring in the province to collect funds for the Ramgarh Congress.[66]

Students' activity was prominent during the Independence Day celebration at Patna, Muzaffarpur, Arrah, Bhagalpur and Monghyr. At Monghyr, Anil Mitra was prosecuted for taking out an unlicensed procession on the Independence Day and was sentenced to several months' rigorous imprisonment. So penalisation of the students for patriotism then naturally produced considerable indignation in the student world.[67] A largely attended Monghyr District Students' Conference was held at Begusarai on the 3rd February, 1940, with Rahul Sankrityayana in the chair. The principal speaker was Subhas

Chandra Bose, who was touring Bihar in that month.[68] In one of the resolutions the students were congratulated for their worthy conduct on the Independence Day. The Congress Working Committee met at Patna from the 28th February to 1st March, 1940. Two meetings were then organised at Patna by the Students' Federation and these were addressed by some prominent leaders.[69]

The arrest of a respected leader like Jaya Prakash Narayan under the Defence of India Rules, for a speech delivered at Jamshedpur on the 18th February, 1940, roused the feelings of people. A meeting in protest of his arrest was held at Patna on 10th March and the 14th March was observed as 'Jaya Prakash Day', meetings being held throughout the Province at which the students most enthusiastically participated.[70]

The Bihar Students' Conference met at Darbhanga on the 27th and 28th April, 1940. Muquimuddin Faraqi, Chairman of the Reception Committee of the All India Students' Federation Conference at Delhi, presided over it. The objects of the Students' Federation included among other things the safeguarding of the students' rights and the development of political consciousness among them.[71]

When the Axis powers were getting victories over the Allied powers and when the Second World War was rather taking a serious turn, the 53rd Session of the Indian National Congress was held at Ramgarh in South Bihar in March, 1940. Preparations for the session were started from the latter half of the year, 1939. Every district contributed much to make the session a success. Prominent ladies coming from the middle class families, such as, Sail Kumari Devi, Sharda Devi, Shanti Ojha and Janak Dulari Devi, Miss Prema Ben and several others worked as volunteers on the occasion of the Ramgarh Congress.[72]

The Ramgarh Session met under the presidentship of Maulana Abul Kalam Azad on the 19th and 20th March

1940.[73] When the Congress Session at Ramgarh was about to commence at 5.30 p.m. on the 19th March, there was a heavy downpour of rain and the whole pandal, picturesquely decorated, became a vast sheet of water. But in spite of the incessant rains, the proceedings of the Congress went on without any let or hindrance.[74] Rajendra Prasad as the Chairman of the Reception Committee, welcome the delegates.[75] Rajbanshi Singh of village Kelharua, Police Station Guthani, Saran, was incharge of the 'Tirhut Division's Volunteer Organisation' and he was also the Field Officer at Ramgarh Congress.[76]

At Ramgarh, Jawaharlal Nehru moved the resolution on Satyagraha which the Congress Working Committee had already passed. The resolution after being seconded by Acharya Kripalani was voted upon and declared passed.[77]

On the 4th April, 1940, in pursuance of the decision of the Ramgarh Session, the Bihar Provincial Congress Working Committee met at Sadaqat Ashram, Patna, under the presidentship of Rajendra Prasad. It resolved that every Congress Committee be transformed into Satyagraha Committee. It also resolved that in order to fulfil that programme it is necessary that work at khadi and charkha be taken up in right earnest. All the office-bearers and members of the Congress Committees should begin spinning regularly and thus set an example to others. This Committee also resolved that a list of those who believe in the efficacy of this programme should be prepared and a camp should be opened for them to give them training and instructions regarding this programme. In the opinion of this committee, the first camp should be held for the members of the Provincial Congress Committee and of those who believe in this programme and are prepared to abide by the rules of the camp. Having received training in the camp they should go to their respective places and start other camps, thus creating an atmosphere in the entire province which may be convincing to Mahatma Gandhi. By another resolution, this Committee selected Sonepur[78] as the site for the training camp of Satyagrahis which was scheduled to be held from the 20th to 26th April, 1940.[79]

The Khadi Exhibition was well organised by Lakshmi Narayan, Secretary of the Charkha Sangh.[80] On the 14th March, Mahatma Gandhi opened the Khadi and Village Industries Exhibition at Ramgarh. He observed on this occasion, "We have to awaken them to a sense of these treasures and dispel their ignorance and darkness. That is the function of these exhibitions."[81]

Some Indian nationalists of radical political views, mostly of the Forward Bloc, were not then at one with the Congress standpoint regarding the war crisis. To them it appeared to be leaning towards compromise with the British Government and they demanded an absolute non-compromise with the imperialist forces. To organise a movement in support of their attitude and policy they held the All India Anti-Compromise Conference at Ramgarh during the Congress Session, The proceedings of this Conference were not impeded by rains, as it had been over before the rains set in. Sahajanand Saraswati was Chairman of the Reception Committee, Dhanraj Sharma, Sheel Bhadra Yajee and some others, belonging to the middle class of Bihar, played a prominent role in it. Subhas Chandra Bose was President of this Conference. Besides containing a strong criticism of Congress policy and after affirming the inalienable and indefeasible right of the Indian people to complete independence, the resolution laid down that from April 6, the date for the beginning of the National Week, there should be the signal for the intensification of local struggles and commencement of a struggle on all India front and added that this movement should symbolise the resolve of the Indian people to withdraw themselves from participation in the war and make final efforts for the achievement of India's independence.[82]

After about two weeks of the Ramgarh Congress, the country celebrated the National Week (6th to 13th April) with more than usual enthusiasm. At all public meetings held during this period emphasis was laid on the importance of the constructive programme in the country's preparation for the struggle under the leadership of Mahatma Gandhi.[83] In an article in the *Harijan* under the caption 'Every Congress

Committee a Satyagraha Committee', Mahatma Gandhi called upon every Congress Committee to become a Satyagraha Committee and register such Congressmen who believed in the cultivation of the spirit of goodwill towards all, who have no untouchability in them in any shape or form, who would spin regularly and who habitually use khaddar to the exclusion of all other cloth.[84]

On the 20th April, 1940, Rajendra Prasad arrived at Sonepur from Wardha.[85] At 10 a.m. with the hoisting of the National Flag by him, the Satyagraha Camp was opened at Sonepur in the mango grove near the Dak Bungalow, about half a mile from Sonepur railway station.[86] Speaking on satyagraha, Rajendra Prasad observed, "As soon as we acquire strength we shall achieve our objectives. That strength of heart comes through the cultivation of self-discipline and charkha was a means to that end. It was possible to acquire that strength through other sources but charkha had the additional advantage of supplying this with cloth. During one week at the camp, every one should spin yarn for one yard of cloth. In this way, if they spin for fourteen weeks, at least one hour daily, they would be able to get yarn for fourteen yards of cloth which was the average requirement per head.[87]

A member of the educated middle class, Mahamaya Prasad Sinha, President, Saran District Congress Committee, paid glowing tributes to Rajendra Prasad. He said, "We are proud of you, who is one of the highest rank satyagrahi in India and we assure you that there are persons in the land of your birthplace to follow you.[88] You are fifty-six but Kunwar Singh, who achieved wonders at the age of eighty, belonged to this very province. Of course his was the strength of sword and yours is that of satyagraha. You have acquired mastery in the use of that weapon so that you are now Mahatmaji's right hand. It is our fervent hope that under your leadership here we shall be able to give a good account of ourselves."[89]

At the Sonepur Satyagraha Camp, 436 miles and 1100 yards of yarn was spun by the satyagrahis enrolled there. Out of this, 39 miles and 758 yards of yarn was spun by thirty-five trainees belonging to the district of Saran.[90]

Among the satyagrahis mention may be made of the name of Prabhawati Devi and Shanti Devi of Saran.[91] Another characteristic feature of the satyagraha camp was that amongst trainees there were some Muslims also. Prominent amongst the Muslims were Rafiuddin Rizvi, Manzoor Hasan Ejazi, Razaq and Sajjad of Chapra.[92]

The constructive programmes of the Congress were given effect to by the leaders of the District Congress Committees. Spinning was one such item of the programmes. In the first week of July, 1940, 'Spinning Day' was observed at different places. On this day Congress spun hundreds of yards of yarn symbolising the unity and the strength of the Congress.[93]

The total number of Satyagrahis enrolled in Bihar up to the 1st of May, 1940, was 2,000. The Provincial Satyagraha Training Camp started at Sonepur from 20th April lasted for a week. It was attended mostly by the middle class people of Saran district. Similar camps were started in other districts also, viz., Patna, Shahabad (at Behea), Gaya, etc.[94] Towards the end of November, 1940, the Congress leaders of the Santhal Parganas held a Satyagraha camp at Saraiyahat.

Unfortunately, communal bitterness was growing between Congress and the Muslims. In his Presidential address at Ramgarh Session of the Congress, Maulana Abul Kalam Azad, while emphasizing the heritage of common nationality between Hindus and Muslims in India, also observed, "This thousand years of our joint life has moulded us into a common nationality. This cannot be done artificially. Nature does her fashioning through her hidden processes in the course of centuries. The caste has now been moulded and destiny has set her seal upon it. Whether we like it or not, we have now become an Indian nation, united and indivisible."[95]

But within a few days in its 27th Annual Session, held at Lahore, the Muslim League enunciated the theory that the Muslims are not a minority but a 'nation' and they must have their homeland, their territory and their state (Pakistan), that is, the areas in which the Muslims are numerically in majority as in the north-western and eastern zones of India, should be grouped to constitute independent States in which the constituent elements shall be autonomous and sovereign.[96]

Many Muslims from Bihar attended the Lahore session of the League and there was a conference of the Muslim League at Chapra on the 13th and 14th April, 1940. On the 19th April, meetings were held at different places in Bihar to observe Pakistan Day, in which the Lahore resolution about partition of India was read and passed.[97] At many centres, however, meetings were also held by the Ahrar Party and the Momins on the same day to observe it as Hindustan Day and the Lahore resolution and the Muslim League activities were condemned.[98]

In response to the Congress offer of co-operation, the Viceroy issued a new statement on 8th August, 1940 (afterwards known as the 'August Offer'). After reiterating the October statement about Dominion Status, it proposed an immediate expansion of the Governor-General's Executive Council and the establishment of a War Advisory Council. It conceded the Congress demand for a Constituent Assembly to frame the Indian Constitution, though it was to meet after the war was over. At the same time it also accepted Jinnah's demand by saying that the British would accept any system of Indian Government whose authority is directly denied by large and powerful elements in India's national life.[99]

The 'August Offer', however, failed to satisfy either the Congress or the Muslim League. So the Mahatma proposed to begin the Individual Satyagraha campaign by selecting one individual at a time to go out in the street shouting anti-war slogans and get arrested.[100]

A conference of the Presidents and Secretaries of the Provincial Congress Committees and Congress Ex-Ministers was held in Bombay on the 17th September, 1940, at the instance of the Congress President, Maulana Abul Kalam Azad. The President in his opening remarks explained the situation arising from the Congress resolution on Satyagraha and the assumption of leadership by Mahatma Gandhi and enjoined upon all present to follow strictly the instructions issued from Mahatma Gandhi and the Working Committees.[101] Satyagraha was started on 17th October by Vinoba Bhave at the village of Paunar, about seven miles from Wardha. He was arrested on the 21st October and sentenced to three months' imprisonment. Jawaharlal Nehru was to be the second Satyagrahi. But he was arrested by the Government at Cheoki on the 31st October and was sentenced to four years' imprisonment.[102]

While the Working Committee was taking the momentous decision for the new phase of Satyagraha, the Congress leaders, most of whom belonged to the educated middle class, of Bihar, were moving from place to place popularise their point of view among the people. On the 3rd and 4th September, 1940, the Provincial Congress Committee met at Gaya and a public meeting was addressed by some of the leaders. The chief speakers were Shrikrishna Sinha and Professor Abdul Bari. A similar meeting was held in the Patna Maidan on the 12th September, the principal speakers in it being Shrikrishna and Satya Narayan Sinha. During the second half of September, Shrikrishna delivered an impressive speech in this connection at Darbhanga and Prajapati Mishra toured in Darbhanga and Madhubani districts for a similar purpose. Gandhi Jayanti was celebrated all over the Province by pushing on the sale of Khadi. Pattabhi Sitramayya made a tour of the Province in connection with these celebrations and addressed several meetings.[103]

Bihar responded to the call of Individual Civil Disobedience with alacrity, as she had done during the previous phases of the national movement. The Santhal Parganas Congress Committee passed a resolution congratulating Vinoba Bhave on his arrest and conviction and condemning the action of the Government.[104] The arrest of Jawaharlal Nehru and the severe sentence passed on him naturally caused much resentment in Bihar. As a protest, hartals were observed and meetings were held at different places on the 2nd November, 1940. On that date, one such protest meeting presided over by Acharya Badrinath Varma was held in the Bankipore Maidan, prominent speakers were Anugraha Narayan Sinha, Abdul Bari and Jagat Narayan Lal. A similar meeting was held on the same day at the Mangles Tank in Patna City, and at Arrah presided over by Rang Bahadur Prasad.[105] An emergency meeting of the Provincial Congress Committee was held at Patna on the 11th November, 1940, in connection with the Satyagraha.[106]

In Bihar, on the 28th November, 1940, individual Satyagraha was started by the ex-Premier, Shrikrishna Sinha, with an anti-war speech before a large crowd at Patna. When he was arrested and was being taken to jail, the crowd disregarding the instructions followed him to the jail gate and the situation became very tense.[107] Students were prominent among the demonstrators, and they were dispersed by the police by a lathi charge.[108] Rajendra Prasad issued a statement condemning the demonstration and laying down instructions for future guidance. Anugraha Narayan Sinha, who was to offer Satyagraha in another part of the city, at the same time was asked by Rajendra Prasad not to do so till they were assured by the people of proper behaviour and strict observance of the prescribed instructions. This produced the desired effect. Assurances of good behaviour poured forth and Civil Disobedience was renewed after two days. Anugraha Narayan Sinha was arrested for a speech at Patna City.[109]

In Saran, on the 28th November 1940, individual Satyagraha was started by the District Congress President, Mahamaya Prasad Sinha. He started from his village Patheri where he was garlanded by his old mother and walked upto Maharajganj. He uttered anti-war slogans and appealed to the people to march forward under Mahatma Gandhi's leadership.[110] Later on, Mahamaya Prasad Sinha was arrested and sentenced to one year's rigorous imprisonment for offering satyagraha at Maharajganj and was transferred from Chapra to Hazaribagh Jail.[111]

The Government of Bihar did not fail to take time by the forelock and at once arrested those who offered Satyagraha after the two leaders, Shrikrishna Sinha and Anugraha Narayan Sinha. A large number of members of the Legislature and leading Congressmen were convicted and sent to jail in quick succession. Gauri Shankar Singh offered Satyagraha in Gaya on 4th December and Shyam Narayan Singh, M.L.A., offered Satyagraha on the 9th December, 1940, at Silao (Bihar Sub-division). All were arrested and convicted under the Defence of India Rules and were sentenced to one year's rigorous imprisonment each. Sarangdhar Sinha, M.L.A., Punyadeo Sharma, M.L.C., Jagat Narayan Lal, M.L.A., who offered Satyagraha at Patna, and Ramayan Prasan, M.L.A, who offered Satyagraha at Patna on the Patna-Arrah border at Koilwar bridge, were arrested and convicted. Kumar Kalika Prasad Singh and Mazhar Faridpuri, son of late Mazhar-ul-Haque, were also arrested and sent to jail during the second half of December, 1940. According to a chart, released by the All India Congress Committee Office on the 3rd March, 1941, nine hundred and seven Satyagrahis were arrested till then in Bihar and the total amount of fines imposed here on the Satyagrahis was Rs. 33,699. This figure did not include many others who offered Satyagraha but were not arrested.[112]

The Congress President, Maulana Abul Kalam Azad, came to Patna in December, 1940. At a meeting of the Provincial Congress Committee, held on the 8th December, he emphasized the need of enlisting more Satyagrahis from the members of the Provincial and subordinate Congress Committees, and at a public meeting held at Patna on the same day. Many local bodies in Bihar passed resolutions applauding the action of the Satyagrahis and condemning Government policy and adjourned their meetings as a mark of protest against Government measures. Shrikrishna Sinha and Krishna Ballabh Sahay, then in jail, refused to see their relatives in the presence of Criminal Investigation Department Officer.[113]

Mahatma Gandhi suspended Satyagraha during the Christmas week. But the Government arrested Maulana Abul Kalam Azad, the Congress President at Allahabad on 30th December, 1940, and sentenced him to 18 months' imprisonment. Mahatma Gandhi issued another statement now emphasizing the qualitative aspect of the movement.[114]

As a mark of protest against the arrest of the Congress President, there were hartals at different places in Bihar. A protest meeting organised by the members of the middle class was attended by a large number of people, was organised in the Whitty Park at Gaya on the 5th January, 1941, and such meetings were arranged at some other places too.[115]

On the same day commenced the second phase in Satyagraha. Lists of Satyagrahis, prepared by local Congress Committees, were sent to Mahatma Gandhi and those selected by him started work according to his instructions.[116] A number of persons offered Satyagraha in Bihar and some ladies also were arrested at Gaya for this. For example, Priyambada Devi, Jagat Rani Devi, and Janki Devi were sentenced to four months' imprisonment each on the 28th and 30th January and 3rd February respectively. In March next, Santi Devi was sentenced to simple imprisonment for one day and to a fine of Rs. 200 in default of simple imprisonment for a further fortnight.[117]

In the district of Santhal Parganas, the following persons were prosecuted and sentenced to various terms of imprisonment till the middle of February, 1941, for offering Satyagraha: (A) In the Godda Subdivision (1) Ulfat Husain (on 12.2.41) and (2) Maisa Paharia (on 15.2.41), and (B) in the Deoghar Subdivision (1) Bhagwan Dutta Rajhans (on 5.2.41) (2) Ayodhya Prasad Misser (on 5.2.41), (3) Bigu Rai (5.2.41), (4) Shrikrishna Prasad (on (15.2.41), Hari Prasad Jayaswal (on 15.2.41), Janki Prasad Singh (on 15.2.41), Narsing Prasad

Roy (on 15.2.41) and Chando Prasad Roy (on 15.2.41).[118] During the week ending the 2nd March, 1941, ten persons were convicted and sentenced to similar punishments in this district for political offences.

On the 22nd February, 1941, a meeting was held in the Dharmasthan at Dumka in which it was announced that Shrimati Kejriwal, wife of Shri Motilal Kejriwal, Vice-Chairman of the District Board and President of the Santhal Parganas District Congress Committee, would offer Satyagraha in Dumka Town. After the meeting a large procession would go round the town. On the 26th February, 1941, Shrimati Kejriwal saw the Deputy Commissioner at his bungalow and offered herself for arrest. But the Deputy Commissioner, instead of arresting her then, arranged for watching her movements.[119]

No one offered Satyagraha on the Independence Day (26th January). This day was celebrated at various places. The National Week was also observed by following Mahatma Gandhi's advice for self-purification by fasting on the 6th and 13th April, and by more concentrated efforts to increase membership, constructive work and propaganda for swadeshi and khadi goods, unity and untouchability.[120]

Satyagraha continued with much vigour. Some Satyagrahis from Monghyr and other parts of Bihar were now (March-April) proceeding to Delhi or United Provinces on foot. To stop this, the Bihar Government passed orders for their arrest as soon as they wanted to cross the provincial frontier.[121]

Regarding Congress constructive works in Bihar at this time, it may be mentioned that a meeting was convened by the All India Spinners' Association on the 24th April, 1941, at the Hindi Sahitya Sammelan Bhawan in Kadamkuan (Patna). Rajendra Prasad presided and exhorted the audience to increase the sale of khadi. The social work of ameliorating the condition of the so-called Depressed Classes was also in progress. The fifth session of the Shahabad District Depressed Classes

Conference, under the chairmanship of Prithvi Singh Azad, opened at Arrah on the 8th November, 1941. The Conference was inaugurated by Anugraha Narayan Sinha. Towards the end of this year, A.V. Thakkar, General Secretary of the All India Harijan Sevak Sangh, toured some districts of Bihar with a view to coordinate the activities of organisations engaged in the upliftment work among the aboriginals.[122]

Unfortunately, reactionary forces were at work under the influence of communalism. The Muslim League in Bihar, as in other parts of India, was trying hard to evoke and enhance greater interest and support for the Pakistan scheme. But intolerance overpowered good sense and, during the summer months of 1941, there broke out serious communal riots at Biharsharif following observance of Pakistan Day on the 23rd March, 1941, and decision of the Hindu Mahasabha to observe Anti-Pakistan Day on the 27th April, 1941. As the situation became serious, the two Secretaries of the Bihar Provincial Congress Committee, Mathura Prasad and Shah Muhammad Ozair, rushed to the riot affected areas and did their best to control the people and quell the disturbances. S.M. Ismail, President of Muslim League in Bihar, alo toured these areas and organised relief through the local branch of the Muslim League. The Magistracy and the Police were also active in taking steps to suppress the trouble.[123]

On returning to Bihar, Rajendra Prasad at once organised Congress Shanti Dals (Peace Brigades) under Abdul Bari, toured the disturbed parts with them and brought the situation under control. With his usual zeal Abdul Bari was working indefatigably to remove communal discord.[124]

The third phase of the Satyagraha had commenced from the middle of April. The Bihar Provincial Congress Committee met on the 17th April to review the progress of Satyagraha in Bihar and to consider what steps should be taken to quicken the pace of the movement. District Satyagraha Officers were appointed and a large number of Congress members now enrolled themselves as Satyagrahis. To keep the Satyagrahis free from the prevailing politics of the local bodies, which unfortunately was not above criticism[125] it was soon decided by the Congress in Bihar under the direction of Rajendra Prasad that all Congressmen should resign from the District Boards and the Municipalities. This order was reaffirmed at meetings of the Provincial Congress Committee held at the Sadaqat Ashram on the 12th August and 2nd September, 1941. The Political Conference, held at Nawadah (Gaya district), on the 18th August was addressed by Acharya Kripalani and passed a resolution urging withdrawal of Congressmen from local bodies except the District Board of Santhal Parganas by the 30th September. Majority of the Congressmen obeyed this order. As a disciplinary measure, the Provincial Congress Committee expelled the recalcitrant members.[126]

Shrikrishna Sinha was released on the 26th August, 1941, on the expiry of his term of imprisonment and Anugraha Narayan Sinha was released at the same time. Shah Muhammad Imam, a prominent Congressman of Gaya, was also released then. Congress activities, naturally, received impetus after the release of such leaders who began to tour the different districts and addressed meetings, particularly during the celebration of the Gandhi Jayanti. By the beginning of October, Satyagrahis released from imprisonment began to come forward to court arrest a second time. Thus in Patna District, Punyadeo Sharma was again sentenced for 18 months' imprisonment for an anti-war speech at Paliganj on the 4th October. Several others courted arrest.[127]

By December 1941, the Bihar Government passed orders for the release of Satyagrahi prisoners whose offences had been either formal or symbolic in character according to Government. From 4th December started general release throughout India. Jaglal Chowdhry, who had been arrested in Purnea district for fresh Satyagraha, was released, as also other civil disobedience prisoners. By the middle of that month, the Government released the members of the Congress Working Committee.[128]

The Second World War had taken a menacing turn for the Allied Powers by the end of 1941. The Japanese forces had penetrated into the South-east Asian countries and they had come much nearer to India. Moreover, the Japanese war planes had started bombing the cities of Assam, Bengal and Vizagapatnam. These had their impact upon the political development in the country. The Congress leaders rightly thought that if the Individual Satyagrah was continued then, it might be that the Congress leaders would be put behind the bar at this critical moment. As a result of it the people at large would be deprived of proper guidance; and, as such, it would militate against the interest of the National Movement. Therefore Mahatma Gandhi suspended the Individual Civil Disobedience Movement and directed the Indian people to remain watchful and to devote themselves to the fulfilment of the constructive programmes of the Congress.[129]

Thus we see that the members of the middle class were chosen in most cases to offer individual satyagraha. Though other groups of the middle class participated in this individual Satyagraha, the educated middle class surpassed all other groups of the middle class.

The Bihar Congress Socialist Party, consisting of members of the middle class, convened a meeting on the 1st of May, 1941, on the Bankipur Maidan in observance of the May, Day. Shibnath Banerjee presided and the other speakers included Ram Briksh Benipuri, Purushottam Trikam Das and Shyamanandan Singh. Fascism, Nazism and British imperialism in India were condemned at this meeting. For the redress of the grievances of the labourers and the Kisans, the speakers advocated remission of rent, increase in wages, grant of dearness allowance and help to the sick, the infirm and the unemployed.[130]

The Bihar Provincial Forward Bloc Conference met at Chapra on the 30th and 31st October, 1941, with V.H. Kamath, Organising Secretary of the All India Forward Bloc, in the chair. Expressing dislike of individual Satyagraha, he advocated a mass movement in the near future. Kamath visited Patna on the 1st November, where he presided over a meeting attended mainly by students. He then made a tour of Bihar accompanied by Sheel Bhadra Yajee and delivered speeches strongly condemning British imperialist policy.[131]

As regards the Kisan Movement, it may be noted that Swami Sahajanand's conviction was a great loss to it. But still it carried on a good deal of activity under the guidance of leaders belonging to the middle class, in the districts of Patna, Shahabad, Muzaffarpur, Darbhanga, Saran, Champaran, Purnea, Palamau and Santhal Parganas. On the 1st September 1940, Kisan Day was observed at various centres of the Province by holding meetings at which resolutions were passed protesting against the arrest of Sohan Singh, President of the All India Kisan Sabha.[132] The attempt of the Congress Socialists to control it did not succeed at the session of the Bihar Kisan Conference held at Dumraon on 8th and 9th March, 1941, and they formed separate organisation under the leadership of Awadheshwar Prasad Sinha with Ram Briksh Benipuri as President.[133] In August next, Jamuna Karjee presided over a meeting of the Council of Action of the Bihar Provincial Kisan Sabha, which decided to suspend all anti-war activities as anti-war propaganda would merely assist the Nazis who were attacking Russia.

The Students' Movement was also on the forward march. No boubt, Narayan Prasad Varma, General Secretary of the Bihar Siudents' Federation, was convicted during the second half of July, 1940, on the charge of possessing a proscribed leaflet.[134] But this did not damp the spirit of the students. They became determined to launch wider agitation against the repressive measures of the Government by organising hartals, strikes, rallies and other demonstrations. A Youth League Conference was held at Laheriasarai on the 18th August, at which a resolution was passed rejecting any compromise with British imperialism.[135] Chandra Shekhar Singh, Secretary of the Provincial Students' Federation, was arrested on the 4th December under the Defence of India Rules. As a protest against it, the Colleges in Patna observed hartal on the 5th December.[136]

On the 23d March, 1941, the students organised a meeting at the Patna Maidan to observe the Security Prisoners' Day.[137] On the 12th and 13th April, 1941, met the Shahabad Students' Conference under the Presidentship of Abdul Bari.[138]

The Farooqui section of the All India Students' Federation held their session at Patna on the 31st December and the following day. Considering that the character of the war had changed after Russia's entry into it, they passed a resolution for unconditional support to war. The majority of the Patna students were opposed to the war-resolution of this meeting.[139]

One new factor at this time intensified distrust of the Indians in various circles about British promises to grant independence to India. The third clause of the Atlantic Charter issued in the month of August, 1941, contained the following significant principles to which the British and American Governments became committed : "They respect the right of all peoples to choose the form of Government under which they will live, and they wish to see sovereign rights and self-government restored to those who have been forcibly deprived." But Winston Churchill's declaration in the House of Commons on the 9th September, 1941, that the Atlantic Charter was not applicable to India, caused much disappointment to the Indians. Discontent, repressed by force, flared up into a mighty conflagration in 1942.[140]

Thus we see that the members of the middle class played a pivotal role in the nationalist movement in the period under study. It is true that in the constructive programmes the masses showed their participative enthusiasm, but the leading role was played by the leaders coming from the middle class, particularly the educated middle class. As regards the celebration of the national occasions, the masses played a commendable role in making such occasions a success, but leadership and direction remained in the hands of the members of the middle class.

Besides, the middle class people played a commendable role in the elections for the Provincial Legistature, and it was due to their ability to mobilise the masses in favour of the Congress that gave it victory with absolute majority. The Ministries formed by the Congress consisted mainly of the middle class educated elites of Bihar.

The part played by the students' and youths' organisations was a role played by the educated middle class as most of them had received education upto degree level. Besides, the middle class people also played a praiseworthy role in the propaganda against Government's War Policy and in making the session of the Ramgarh Congress and the Satyagraha Camp at Sonepur by participating and mobilising the masses to attend these two occasions. The individual Civil Disobedience was mainly a movement of chosen leaders belonging to the middle class, mainly the educated middle class. But the role played by some members coming mainly from the educated middle class in spreading the poison of communalism left a stain on our national integration.

To conclude, it may be said that it was due to the participation, guidance and leadership of the leaders belonging to the middle class that the nationalist movement during this period became a success to a great extent.

Notes

1. Datta, K.K., *Op. cit.*, Vol. II, p. 256.
2. *Ibid.*, p. 260.
3. Fortnightly Report of the Patna Commissioner for the period ending 27th July and 13th August, 1935.
4. *Ibid.*, for the period ending 13th and 27th Sept., 1935.
5. *Ibid.*, for the period ending 14th October, 1935.
6. *The Indian Nation*, October 20, 1935.

7. *Ibid.*
8. *Ibid.*, November 15, 1935.
9. Fortnightly Report of the Patna Commissioner for the period ending June 27, 1935. *The Indian Nation*, October 16, 1935.
10. *The Indian Nation*, November 15, 1935.
11. Datta, K.K., *Op. cit.*, Vol. II, pp. 262-263.
12. *The Indian Nation*, November 27, 1935.
13. *Ibid.*
14. Fortnightly Report of the Patna Commissioner for the period ending January 15, 1935.
15. *The Indian Nation*, November 27, 1935.
16. *Ibid.*
17. Bihar Political Conference Report.
18. *The Indian Nation*, January 18, 1936.
19. File No. 18/1936, Bihar Political (Special) Department.
20. *Ibid.*
21. *The Searchlight*, January 28, 29, 30, 1937.
22. Prasad, Rajendra, *Op. cit.*, pp. 465-466.
23. *Ibid.*
24. Datta, K.K., *Op. cit.*, Vol. II, pp. 278-279.
25. File No. 29/1937, Bihar Political (Special) Department.
26. Report of the Collector of Shahabad to the Commissioner, Patna Division for the period ending 11th September, 1937.
27. Diwakar, R.R., *Op. cit.*, p. 663.
28. *Ibid.*, pp. 663-664.
29. Datta, K.K., *Op. cit.*, Vol. II, p. 287.
30. *Ibid.*, p. 288.
31. *The Indian Annual Register*, 1937, Vol. I, p. 188.
32. Fortnightly Report of the Patna Commissioner for the period ending May 13, 1937.
33. Report of the Magistrate of Patna to the Patna Commissioner for the period ending May 26, 1937.
34. *Ibid.*, for the period ending July 25, 1937.
35. Report of the Magistrate of Shahabad to the Patna Commissioner, August 11, 1937.
36. Prasad, Rajendra, *Op. cit.*, p. 476.
37. *Ibid.*, pp. 663-664.
38. Azad, A.K.. *India Wins Freedom*, p. 150.

39. Letter from the District Magistrate, Patna to the Commissioner, Patna Division, July 25, 1937.
40. *Ibid.*, August 12, 1937.
41. Datta, K.K., *Op. cit.*, Vol.II, p. 299.
42. Bhagwan Vishnoo, *Constitutional History of India and National Movement*, p. 242.
43. Datta, K.K., *Op. cit.*, Vol. II, p. 300.
44. *Ibid.*, Appendix XXIX.
45. File No. 18/21/1938, Home (Political) Department, National Archives of India, New Delhi.
46. File No. 18/5/1938 and 18/6/1938, Home (Political) Department, National Archives of India, New Delhi.
47. Datta, K.K., *Op. cit.*, Vol. II, p. 312.
48. *Ibid.*
49. *Ibid.*, p. 266.
50. *Ibid*, pp. 313-14; Swami Sahjananda Saraswati, *Mera Jeevan Sangharsha* (Hindi), People's Publishing House, Delhi, 1985.
51. Report of the Magistrate, Patna to the Patna Commissioner, December 11, 1937.
52. Datta, K.K., *Op. cit.*, Vol. II, p. 327.
53. *The Annual Indian Register*, 1931, Vol. I, p. 371.
54. Appendix XXVIII of *History of the Freedom Movement in Bihar* by K.K. Datta, Vol. II.
55. The second leaflet was printed in the Vyapar Press, Dehri-on Sone.
56. *The Indian Nation*, January 20, 30, 1939.
57. Sitaramayya, B. Pattabhi, *Op. cit.*, Vol. II, pp. 129-30.
58. *The Indian Nation*, October 17, 1939.
59. *Ibid.*, October 23, 1939.
60. *Ibid.*, November 1, 1939.
61. Zawar Husain was the Secretary, Bihar Students' Federation.
62. Datta, K.K., *Op. cit.*, Vol. II, p. 348.
63. *Ibid.*
64. *The Indian Nation*, January 30, 1940.
65. *Ibid.*, January 20, 30, 31, 1940.
66. Datta, K.K., *Op. cit.*, Vol. II, p. 351.
67. Report on the events in Bihar during the first half of February, 1940.
68. *Ibid.*

69. *Ibid.*, during the second half of February, 1940.
70. *Ibid.*, during the month of March, 1940.
71. *Ibid.*, during the second half of April, 1940.
72. *The Indian Nation*, November 2, 1939.
73. Sitaramayya, B. Pattabhi, *Op. cit.*, Vol. II, p. 166.
74. Datta, K.K., *Op. cit.*, Vol. II, p. 367.
75. Sitaramayya, B. Pattabhi, *Op. cit.*, Vol. II, p. 167.
76. *Ibid.*
77. Datta, K.K., *Op. cit.*, Vol. II, p. 369.
78. Sonepur is a place in the district of Saran (North Bihar).
79. Extract from the Proceeding Book of the Working Committee of the Bihar Provincial Congress, pp. 82-85.
80. Prasad, Rajendra, *Op. cit.*, pp. 545-47.
81. Tendulkar, *Mahatma*, Vol. II, pp. 319-20.
82. Datta, K.K., *Op. cit.*, Vol. II, p. 372-73.
83. *Ibid.*, Appendix XXIV.
84. *Ibid.*, Appendix XXV.
85. Prasad, Rajendra, *Op. cit.*, p. 557.
86. *The Indian Nation*, April 27, 1940.
87. *Ibid.*, April 29, 1940.
88. Rajendra Prasad was born in village Ziradeo (Saran).
89. *The Indian Nation*, April 29, 1940.
90. *Ibid.*, April 28, 1940.
91. She was the daughter of a veteran Congress leader, Brij Kishore Prasad and wife of Jaya Prakash Narayan.
92. *The Indian Nation*, April 21, 1940.
93. *Ibid.*, July 12, 1940.
94. *Congress Bulletin*, May 27, 1940; Prasad, Rajendra, *Op. cit.*, pp. 551-57.
95. Datta, K.K., *Op. cit*, Vol. II, p. 377.
96. *Ibid.*
97. Reports on Political events in Bihar during the second half of April, 1940.
98. *Ibid.*
99. Majumdar, R.C., *History of the Freedom Movement in India*, Vol. III, pp. 605-606.
100. *Ibid.*, p. 607.
101. *The Indian Annual Register*, 1940, Vol. II, pp. 22-24.

102. Datta, K.K., *Op. cit.*, Vol. II, p. 382.
103. *Ibid.*, p. 383.
104. *Ibid.*, p. 384.
105. *Ibid.*
106. Report on the events in Bihar during the first half of November, 1940.
107. Prasad, Rajendra, *Gandhi and Bihar*, p. 114.
108. Report on events in Bihar during the second half of November, 1940.
109. Datta, K.K., *Op. cit.*, Vol. II, p. 385.
110. Patheri village is near Maharajganj Railway Station in Saran district.
111. (a) *The Indian Nation*, November 30 and December 1, 1940.
 (b) *Ibid.*, December 3, 1940.
112. Indian National Congress, Report of the General Secretaries, March 1940, October, 1940, p. 20,
113. Datta, K.K., *Op. cit.*, Vol. II, p. 389.
114. *Ibid.*, p. 300.
115. *Ibid.*
116. Majumdar, R.C., *Op. cit.*, Vol. III, p. 608.
117. Datta, K.K., *Op. cit.*, Vol. II, p. 390.
118. *Ibid.*
119. *Ibid.*, p. 391.
120. *Ibid.*, p. 392.
121. *Ibid.*
122. Report on events in Bihar during the first half of December, 1941.
123. *Ibid.*, during the second half of March, 1941.
124. Prasad, Rajendra, *Op. cit.*, p. 563.
125. *Ibid.*, p. 565.
126. *Ibid.*
127. Not less than forty-five by the end of October, according to the Government Report.
128. Datta, K.K., *Op. cit.*, Vol. II, p. 399.
129. *Ibid.*, p. 400.
130. *Ibid.*, p. 401.
131. *Ibid.*, p. 405.
132. *The Searchlight*, September 3, 1940.
133. *Ibid.*, March 11, 1941.

134. Datta, K.K., *Op. cit.*, Vol. II, p. 406.
135. *The Searchlight*, August 20, 1940.
136. *Ibid.*, December 6, 1940.
137. *Ibid.*, March 24, 1941.
138. *Ibid.*, April 14, 16, 1941.
139. Datta, K.K., *Op. cit.*, Vol. II, p. 410.
140. *Ibid.*, p. 416.

7

The Nationalist Movement between 1942 and 1947 and the Middle Class in Bihar

In this chapter an attempt has been made to review the role of the middle class in educating and preparing the people for irresistible struggle against the British Raj, the Quit India Movement, the underground movement, the constructive works, the communal politics, the elections to the Provincial Legislature and the celebration of Independence Day and other national occasions.

The year 1942 was marked by strenuous political activities in Britain as well as India.[1] The Second World War had taken an ominous term for the allied powers. The Japanese forces were threatening India almost at her very doors. The demand of the Indian people for a national Government at the Centre evoked a countrywide response but it was ignored by the British Government. The Cripp's proposal instead of solving their constitutional deadlock further complicated the situation with the result that the political situation in India became highly explosive. At this critical hour India threw an open challenge to British Imperialism by asking the British Government to quit the country. Rajendra Prasad, a member of the educated middle class, observed, "It was not to embarrass the British people that our whole scheme was planned, but to enable the people to resist whoever wanted to dominate India, whether it be British or Japanese."[2]

India's widespread national challenge to British imperialism seemed inevitable. So, from the end of April and during the months of May and June, Rajendra Prasad, Shrikrishna Sinha and other Congress leaders of Bihar, who belonged to the different groups of the middle class, toured different districts of Bihar to educate and prepare the people for the impending struggle. They addressed numerous meetings in which explicit reference was made to the coming ordeal.[3]

A number of public meetings were already held in the second half of March 1942 in which Congress leaders laid stress on positive action in the political field. Similar view was expressed in a meeting at Sonepur. Another meeting was organised at Zeeradei, home village of Rajendra Prasad, in the district of Saran under the presidentship of Mahamaya Prasad Sinha, who belonged to the educated middle class. He exhorted the people present in the meeting to hoard foodstuffs instead of money since currency notes were likely to lose their value.[4]

The Working Committee of Bihar Provincial Congress Committee met at Patna on the 15th and 16th April, 1942. It endorsed the resolution of the All India Congress Working Committee rejecting the Cripp's proposal. It also accepted the recent resignation of all the members of the Provincial Committee and gave Rajendra Prasad full power to form his own Committee.[5]

On the 11th May, 1942, Rajendra Prasad visited Chapra and addressed a public meeting there on the next day in which he asked the people to carry on constructive works and to arrange for storage of grains. During the first half of May, two well attended Political Conferences were held, one at Ranka in the Palamau district and the other at Kudra in the Shahabad district.[6]

A meeting was held at Patna City on the 30th April under the presidentship of Anugraha Narayan Sinha for organisation of Raksha Dal (Defence Party). Anugraha Narayan Sinha, Jagjivan Ram and Jagat Narayan Lal, all belonging to the educated middle class, visited Mokameh on the 27th June and, besides speaking on the war situation, emphasised the need for forming village defence parties.[7] A meeting of the Congress Party was held at Sonepur on the 30th June in which resolutions were passed reaffirming complete faith in Mahatma Gandhi's leadership.[8]

A largely attended meeting of combined Socialist, Congress and Kisan elements, consisting the bulk of the middle class, was held on the 10th July at Hasanpura in the Saran district at which some speakers exhorted the audience to join the forthcoming mass movement under Mahatma Gandhi's leadership.[9] At the meeting Rambriksha Brahmachari and Ram Bhuwan Singh, both ex-terrorists, called on the audience to join Mahatma Gandhi's forthcoming mass movement. They were supported by Mahamaya Prasad, President of the District Congress Committee, who described the proposed movement of the Mahatma as last bid of freedom.[10]

An important meeting of Congressmen was arranged at Tarapur in the Monghyr district on the 18th and 19th July, 1942, mainly to protest against the unsatisfactory management of the Banaili Estate in relation to its tenants. It was attended, among others, by Acharya Kripalani, Rajendra Prasad, Shrikrishna Sinha and Krishna Ballabh Sahay. Anugraha Narayan Sinha was in the chair.[11]

Thus Bihar was making a psychological preparation for the impending challenge to British imperialism, when the Working Committee of the Indian National Congress met at Wardha on the 6th of July to consider the situation. After a close and careful consideration of the full implications of Mahatma Gandhi's reasons for demanding British withdrawal, the Working Committee passed the 'Quit India' resolution on the 14th July, 1942, which was to be placed before the next meeting of the All India Congress Committee at Bombay.[12] It renewed the demand that the British rule in India must end immediately and reiterated the view that the freedom of India was necessary not only in the interest of the country at large but also for the safety of the world and for the ending of Nazism, Fascism, Militarism and other forms of imperialism and aggression of one nation over another.[13]

With this objective a meeting of the Bihar Provincial Congress Working Committee was called at Patna on the 21st and 22nd July, where the resolution of the Congress Working Committee was endorsed. A plan of Satyagraha was also indicated, which was not fundamentally different from that of the previous Satyagraha but was certainly more forceful.[14]

In a meeting which was addressed by Anugraha Narayan Sinha, a lawyer and so belonging to the educated middle class, at the Anjuman-e-Islamia Hall, Patna, the students were asked to prepare themselves for the coming struggle. Rajendra Prasad remained at the Sadaqat Ashram, Patna, with Mathura Prasad and Chakradhar Saran, who belonged to the educated middle class.[15]

But the matter immediately took a serious turn. The Working Committee met at Bombay on the 5th August and passed the famous resolution, later on called the 'Quit India' resolution, repeating with all emphasis the demand for the withdrawal of the British power from India, which it considered to be an urgent necessity both for the sake of India and for the success of the causes of the United Nations. They must remember that non-violence is the basis of this movement.[16]

This resolution was considered at the historic session of the All India Congress Committee at Bombay on the 8th August and was passed with overwhelming majority. In addressing the Congress after this, Mahatma Gandhi suggested for the people the mantra 'Do or Die'. We shall either free

India or die in the attempt, we shall never live to see the perpetuation of our slavery.[17]

In the morning of the 9th August, 1942, Mahatma Gandhi and other leaders were arrested.[18] On the same day at Patna the District Magistrate, W.G. Archer, appeared before Rajendra Prasad at about 10 a.m. Finding him indisposed, the District Magistrate sought Government instruction as to what should be done in such circumstances. He was advised to consult the Civil Surgeon as to whether Rajendra Prasad would be taken out at any distant place in that state of health. On examining him, the Civil Surgeon, Major Muddock, gave the option that his health did not permit him to be shifted to a distant place (presumably to Hazaribagh Central Jail). Rajendra Prasad was then arrested under section 26(i)(b). Before his departure of jail, a large number of persons had gathered in Sadaqat Ashram and remained standing in torrential rains and, as Rajendra Prasad came out smiling, he was greeted by national slogans—'Quit India', 'Rajendra Prasad Hamare Neta Hain', 'Congress Zinda Bad' and other slogans.[19] Phulan Prasad Varma of village Jigana, Police Station Mirganj (Saran) and Mathura Prasad of Saran were also arrested on the same day (i.e., on the 9th of August, 1942) at Patna.[20]

On the 9th August 1942, the Government of Bihar issued some notifications—1-C(P), 2-C(P) and 3-C(P)—declaring unlawful such bodies as the All India Congress Working Committee and its branches, etc., Bihar Provincial Congress and its branches, etc., Bihar Congress Working Committee and its branches, etc., the Bihar Congress Executive Committee and its branches, etc., all the District Congress Committees, all Subdivisional Congress Committees, all Thana Congress Committees, the Provincial Committee of the Congress Socialist Party, the Council of Action of the Provincial Committee of the Congress Socialist Party and all local Committees of the Provincial Committee of the Congress Socialist Party.[21]

The fire started in the hearts of the students, who played indeed a heroic role in this great and gigantic struggle of India freedom, fully demonstrating to the world how the youths of India could be inspired by the Mantra of 'Do or Die'. Immediately on hearing of Rajendra Prasad's arrest, the Patna students organised themselves to lead a large procession, which was joined by others as well.[22]

On the 10th August, the police seized the Sadaqat Ashram, the Kisan Sabha Office (Kadamkuan Road, Kotwali P.S.), the District Congress Office, New Kadamkuan and the Congress Socialist Party Office, New Kadamkuan. At the Sadaqat Ashram all its inmates were asked by the police to vacate it, and Amar Kishore Sinha, a member of the educated middle class and Publicity Officer of the Bihar Provincial Congress Committee, was taken into custody for refusing to do so. The police took possession of the building of the Bihar Vidyapith.[23]

In the Patna Medical College, not only the students went on strike but their example was followed by the nursing staff, housemen and others who constituted the bulk of the educated middle class. The authorities failed to persuade them to do their normal duties. It is mentioned in a Government report and also in the *Searchlight* that Captain Ghos of the Patna Medical College produced a letter from Rajendra Prasad to the effect that the nursing staff of the Hospital should join their duty in the interest of the patients.[24]

On the same day (10th August), students of the Nalanda College and of the schools at Biharsharif and those of Barh, and Mokameh, went on strike, took out procession through the town and hoisted national flag on several buildings. There were hartals at all those places. In Gaya too, majority of the students acted similarly. There was a complete hartal in the Gaya Cotton and Jute Mills and at Hajipur.[25]

On the 10th August, there was complete hartal at Muzaffarpur. Students of the G.B.B. College (now called the L.S. College) and of the local schools formed a procession near one of the hostels of the college at 7 a.m. and they were soon joined by thousands (more or less 5000 according to Government estimate).[26] At Darbhanga, the students of the C.M. College and the Medical School took a leading part in organising hartals and processions on the 10th August. At Darbhanga there was almost complete strike of students and processions moved through the towns.[27] In Dhanbad area, there were hartals at Jharia and Katras, strikes of students and their processions and meetings. At Jamshedpur, John and Treta Singh addressed a meeting of thousands of workers on the 9th August and asked them to observe a strike on the next day.[28] At Ranchi, there was hartal on the 9th August and the police seized the office of the District Congress Committee there in the evening of that day.[29] At Dalmianagar, the labour force of the Rohtas Industries came out on the 9th August at the suggestion of Reyasat Karim.[30] At Bhagalpur a large procession of students, who had gone on strike, joined also by others, moved throughout the city, made demonstrations before the Courts, hoisted national flag on the buildings of the Zila School and the Office of the Divisional Inspector of Schools and shouted slogans appealing to the police and other government servants to join the Movement. There was almost general hartal in the city.[31]

On the 10th August, there was a complete hartal in Chapra town. Even vehicular traffic had seized plying on the streets. Manick Chand Singh, Secretary of the Chapra Town Congress Committee, Pandit Jagannath Mishra alongwith some others named in the list were arrested by the 10th August, 1942. The officers of the District and Town Congress Committee as also the officers of the District Congress Socialist Parties were seized. Hartals, meetings and processions were organised on that day at several other places in the Saran district, such as, Revilganj, Sonepur, Marhowrah, Amnaur, Maharajganj, Gopalganj.[32] On the 11th August, 1942, there was an angry and violent demonstration at Chapra.[33] There was a complete strike in the D.A.V. College and the high schools of the town. The students paraded in procession which terminated in a meeting addressed by Basudeo Narain Sinha, a member of the educated middle class.[34]

A very serious situation developed at Patna, and certain events took place here on the 11th of August for which it will be ever reckoned as a memorable day in the history of Bihar's struggle for freedom. Seven persons, who came from the families of the middle class landed interest of Bihar, were martyred. These were—Uma Kant Prasad Sinha, s/o Ram Kumar Sinha of village Narendrapur, P.O. Husainganj, P.S. Darauli, District Saran and a student of Class XI of the R.M.R. Seminary, Patna; Ramanand Singh, s/o Lakshman Singh of village Shahadatnagar, P.S. Masaurhi, District Patna and a student of Class XI of R.M.R. Seminary, Patna; Satish Prasad Jha, s/o Jagdish Prasad Jha of village Kharhara, P.S. Banka, Bhagalpur and a student of class XI, Patna Collegiate School; Jagpati Kumar, s/o Sukhraj Bahadur of village Kharathi, P.S. Obra, District Gaya and a student of 2nd year class, B.N. College, Patna; Devi Pado Chaudhary, s/o Devendra Nath Chaudhary of village Jamalpur, P. S. Biswanath, District Sylhat and a student of Class IX of Miller H.E. School, Patna (his father was then serving as a teacher in Punaichak L. P. School, Patna); Rajendra Singh, s/o Sheo Narain Singh of village Banwarichak, P.S. Sonepur, District Saran and a student of Matric class in Patna H.E. School; and Ramgovind Singh, s/o Devaki Singh of village Dasratha, P.S. Phulwari, District Patna and a student of Matric Class in Poonpoon H.E. School.[35]

Out of the processionists, fifty students were arrested and confined in the Bankipur Jail. The Secretariat tragedy made the situation extremely grave. The news reached the town within five minutes and, at once, all shops both of Hindus and Muslims, were closed. There was an acute tension throughout the city and this dastardly action on the part of the Patna executive brought about a spell of hatred, excitement and indignation. A procession of many Secretariat Assistants and Chaprasis moved in the Gardanibagh area in the evening headed by D.P. Tripathi, a Store-Keeper of the P.H.D., shouting slogans as a protest against the firing. A mass meeting was held in the Medical College compound condemning this bloody action of the Government.[36]

In Bihar, the situation took a serious turn after the police firing near the Secretariat building on the 11th August. Thereafter trouble spread out from district to district and within a week extensive damage was done to railway tracks, railway stations and trains in North as well as South Bihar. A number of police stations were attacked, post and sub-registry offices looted and attempts were made to hoist the Congress flag on district and sub-divisional offices, buildings of local bodies and schools. Hartals and picketing of schools and law courts became common. Curfew was imposed in Patna and Arrah where the situation seemed serious.[37] Describing the situation in Bihar, the Governor, T. Steward, wrote to the Viceroy, "Though (Patna) firing checked the attack, the crowd went back in an ugly mood in the evening and through the night engaged in widespread sabotage and road obstruction, the thoroughness of which had to be seen to be believed. Telegraph poles, complete with their full equipment of wires, were pulled over and branches of trees a feet and over in diameter were chopped down. This was not the work of 5 minutes or an hour but nevertheless no information came into headquarters that the wholesale destruction was going on."[38] Roads were cut and culverts and bridges damaged. That is the sight, as the *Searchlight* Staff Reporter mentioned on the 13th August. On the 13th August, there was incendiarism at the Patna City, Gulzarbagh, Barh, Lohanda Road and Taregna Railway Stations. Many students gathered at the Bihta Railway Station and held up a train. The Sadisopur Railway Station and the Naubatpur Dak Bangalow were damaged by a large number of students workers. Murli Manohar Prasad, a member of the educated middle class and Editor of the *Searchlight*, was guiding the people in that area.[39]

Large scale arrests,[40] deployment of military force, and other rigorous measures adopted by Government till about the middle of August, could not check the Movement at all. In fact, growing severity of Government policy and measures added fuel to the fire and aggravated intensity of the popular upheaval. Large mobs moved, assembled here and there, and continued to attack the police stations, railway stations, post offices, liquor shops, excise offices and other offices considering these to be the symbols of British imperial authority.[41]

Indeed, events in Bihar took the form of rebellion, spreading fast from urban to rural areas. By 12th August, Patna was completely cut off from the rest of India. On the 13th August, at Fatwah, two Royal Air Force Canadian officers were dragged out of a train and killed. Planes armed with machine guns were used on crowds dismantling rail-lines, roads and bridges at Kajra. All official residences at Dehri-on-Sone were burnt by the mob on the 14th August. At Bihta, on the 15th August, 14 wagons of British troops' rations were burnt. Railway traffic was completely dislocated. On 18th August, a military aircraft crashed at Narayanpur. According to the official report, the surviving members of the crew were killed by the mob. On the 19th August, the crowd even captured trains and drove them. On 3rd September, the town police at Jamshedpur went on strike. On the 4th September, prisoners of Bhagalpur Central Jail murdered the D.S.P., the Carding Master and a Warder. The armed police killed 28 prisoners and wounded another 87 of them. In Darbhanga district all police stations except 5 were attacked and looted. On the 11th September, 5000 copper miners went on strike at Mushabani.[42]

The people of Bihar handled all sorts of weapons in their fight with the police. Generally they used their own indigenous weaponry, which included spears, bows and arrows and other local products. After looting the police armoury, they used to handle police muskets, .303 rifles and shot guns and sometimes revolvers too. Spears and other weapons were being manufactured by village blacksmiths from fish-plates and other pieces of metal taken from the railway lines. All classes of people took part in the movement—intellectuals, students, factory workers, miners, peasants, policemen, 'C' class apprentices and sweepers. 205 policemen defected. In October, the jail population in Bihar rose to 27,000.[43] Violent mobs killed some military personnel at Saran and some other government and police officials at Sitamarhi and Minapore in the district of Muzaffarpur, Singhia in the district of Darbhanga and Rupauli in the district of Purnea.[44]

During the heat of the movement, the Government had almost lost control over Patna, Arrah, Bhagalpur and Darbhanga districts. Communications were maintained only through aeroplanes. As regards postal and telegraphic communications, the most affected areas in India were Bihar, Eastern U.P., Eastern Bengal. All the communication lines connected with Patna were completely cut off; only through military wireless communication system could the officials at Patna maintain contact with the rest of India.[45]

The Government was particularly disturbed by the long strike in the Tata factories. Tata Iron & Steel Company was on strike from 21st August to 3rd September, 1942.[46] Linlithgow, in a secret letter to Amery, wrote on 22nd August, 1942, "In some ways the most disturbing a development is the openly declared political strike in the Tata Factories and the serious interruption of vital war industries which this involves and to which for obvious reasons we have done our best to deny publicity."[47]

The strike in the Tata factories, according to official intelligence, was instigated by the foremen and supervisory staff who numbered about four hundred. Also A.R. Dalal, a Director and Jahangir Ghandy, the General Manager, were in favour of the strike.[48] This shows the role of the industrial middle class in the 'Quit India Movement'.

The youth, both educated and uneducated, played a leading role in the mass upsurge. The 1942 movement was, indeed, a movement of the youths. They took the arrest of top Congress leaders as a national affront. The youth accepted the challenge. Soon they were in command everywhere. The Bihar Chief Secretary wrote, "Students were very prominent, specially in the early stages and were much to the fore in organising and carrying out sabotage."[49]

Students, to whom patriotism became a virtue, played a very noble role in the history of our country's freedom. What they did in the earlier phases of it, has been already noticed. In the Movement of 1942, they were in the vanguard regardless of personal considerations and made profound sacrifices for the cause of liberty, some of them courting martyrdom like great heroes.[50]

Indeed, the students' movement was not dead. For sometime it went underground. Several student leaders had been sent to jail. But others formed a secret society named the Bihar Central Students' Council from about the month of December, 1942, and started their work. Late Anirudh Kumar Sinha, a youth of exemplary character, whose life was a noble sacrifice for the service of the motherland, was the Chairman of this Council. Hardeo Narayan Singh and Sambhu Nandan were its Joint Secretaries. The Central Office of the Students' Council was at Patna and branches of it were started in different parts of the province. This body published one fortnightly paper called 'Hamara Sangharsa' (Our Struggle) and other revolutionary leaflets were distributed by them here and there.[51]

Though the national uprising of Indian people in August 1942 was ruthlessly crushed by the British Government on the point of gun and bayonet, still the movement did not die out completely, rather it became underground.

In order to prevent the recurrence of attacks on the lines of communication, the Government imposed collective fines on the inhabitants of certain areas. The Viceroy believed that, in the existing circumstances, collective fines would provide a potent deterrent.[52] He rebuked the Governor of Bihar for granting remissions to some localities and reminded him that the imposition of collective fines was an objective method of keeping up pressure on the Congress and its supporters.[53]

It seems the Congress Socialist Party had formulated some plan even prior to August, 1942. According to report reaching the Government, the Party had organised a secret Congress Corps in Bombay, Bihar, U.P., Bengal and the Punjab. Ram Nandan Mishra in Bihar had to act as secret dictator.[54]

While the underground activities against the Government were carried on by the Indian revolutionaries, there occurred an incident which put the Bihar Government to great embarrassment and that was the escape of Jai Prakash Narayan, the Socialist leader, along with his five comrades from the Hazaribagh Central Jail.[55] On the 9th November, 1942 (i.e., on Deepawali Day), Jai Prakash Narayan with five political prisoners escaped from the Hazaribagh Jail. According to Government report, the escape was facilitated by laxity of supervision in the jail, but the possibility of help from the outside is not excluded.[56] After his escape from the jail he moved from place to place, contacted hiding Congress workers and inculcated in them a fighting spirit to prolong and intensify the struggle against the British Raj without loosing much time. All of them were of the Congress Socialist Party. After their escape, Jai Prakash Narayan and his associates entered the Gaya district. They divided themselves into two groups—one consisting of Jai Prakash Narayan, Ram Nandan Mishra and Saligram Singh who proceeded towards Benares, and the other consisting of Jogendra Shukul, Suraj Narayan Singh and Gulali Sonar who went to North Bihar. From Benares, Jai Prakash Narayan went to Delhi to chalk out the programme of action. From Delhi he proceeded to Bombay and stayed there for three months. From Bombay he went to Madras and from Madras he came to Calcutta. He, with Suraj Narayan Singh, proceeded to Nepal. Nepal was to be made all-India Centre of the Azad Dasta.[57] On suspicion of being connected with the plot for this escape, Ram Narayan Singh, Krishna Ballabh Sahay and Sukh Lal Singh were secretly transferred to Bhagalpur Jail.

In the night of the 4th December, 1942, four political prisoners escaped from the Muzaffarpur Jail and a police report notes that Yogendra Shukul was at Muzaffarpur that day. Soon at Akharaghat, two persons recognised him and on their secret information the Police Superintendent of Muzaffarpur, who had already made sufficient preparations to watch his movements, arrested him there along with another person who was identified to be Balgovind Singh of Karnauti.[59] Suraj Narayan Singh and Gulali had, however, proceeded towards Darbhanga and remained engaged in carrying on their secret activities.

Already in the month of December 1942, the Bihar Government had traced a circular said to have been issued by Basawan Singh and containing instructions for the destruction of Government buildings and communications, opposition by direct action to the levy of collective fines, creation of dissatisfaction in the army and police, collection of arms and ammunition, etc.[60]

The underground resistance movement made some dents in Bihar, U.P., Bengal, Delhi, Orissa and Assam. Jai Prakash Narayan selected Bihar as his chief operational base. The close proximity of Nepal enabled him to operate here from his headquarters in Nepal Terai region. He started a regular guerilla training school. Gulali Sonar and Suraj Narayan Singh also were connected with this enterprise. Their centre was located in the jungles north of Jaleshwar. They had, in all probability, built up a strong guerilla force.[61]

Under the leadership of Jai Prakash Narayan the network of the underground resistance movement spread out widely in Bihar. With the growth in the intensity of guerilla warfare, a number of dormant terrorist groups became active in north and central Bihar. Former terrorists like Suraj Nath Chaubey, Prasuram Singh and Parath Brahmachari and Siyaram Singh became the leaders of local guerilla bands. The Bengal groups were also active in place like Jamshedpur. In the Santhal Parganas, Sabha Hor's group was assisting the underground resistors. In northern Bihar, Jogendra Shukul was the leader of the local guerillas. This group indulged in many political dacoities to augment its funds. Many of its members were trained in Nepal. Another group of armed rebels was active in the Dumaria and Imamganj areas. Their groups had widespread ramification. The guerillas were most concentrated in the district of Bhagalpur, Monghyr and Santhal Parganas.[62]

Besides these, the northern strip of the Hazaribagh district and eastern part of Gaya district were also centres of underground activities.[63] A training camp for the guerilla was also set up in the jungles of the Banka subdivision. It had wireless sets and a charging machine. Some army deserters too had joined the camp. They were imparting training in the use of weapons to the recruits. In Chhotanagpur, the guerillas were inciting the aboriginals to participate in the movement.[64] Swaraj Panchayats were formed at Sonbarsa in the Tirhut Division and at Bhagalpur.[65] About 44 prisoners escaped from the jail during the last part of October 1942 to join the guerilla bands.[66] A destructive party was formed at Monghyr to go for action at short notice. This party had also seized large quantity of hand grenades from a military depot. The Bihar Government reported that raids were contemplated on armouries and magazines in order to acquire arms and explosives after which roads and railways would be wrecked on a date to coincide with either Japanese invasion or an attempt to recapture Burma. A party was formed to assassinate Government officers and plans were made to kidnap them.[67]

The guerillas in Muzaffarpur were trying to form a parallel Government there. The leaders were Govind Singh, Ram Bahadur Singh and Krishna Singh. The whole village in Dhanduar in Muzaffarpur was under the control of the guerillas. The underground resisters brought out their own paper 'Baghi'in Hindi from the Gaya district.[68] On 29th October,a live bomb and ingredients for the manufacture of explosives were found by the police during the search of a Homoeopathic dispensary at Gaya.[69] On the 14th November, 1942, Narsingh Narayan Azad, a prominent absconding Socialist, was arrested at Gaya and the police got six live cartridges from him.

Considerable underground activities were continuing in the Shahabad district.[70]

In praise for the working of the guerillas, a Government official stationed at Sahibganj reported, "The political organisation around this district is such that the like of it has never been seen. They have a code of signal by whistle, tick-tacking similar to book-makers tour at Epsom and at night signalling by light both flash light and oil. The rapidity of the movement and operation of them is incredible. I am not an alarmist or a defeatist but the restoration of services, both rail and telephonic, will not be an easy matter due to amount of materials required."[71]

As has been mentioned earlier, Nepal provided a base for the guerilla from Bihar. Particularly the area between Raxaul and Jaleshwar, where there were passes into Nepal, provided them with a springboard. Without the co-operation of the Nepalese authorities, the Government of India could not carry out a combing operation in this area. But the Maharaja of Nepal was not in favour of carrying out a joint operation of troops to mop up Indian rebels from their hide-outs. As a result only one man could be arrested out of 435 wanted men. The Nepalese Government's obvious lack of interest in this matter led to compelete failure of the mopping up operations.[72]

It was from a bamboo hut at Bakro-ka-Tapu that Jai Prakash Narayan guided the Central Organisation of the Azad Dasta. In front of the hut was a hillock which was utilised as a wireless. Ram Manohar Lohia, who had come there with Shyam Nandan Singh, became the Director of the Radio and Publicity Department. The office of the Bihar Provincial Azad Dasta was also located at a nearby place. The first Military Camp was started in Nepal with 35 people, Sardar Nitya Nand Singh being the Chief Instructor.[73]

On 21 May 1943 the Nepalese Police arrested Jai Prakash Narayan, Ram Manohar Lohia and three others. The arrested people were kept at Hanumannagar Police outpost.[74] On 22 May 1943, a batch of about 50 guerillas came and attacked the Police Outpost. After an exchange of fire, the prisoners were rescued.[75] The Government of India felt much disappointed since the arrest of those five people would apparently knock the bottom out of such underground activities and might lead to information which would enable them to assess the responsibility for the rebellion with some finality.[76]

Immediately after the Hanuman Nagar incident, Jai Prakash Narayan and other top leaders left Nepal and entered Bihar. They sent their men to military cantonment areas to tamper with the loyalties of Indian soldiers and to procure dynamites from nearby coalfields to blow up bridges and dislocate communication lines. The police again failed to arrest Jai Prakash Narayan on the 30th July 1943, when, along with Gulali Sonar, he came to Muzaffarpur to collect money from the local Zamindars.[77] According to an official report, Jai Prakash Narayan had at that time at his disposal a band of 50 youngmen who were ready to sacrifice their lives to protect him. On the 9th August 1943, about 150 to 250 guerillas attacked the police outpost in Sonbarsa Diara in the Bhagalpur district. In the gun dual, 4 rebels were killed and some more were drowned in the river. Four policemen suffered serious injuries.[78]

In Bihar proper, some revolutionary groups were still engaged in disruptive activities to paralyse administration and to foster the progress of the revolution. The most active of these was that known as the 'Siaram Dal' after the name of its leader Siaram Singh. This party had three objects in view: collection of money, collection of arms, training of the people to be able to oppose the British Government effectively.[79]

The adventures of Siaram Singh and his party in 1943 and 1944 were indeed highly daring. Moving from place to place in Bhagalpur, Monghyr, Purnea and Santhal Parganas districts though hills, jungles, rivers and hamlets, they organised their bands of workers and continued their activities defeating the utmost vigilance and much concerted measures of the police and executive to arrest them.[80]

At about 5.30 a.m. in the morning of the 29th August, 1943, Siaram Singh with about 150 young followers raided the Sonbarsa Police Station, the staff of which were very oppressive on the people and where arms had been kept. An exchange of gun fire from both sides continued for some time, as a result of which Sardar Nityanand Singh, Arjun Singh, Faudi Mandal, Ladoo Sharma and Ram Avtar Jha died on the spot.[81]

The Bihar Police administration stated, "There was a series of armed encounters between the police and elusive guerillas operating in jungle terrain favourable to the latter. A number of rebels were killed and quantity of arms and ammunitions recovered. About 1,200 arrests were made. In fact it was the political glamour that attracted to the terrorist ranks so many disgruntled or unemployed youths." The report alleged that gruesome crime and attrocities were committed by the guerillas against informers and defectors. Few people consequently like to bear witness against the underground resisters.[82]

Jai Prakash Narayan was at last arrested in the Punjab towards the end of September 1943; though for some time, the Congress Socialist Party went on announcing that he was still at large.[83] This upset seriously the plans of the underground resistance movement, and completely dislocated the Congress Socialist Party's strategy. There was none who could replace Jai Prakash Narayan. Already a cleavage had appeared among the underground resisters on the issue of violence. The rift now widened further. The pro-non-violence group was now engaged to renounce violence by starting individual Satyagraha and by reviving Khadi spinning and organising Gram Sangathan for settlement of village disputes.[84]

On 28th February 1944, at a secret meeting of the inner circle of the underground resisters in Darbhanga it was decided to organise the Azad Sena with an active and reserve branch. The purpose was apparently to organise an effective force in each thana three times stronger than the local police force to ensure success in future attacks on police stations. There was a plan for the creation of two dictatorships for North and South Bihar. The plan, however, did not materialise.[85]

Among the important guerilla leaders, Siya Ram Singh was to switch over from violence to non-violence. Seeing this rift in the underground resistance camp, the police intensified their operation against the guerillas. The whole of the north Bhagalpur was cordoned off by the police. Collective fines were imposed on the affected villages. This had the desired effect. Certain villagers and people of certain castes rendered help to the police, and were in turn granted exemption from the fines. Another method of the government was the detention of relatives of the guerillas, especially those who used to offer them shelters.[86]

These measures facilitated the arrest of the leaders of the guerillas such as Shyam Nandan Singh, Suraj Nath Chaubey, Mahendra Gope, Suraj Narain Singh, Gulali Sonar and Bindu Bashini Singh. Birinchi Missir and Kare Tanti were shot dead by the police in North Bhagalpur and North Monghyr respectively. With the arrest of so many leaders, the guerillas, activities naturally came to an end. Later, Aruna Asaf Ali, in February 1945, made an unsuccessful bid to revive the movement with the help of Badri Narain Sinha.[87]

Village teachers, doctors surviving the rural dispensaries, station masters of the railways and officials in the postal department did not extend full co-operation to the Government in suppressing the disturbances. Particularly in Bihar, the constabulary, the magistracy and the revenue officials were very much affected.[88] The Bihar Government was constrained to observe, "In a sudden or extensive popular upheaval like this one we have no Government servants in the Mufassils other than the regular police and our sources of information dried up and local support undergoes severe diminution. We could have expected some support from the employees of the local bodies but they have in recent year been almost all under Congress control."[89]

The Bihar police struck work on two occasions. About 150 recruits deserted from Nathnagar Police Training Centre. At Jamshedpur, one head constable led a strike of 120 policemen on the 10th August, 1942.[90] Most of them, however, rejoined duties by the 6th September, 1942. The Government prosecuted 33 of them. During the trial, these policemen consistently shouted Congress and Anti-British slogans. 17 of the accused refused to be tried under the existing law and the evidence had to be recorded in their absence.[91] Regarding the morale of the police, the Superintendent of Police, Chapra, Bihar, reported on the 15th August, 1942, "We have been watching the attitude of constabulary for the last two days and regard their attitude with grave apprehension wherein we have attempted to clear crowds by lathi charge, they have done the minimum that is possible and it is only the officers who have done all that is possible,"[92]

In September 1943, the Gandhian group decided to break away, and Sucheta Kripalani resigned from the Central Directorate. The formation of the new group called the All India Satyagraha Council sealed the split in the underground resistance movement. The organisational set up of the new body was modelled on the same line as that of Central Directorate. It was established mainly by the efforts of Sucheta Kripalani. The other important leaders of the organisation were Anand Prasad Chowdhary of Bengal, R.R. Diwakar of Bombay, G. Ramchandran of Madras, Baldeo Narain Verma of Bihar and R.S. Dhotre of the All India Spinners' Association. Their activities were largely confined to the provinces of Bengal, Bihar, Bombay and Madras.[93]

Besides the activities of the Congress Socialist Party, and underground revolutionary activities of the Azad Dasta and other groups, to which reference has already been made, silent constructive works were being continued here and there and efforts were being made by some belonging to the middle class, who were outside the prison bars, to carry on national activities. Manuscript leaflets were frequently distributed asking all classes of people to observe the 'Independence Day', emphasising the Congress programme of starting 'Swaraj Loan Fund', exhorting the people to stop payment of rent and revenue, to boycott courts, to organise panchayat system and appealing to the police and the soldiers not to do any act against their own countrymen. To keep up enthusiasm, special arrangements were made on an occasion like the 'Independence Day', which was celebrated on the 26th January, 1943, at different places in Bihar with solemnity by Prabhat Pheries, processions and hartals.[94]

A significant event soon caused widespread agitation in the country. It was Mahatma Gandhi's decision to begin 'Epic Fast' from the 10th February 1943 as a moral protest against Government excesses. Mahatma Gandhi's fast at the age of seventy-three caused immense anxiety throughout the country and there was widespread demand for his unconditional release.[95]

Throughout the country there was intense anxiety for Mahatma Gandhi's fast. In Bihar, it produced considerable reaction and public concern about it continued to be acute during the period of the fast. There were hartals at different places on the 17th and 19th February. Meetings were held at various centres by the students and the other sections of the people belonging to the middle class, prayers were offered for the life of Mahatma Gandhi and sympathetic fasts were observed in jails and elsewhere. Individuals and public bodies sent numerous telegraphic appeals to the Viceroy for the release of Mahatma Gandhi.[96]

During the National week from the 6th April to the 13th April, 1943, the national workers of this province followed a programme, which included holding of meetings, taking out of processions, hoisting of the national flag and the observance of Labour Day, Quiet India Day, Fasting Day, Students Day and finally the Martyrs Day,[97]

The workers of the Kisan Sabha were also active in this period. They secretly encouraged the movement. On the 12th, 13th of June 1943, the 10th Bihar Provincial Kisan Conference was held at Sonepur under the presidentship of Swami Sahjanand Saraswati. Several resolutions were adopted which included a protest against the imposition of tax on tobacco, advice to Kisans not to sell their cattle for military food, advice to labour to demand increase in their wages and payment of the same in kind, a protest against the removal of the embargo on the export of foodgrains and opposition to the formation of coalition ministry. The government was held responsible for the August disturbances and the release of Congress leaders was urged.[98]

Rajendra Prasad's 59th birthday was celebrated on the 8th December, 1943, at different places in the province by public meetings of all-party character, one of the largest being at Chapra with Rajandhari Singh in the chair. To popularise Congress activities, leaflets were in circulation in several districts. One such leaflet was issued by a recently formed organisation, called the All India Satyagraha Samiti, which aimed at evolving a programme of struggle to prepare the masses for a nation-wise non-violent revolution with the object of paralysing the machinary of Government and replacing it by a people's government. The programme included the signing of a satyagraha pledge, paralysing of the work of the law courts, contact with Government servants, distribution of literature and intensive propaganda. Thus, the nation's struggle was being kept alive against overwhelming ruthlessness of the ruling authorities in a period of constitutional stalemate, under the leadership and guidance of the members of the middle class.[99]

As in the immediate past, so in the year 1944 the 'Independence Day' was celebrated on the lines of the old programmes, and the Government following their usual policy, made arrests and convictions at different places in the province. There was a good deal of criticism in the *Searchlight* regarding Government ban on the Independence Day pledge and on

Shrimati Naidu's speech and appeal that it was not to ceremony but to sacrament they were bidding the year on the 26th January.[100]

But, unfortunately, the gulf of the communal separatism was widening and, with the Congress demand of 'Quit India' was matched the Muslim League's new slogan 'Divide and Quit'. The Provincial Muslim League in Bihar had been enthusiastic about it. The few Bihar delegates who attended the Muslim League Conference at Karachi from the 24th to the 27th December, 1943, returned full of enthusiasm, was considered likely to revitalise the Provincial Organisation of the League. Urdu Day was observed in Bihar on the 4th February, 1944 and several telegrams were sent to the Viceroy against the alleged encouragement of the Hindustani as opposed to Urdu. Under directions from the Provincial Muslim League in Bihar, all district branches observed 'Pakistan Day' on the 23rd March 1944, at which the Lahore resolution of 1940 was read and all present declared that they stood for the ideals undertaken by that resolution.[101]

A Pakistan Conference was held at Gaya on the 9th and 10th April 1944 under the chairmanship of Khwaja Nizamuddin, Premier of Bengal. Resolutions were passed in it reiterating the demand for Pakistan and faith in the Lahore Resolution and expressing concern at the situation in Palestine. Addressing the second day's sitting of this Conference, Liaquat Ali Khan, General Secretary of the All India Muslim League observed, "Pakistan is our birthright and we have once for all decided to achieve it." A Pakistan meeting was held in two sittings at Jamui in the Monghyr district on the 29th and 30th April, 1944. Khwaja Nizamuddin presided over it.[102]

As regards the general affairs of the Congress in Bihar in 1944-45, there were, along with the observance of special occasions, renewal of efforts for constructive and social service works with the gradual release of the Congress leaders and other workers of the province belonging to the middle class in most cases. The National Week was celebrated here almost as in the last year. Many Congress workers took active part in collections for Kasturba Fund and in sale of khadi. They were also engaged in anti-Savings Drive. The serious illness of Mahatma Gandhi in April 1944 caused immense anxiety among the people of this province as elsewhere. Though the Government asked the local press to exercise restraint in dealing with the subject, the news about it spread with rapidity. With deterioration in Mahatma Gandhi's condition from the end of April to avoid possible repercussions in this province, the local Government took several precautionary steps and sent instructions to all District Officers to deal with the emergency. Some important Congress workers, who had been absconding, were arrested in Bihar in this month. They were Secretaries of the Purnea and Darbhanga District Congress Committees and others. Sucheta Kripalani was arrested at Patna on the 28th April, 1944.[103]

The release of Mahatma Gandhi on the 6th May, 1944, gave a sense of relief to all who were passing their days in intensive anxiety. A meeting was held at Patna, presided over by Shyamnandan Sahay, a member of the educated middle class, at which demands were made to the release of Jawaharlal Nehru and the formation of a Congress Ministry. The 15th of June was observed as 'Gandhi Day' in Bihar.[104]

After this release, Anugraha Narain Sinha concentrated his attention on social service activities relating principally to sanitation and health of the people, particularly in North Bihar. Thakkar Bapa visited several places in this province to stimulate collections. Shrikrishna Sinha gave them much encouragement and help in these matters. There was also a widespread demand for the release of Rajendra Prasad for facilitating such activities against epidemics as he had organised to cope with the ravages of the Earthquake in 1934.[105]

Notwithstanding all precautionary measures on the part of the Provincial Government, anniversary of the Revolution of 1942 was celebrated on the 9th August, 1944 by holding meetings, organising processions and in other ways as in the last year. At Patna, wreaths were laid on a tablet in the Congress Maidan to commemorate the martyrs, who had fallen victims of the Police firing in front of Patna Secretariat in August 1942. On the 11th August, about seven persons were arrested at Patna for trying to repeat this function.[106]

On the 13th August 1944, a meeting of all party leaders was held at the residence of Anugraha Narain Sinha at Patna in which a resolution was passed demanding the immediate release of Rajendra Prasad in view of the spread of epidemics in north Bihar. It was expected that his release would facilitate the organisation of effective relief measures in the affected areas. Shrikrishna Sinha, who presided over the meeting, requested the government to release Rajendra Prasad, who, by virtue of the position which he held in the country, would be able to collect money that was necessary for the purpose of giving relief to the affected persons of north Bihar.[107]

The main work of the Congress workers at this time was intended to be the fulfilment of the constructive programme on the 16th of January, 1945, a meeting of Bihar Constructive Workers Conference was held in the Aujuman-e-Islamia Hall at Patna. The convener was Professor Abdul Bari, and at this meeting an Advisory Committee was appointed to take steps for fully implementing the constructive programme. The Committee consisted of Shrikrishna Sinha, Anugraha Narayan Sinha, Murli Manohar Prasad, Prajapati Mishra and Abdul Bari. The Conference decided to send workers into the villages.[108]

During the month of April, the National Week was observed in the province on the usual lines. Atul Chandra Ghosh, an educated middle class leader of Manbhum and a prominent Congress leader of the province, was arrested for hoisting national flag. This led to a Flag Satyagraha in this area, and, in the month of May, five persons including three ladies were arrested in Manbhum for hoisting the national flag.[109]

During April and May 1945, Shrikrishna Sinha was touring in the Bhagalpur Division and got much evidence about police excesses in thal area. Binodenand Jha was also collaborating in this work in that area. Srikrishna Sinha published an article in the *Searchlight* severely criticismg the pollce actions of repression and blackmail under the threat of arrest in the Eastern Range.[110]

The national movement of India took a new turn when on the 14th June, 1945, the Viceroy announced his decision for the release of the members of the Congress Working Committee.[111] Rajendra Prasad was released in the early morning of the 15th June. On the same day the ban on the Congress Working Committee was also withdrawn and the display of the Congress flag in public was allowed.[112]

The Bihar Provincial Congress Committee decided to celebrate the 9th August 1945, in the following manner:

1. Private meetings of Congress workers at 6 p.m. in which the All India Congress Committee Resolution of August 1942 would be read out and reiterated. If the local workers so choosed, they might hold a public meeting with the permission of the authorities instead of a private meeting.
2. Peaceful strikes in schools, colleges and labour concerns, i.e., factories.

The above was rather different from the general and more public instructions having been issued as follows: (a) Prabhat Pheries (early morning processions), (b) Flag hoisting and salutation ceremonies, (c) Reading of 'Quit India' resolution by every individual, (d) Spinning demonstrations, (e) Khadi sale, (f) Furthering the constructive programme, (g) Collection of funds towards prisoners' relief, Defence Committee and Kasturba Fund, (h) Prayers for peace to all souls of martyrs. These programmes would be followed from the 9th ,o the 15th August, 1945.[113]

The Bihar Government decided not to allow public meetings for the purpose of reading the resolution or of eulogising the martyrs who had lost their lives in the movement of 1942. However, the celebrations were held peacefully throughout the province.[114]

Rajendra Prasad issued an appeal to his countrymen for liberal donation so that with the amount so collected necessary relief would be given to the families of those who had suffered in the political movement of 1942 and also to meet the expenses incurred in connection with contesting the cases of those persons who were in prison and were unable to meet their own expenses over the cases pending in the court on account of their poverty.[115]

On the 19th September 1945, the British Prime Minister Attlee and Viceroy, Wavell made simultaneous announcement regarding steps to be taken by them to solve the Indian constitutional problem. Expressing the hope that ministerial responsibility will be accepted by political leaders in all provinces after elections to Central and Provincial Legislatures which were to be held during the winter season of 1945-46, Lord Wavell announced the intention of His Majesty's Government to convene, as soon as possible, a Constitution making body for which he had been authorised to hold preparatory discussions with elected representatives in British India and with Indian States immediately after the elections. He further observed that His Majesty's Government were proceeding to the consideration of the content of the treaty which would require to be concluded between Great Britain and India and that, as soon as the result of the elections were published, to take steps to bring into being an Executive Council which would have the support of the main Indian parties.[116] The announcement of Lord Wavell had its effects on the political movement in Bihar. The people of Bihar began to feel that political impasse would come to an end and now the political movement would bear some concrete fruits.[117]

In September 1945, the Working Committee of the All India Congress Committee met at Bombay and declared the proposals of the British Government 'inadequate and vague'.[118] However, the Indian National Congress decided to contest the ensuing elections. Accordingly, an Assembly Sub-Committee was constituted to organise the elections. The Committee considered of Maulana Abul Kalam Azad, Sardar Vallabhabhai Patel, Rajendra Prasad, Pandit Govind Vallabh Pant, Asaf Ali, Pattabhi Sitaramayya and Shankarrao Deo. Soon an Election Manifesto was drawn up for the Centre and provinces.[119]

Towards the end of September 1945, Rajendra Prasad issued a statement to the press in which he criticised the orders of the Provincial Government regarding the revision of the electoral rolls and said that the Bihar Government should at least take their clue from the Bombay Government which had ordered new electoral rolls to be prepared suo motu. He also urged that the ban on individuals and societies should be removed. He further complained that over 1,000 Congress-men of Bihar were behind the prison bars as detenues or political convicts.[120]

Rajendra Prasad and the other Bihar leaders now devoted themselves to election works and began to tour in different parts of the province. During the month of September 1945, Shrikrishna Sinha made a tour of Bhagalpur Division where he addressed a number of meetings and delivered stirring speeches with his remarkable oratory. On the 29th September 1945, a Political Conference was held at Hajipur in the Muzaffarpur district. It was addressed both by Shrikrishna Sinha and Anugraha Narayan Sinha. Shrikrishna Sinha made a highly suggestive and inspiring speech pointing out that the time had come when every Indian should challenge the British Government.[121]

In another speech at Patna, Rajendra Prasad stated, "What people had done in 1942 is the brightest chapter in India's history and coming generation will read it with feelings of pride." He further said, "We kept the people ready for action. After the arrest of the leaders, people did what they liked in the absence of any complete programme before them." He again said, "The August Resolution cannot be altered nor can even a comma of it be omitted till complete independence has been achieved."[122]

On the 12th February 1946, the Patna students observed 'Jai Prakash Day'. Shops of the city were decorated with national flags. Students moved about with small photographs of Jai Prakash Narayan. Mahamaya Prasad Sinha, President of the Saran District Congress Committee, addressed the audience at Bankipore Maidan (Patna) and said that Jai Prakash might be a rebel in the eyes of the British Government but to Indians he was as great as Washington was for Americans and Lenin to the Russians.[123]

The election campaign was in full swing since the polling day of the election was drawing nearer. On the 12th February 1946, Anugraha Narayan Sinha visited Kateyan and Kuchaikote thanas af Saran district and explained the significance of the Congress manifesto issued on the eve of election.[124]

Since the Congress Party won the majority of seats in the Provincial Legislature, the leader of the party was asked to form government in the province of Bihar. Thus, on the 2nd April 1946 at 11 a.m. the popular Congress Ministry was sworn in at the Government House. The oath of office was administered to Shrikrishna Sinha, Anugraha Narayan Sinha and Syed Mahmood by the then Governor. Immediately after taking over the charge of the administration, Shrikrishna Sinha, who was incharge of law and order, passed orders for the forthwith release of several political prisoners.[125] The Additional members took the oaths of office and secrecy on the 6th April, 1946. They were Ram Charitra Singh, Acharya Badrinath Verma, Krishna Ballabh Sahay, Binoda Nand Jha and Abdul Qaiyum Ansari.[126]

In the meantime, the ban on the Congress Socialist Party was lifted on the 11th April, 1946. Jai Prakash Narayan along with Ram Manohar Lohia were released from Agra Jail.

Prabhawati Devi, wife of Jai Prakash Narayan was also present at the gate of Agra Jail to receive her husband. After release from the jail, Jai Prakash Narayan and Ram Manohar Lohia left for Delhi along with Prabhawati Devi to meet Mahatma Gandhi.[127] After they were released, the Independent Labour Party of London sent the following telegram to Jai Prakash Narayan and Ram Manohar Lohia: "The Independent Labour Party welcome you to freedom and pays tribute to your courageous record."[128]

The Cabinet Mission reached Karachi by air on 23rd March, 1946. After discusssions with the Viceroy and the Governors of the Provinces and interviews and prolonged negotiations with the leaders of different parties and groups, the mission met at Simla in a Tripartite Conference with the Congress and the Muslim League delegates from the 5th May.[129]

The Cabinet Mission proposals and reactions of different parties thereto naturally produced mixed feelings of optimism, and there were varying comments in the local press about it. The Left wing leaders of the forward bloc and the I N.A., who were touring the province continually, attacked these proposals and similar was the standpoint of Jai Prakash Narayan who was also touring here.[130]

The Interim Government of 12 members with Shri Nehru as Vice-President took office on the 2nd September, 1946, at the Centre. The cabinet was composed of 12 leaders including Rajendra Prasad and Jagjivan Ram from Bihar.[131]

East Bengal massacres and other tortures on the Hindus produced repercussions in Bihar causing, from the end of October 1946, widespread communal disturbances in the provinces in which the Muslims suffered heavy casualties. On the 25th October, there were fairly complete hartals at Patna, Chapra and other towns of the Province, followed by a serious communal riot at Chapra town. On the 26th October, mobs from the villages in the Diara, north of Chapra began invading Muslim tolas. Some Muslims were killed and many houses were burnt. By the evening that day, the situation was brought under control by Government officers, but on the 27th October there were attacks on the Muslims in the outlying villages in the Sadar Subdivision. The Government officers soon controlled the situation. The visits of the Premier and S. Mahmood to Saran and Muzaffarpur produced a sense of relief among the general public and gave encouragement to the officers. Unfortunately, however, widespread riotings soon took place in the Patna district. It quickly spread through the east and south-east of the district into the Jehanabad Subdivision of Gaya district and in the western part of the Monghyr district. Trouble occurred simultaneously in the south-east of Monghyr district. Rioting had started in Bhagalpur town on the 28th October, from where it spread south into the Banka Subdivision and also to the edge of the district of Santhal Parganas, where it was quickly suppressed. Troops were promptly requisitioned and sent to the affected areas to bring the situation under control. Rajendra Prasad and others began touring the affected areas to calm the people.[132]

The opening session of the Indian Constituent Assembly met at Delhi on the 9th December 1946, under the presidentship of Sachchidanand Sinha, an Indian leader of repute and a great son of Bihar belonging to the educated middle class. The elected Muslim League members absented themselves from the meeting, though representatives of other communities took part in its deliberations.[133]

On December 11, 1946, Rajendra Prasad assumed the chair. He was elected as the permanent President of the Constituent Assembly.[134] Naturally this produced feeling of pride and profound satisfaction among the people of the district of Saran as Rajendra Prasad belonged to the soil of this district.

On the 20th February 1947, Mr. Attlee made the momentous declaration that it was British Government's definite intention to take necessary steps to affect the transfer of power to responsible Indian hands by a date not later than June 1948. Lord Mountbatten came to India as successor to Lord Wavell in March 1947 and he accelerated India's march to a new status. In his plan of 3rd June, 1947, he outlined the procedure for transfer to power to Indian hands. The plan had no doubt certain defects, the most serious being the proposed partition of India. While expressing regret that the plan of June 3, 1947 was likely to lead to the secession of certain parts of the country from India, the All India Congress Committee accepted these out of very practical considerations in view of the distressing political conditions in the country.[135]

The All India Congress Committee met at Delhi on the 15th June, 1947, and resolved that the committee welcomes the decision of the British Government to transfer power completely to the Indian people by next August.[136]

On the 4th July, 1947, the Indian Independence Bill was introduced in the House of Commons. High tributes were paid to both Mr. Attlee and Lord Mountbetten by members of the British Parliament. The Bill was passed without any amendment on July 15, and by the House of Lords on the following day. It received the Royal Assent on July 18, 1947. One of the main provisions of the Indian Independence Act, 1947, was two independent Dominions known respectively as 'India' and 'Pakistan' set up as from the 15th day of August, 1947.[137]

Really, the Act was the last milestone on the highway to the ultimate destination of a subject nation. It was the noblest and greatest law ever enacted by the British Parliament. It was said to be a gracious and dignified farewell. Rajendra Prasad said: "The period of domination of British over India ends today and our own relationship with Britain is henceforth going to rest on a basis of equality and mutual goodwill."[138]

At last, the historic day of August 15 arrived—the last day of the one hundred and fifty years of British rule in India, the first day of freedom for the three hundred and fifty million Indian people, the day on which men and women were understandably besides themselves with joy, when countless delirious crowds flooded the streets breaking down all restraints, obstructing the Viceregal and ministerial processions, pressing round the Assembly Hall, shouting slogans of victory to India and its leaders and indulging in a carnival of noisy and riotous rivalry.[139]

In Bihar, there was tremendous enthusiasm over the Independence Day celebration throughout the Province. Party differences were forgotten in mass jubilation and there was universal rejoicing that India had attained freedom.[140] Muhammadans generally joined the celebrations. A few members of the Hindu Mahasabha were against the celebrations, but their voice was drowned in the general spontaneity of mass fervour and enthusiasm.[141] Jairamdas Daulatram, appointed Governor of Bihar, took the oath of office on the night of 14th August. In the afternoon of 15th August he laid the foundation stone of the Martyrs Memorial to be erected to commemorate the memory of the students who had been killed by police firing in August, 1942. The Prime Minister performed the foundation ceremony of the memorial at Arrah to Babu Kunwar Singh, the Bihar hero of the Indian Movement of 1857-59. The Congress organisation, with Mahamaya Prasad Singha as President, showed unprecedented enthusiasm in Independence Day celebrations. There was generally happy fraternisation between them and their political opponents. The attitude of the Provincial Muslim League, which made them participate in the celebrations, was welcome in political circles.[142]

Thus we see that the members of the middle class played an important role in the national movement during the period under study. Leaders like Rajendra Prasad, Anugraha Narayan Sinha, Shrikrishna Sinha, J.B. Kripalani, Mathura Prasad, Jagat Narayan Lal and others, who were instrumental in educating and preparing the people for Gandhi's mass movement, belonged to the educated middle class of Bihar. It is true that prominent leaders belonging to the middle class were arrested before the movement started, but we should not forget that it was this abrupt official action that excited the people and that excitement gave birth to 'Quit India Movement'. Besides, in their absence, the other members of the middle class who remained outside the prison bars, led the people to the path of revolution. The youth belonging to the different groups of the middle class, both educated and uneducated played the leading role in the mass upsurge. In urban centres mainly college students and local leaders coming from the middle class remained in the vanguard. In rural areas, the members of the middle class landed interest took the lead. The underground revolutionary movement was carried on mainly under the leadership of Jai Prakash Narayan, a member of the educated middle class. There were several leaders belonging to the landed, industrial and commercial middle class who also played a commendable role in the underground movement.

Besides these activities, silent constructive works and other national activities were carried on under the leadership and guidance of the members of the middle class who were outside the prison bars. They also organised meetings at which demands were made for the release of the national leaders. Prominent leaders of Bihar, who came from the middle class, devoted their best efforts for the constructive works and celebration of national occasions after their release.

One disquieting feature of this period was that communal separatism became stronger ultimately leading to the 'Two Nation Theory'. Some members of the middle class of both the communities were responsible for this sad development.

Notes

1. Sitaramayya, B. Pattabhi, *Op. cit.*, Vol. II, p. 310.
2. Diwakar, R.R., *Op. cit.*, p. 667.
3. Home Political File No. 18/7/1942, National Archives of India, New Delhi.
4. Home Political File No. 18/3/1942.
5. Home Political File No. 18/4/1942.
6. Home Political File No. 18/7/1942.
7. Datta, K.K., *Op. cit.*, Vol. II, p. 20.
8. Home Political File No. 18/7/1942.
9. Report on the events in Bihar during the second half of July, 1942.
10. Home Political File No. 18/7/1942.
11. Datta, K.K., *Op. cit.*, Vol. II, pp. 20-21.
12. Sitaramayya, B. Pattabhi, *Op. cit.*, Vol. II, p. 340.
13. *Ibid.*
14. Prasad, Rajendra, *Op. cit.*, pp. 588-89.
15. *Ibid.*, pp. 589-90.
16. Sitaramayya, B. Pattabhi, *Op. cit.*, Vol. II, p. 343.
17. Datta, K.K., *Op. cit.*, Vol. *III*, p. 28.
18. Majumdar, R.C., *Op. cit.*, Vol. III, p. 646.
19. *The Searchlight*, August 10, 1942.
20. *Ibid.*
21. *The Bihar Gazette*, Extraordinary, Aug. 9, 1942.
22. Fortnightly Report, Bihar, August, 1942.
23. *Ibid.*
24. *The Searchlight*, August 11, 1942.
25. Reports on events in Bihar during the first half of August, 1942.
26. *Ibid.*
27. *Ibid.*
28. *The Searchlight*, August 11, 1942.
29. *Ibid.*
30. *The Indian Nation*, August 11, 1942.
31. Datta, K.K., *Op. cit.*, Vol. III, pp. 36-37.
32. *The Searchlight*, August 11, 1942, and *The Indian Nation*, August 13, 1942.

33. *The Indian Nation*, August 13, 1942.
34. *The Searchlight*, August 14, 1942.
35. Chopra, P.N., Chief Editor, *Who is Who of Indian Martyrs*, Vol. I, 1916, Government of India, pp. 288 and 341; Rajendra Prasad, *Op. cit.*, p. 624.
36. Fortnightly Report, Bihar, August 1942.
37. Home Political File No. 3/22/42.
38. T. Steward to Linlithgow, Aug. 22, 1942, Mansergh, N. 2, p. 787.
39. *The Searchlight*, August 14, 15, 16, 1942.
40. 243 at Patna till the 18th August, according to a police report.
41. Narayan, Baldeo, *August Kranti* (Hindi), pp. 12-18.
42. Fortnightly Reports, Bihar, August-November, 1942.
43. Home Political File Nos. 18/8/42, 18/11/42 & 3/30/42.
44. *Ibid.*, 3/107/42.
45. *Ibid.*, 3/16/42.
46. *Ibid.*, 3/26/42.
47. *Ibid.*, 3/16/42.
48. *Ibid.*, 140/42.
49. The Chief Secretary of Bihar's letter addressed to Home Secretary, Government of India, dated Sept. 1942; Home Political File No. 3/34/42.
50. Datta, K.K., *Op. cit.*, Vol. III, p. 256.
51. *Ibid.*, p. 265.
52. Home Political File No. 3/48/42.
53. *Ibid.*, 3/106/42.
54. *Ibid.*, 3/31/42.
55. *Ibid.*, 18/11/42; and Fortnightly Report, Bihar, November, 1942.
56. Reports on the events in Bihar during the first half of November, 1942.
57. Datta, K.K., *Op. cit.*, Vol. III, pp. 269-73.
58. *Ibid.*, p. 269.
59. Report of the Superintendent of Police, Muzaffarpur, December 9, 1942.
60. Report on the events in Bihar during the first half of December, 1942.
61. *Ibid.*, 18/6/43; Fortnightly Report, Bihar, June, 1943.
62. Bihar Police Administration Report—Terrorism, 1943, Home Political File No. 3/19/44.
63. Home Political File No. 18/3/43; Fortnightly Report, 3/43.

64. Home Political File No. 18/11/42.
65. Home Political File No. 18/9/42, 18/10/42, 18/11/42; Fortnightly Report, Bihar, Sept.-Oct., 1942.
66. Home Political File No. 18/12/42; Fortnightly Report, Bihar, December, 1942.
67. *Ibid.*, 18/11/42, 18/12/42; Fortnightly Reports, Bihar, November-December, 1942.
68. *Ibid.*, 18/4/42, 18/16/42; Fortnightly Reports, Bihar, April-June, 1942.
69. Reports on the events during the first half of November, 1942.
70. *Ibid.*, second half of November, 1942.
71. Home Political File No. 3/3/42.
72. *Ibid.*, 3/39/42.
73. atta, K.K., *Op. cit.*, Vol. III, p. 274.
74. Majumdar, R.C., *Op. cit.*, Vol. III, p. 671.
75. Home Political File No. 18/5/43.
76. *Ibid.*, Nos. 3/39/43, 3/68/43.
77. *Ibid.*, No. 18/7/43.
78. *Ibid.*, No. 18/8/43; Fortnightly Report, Bihar, August 1943, also Political File No. 3/68/43.
79. Datta, K.K., *Op. cit.*, Vol. III, p. 275.
80. *Ibid.*, pp. 280-81.
81. Report on the events of Bihar during the second half of August, 1943.
82. Bihar Police Administration Report, Terrorism, 1943. Home Political File No. 3/19/44.
83. Home Political File No. 18/10/43; Fortnightly Report, Bihar, October, 1943.
84. Home Political File Nos. 18/11/43, 18/5/44.
85. *Ibid.*, No. 18/3/44.
86. *Ibid.*
87. *Ibid.*, Nos. 18/4/44, 18/9/44, 18/11/44.
88. *Ibid.*, No. 18/2/45.
89. *Ibid.*, No. 3/34/42.
90. Datta, K.K., *Op. cit.*, Vol. III, p. 220.
91. Home Political File Nos. 3/34/42, 18/10/42; Fortnightly Report, Bihar, October, 1942.
92. Datta, K.K., *Op. cit.*, Vol. III, p. 60.
93. Home Political File No. 4/4/44.
94. Reports on events during the second half of January, 1943.

95. *Ibid.*, during the first half of February, 1943.
96. *Ibid.*, during the second half of February, 1943.
97. Datta, K.K. *Op., cit.*, Vol. III, pp. 297-98.
98. Home Political File No. 18/6/43.
99. *Ibid.*, No. 18/12/43.
100. *The Searchlight*, January 27, 1944.
101. Datta, K.K., *Op. cit.*, Vol. III, p. 312; *The Searchlight*, March 24, 25, 26, 1944.
102. Report on events during the first and second half of April, 1944,
103. Datta, K.K., *Op. cit.*, Vol. III, p. 314.
104. *Ibid.*, p. 314.
105. *Ibid.*, p. 315.
106. Fortnightly Report, Bihar, August, 1944.
107. *The Indian Nation*, August 14, 1944.
108. Fortnightly Report, Bihar, January, 1945.
109. *Ibid.*, May, 1945.
110. *The Searchlight*, June 3, 1945.
111. Datta, K.K., *Op. cit.*, Vol. *I*II, pp. 325-26.
112. Home Political File No. 18/6/45.
113. *Ibid.*, 18/7/45.
114. Report on the events in Bihar during the first half of August, 1945.
115. *Ibid.*
116. Diwakar, R.R., *Op. cit.*, pp. 671-72.
117. *The Indian Nation*, September 25, 1945.
118. Sitaramayya, B. Pattabhi, *Op. cit.*, Vol. *II*, p. 672.
119. *Ibid.*, p. 673.
120. Home Political File No. 18/9/45.
121. Datta, K.K., *Op. cit.*, Vol. *III*, p. 329.
122. Home Political Eile No. 18/9/45.
123. *The Indian Nation*, January 26, 1946 (Dak Edition).
124. *Ibid.*, February 14, 1946.
125. *The Indian Nation*, April 3, 1946 (Oak Edition).
126. Datta, K.K., *Op. cit.*, Vol. *III*, pp. 332-33.
127. *The Indian Nation*, April 13, 1946 (Dak Edition).
128. *Ibid.*, April 16, 1946 (Oak Edition).
129. Datta, K.K., *Op. cit.*, Vol. *III*, p. 334.
130. *Ibid.*, p. 338.

131. *Ibid.*, p. 342.
132. Report on events in Bihar during the second half of October, 1946.
133. Datta, K.K., *Op. cit.*, Vol. III, p. 350.
134. *The Searchlight*, Decembe, 12, 1946.
135. Diwakar, R.R., *Op. cit.*, pp. 674-75.
136. Majumdar, R.C., *Op. cit.*, Vol. III, p. 808.
137. Diwakar, R.R., *Op. cit.*, pp. 674-75.
138. Majumdar, R.C., *Op. cit.* , Vol. III, p. 814.
139. Bhagwan, Vishnoo, *Op. cit.*, p. 310.
140. Tara Chand, *History of the Freedom Movement in India*, Vol. III, p. 550.
141. Report on the events in Bihar during the first half of August, 1947.
142. *Ibid.*

Conclusion

The middle class in Bihar as elsewhere in India played a very significant role in the various phases of the national movement. Under the leadership of the middle class the smouldering discontent of the people found expression in the form of a mass upsurge before which the British imperial machinery had to bow down. Various factors influenced the emergence of the middle class.

The second half of the 19th century was marked by the growth of patriotic and national sentiments chiefly due to English education and the contact with the Western culture. Western ideas of patriotism and nationalism gradually made their influence felt, as the ideal of the British democratic system of government animated the people. Under the influence of the British administration and English education some of the features of Western Social Organisation were introduced in the Indian Society, which shook its very foundation. As a result of the social change, inaugurated by the British, a new social class, the Indian Middle Class, came into existence, which, in relation to the rest of the Indian population, occupied the elite position in all spheres of social life and activities.

There are several views regarding the bases of class. But as a working concept of social research mainly two views have been effectively employed. One is based on economic factors, such as, income, economic functions or relation to a system of production which renders class into a socio-economic aggregate; and the other is based on subjective considerations of class-consciousness which changes the class into a socio-psychological phenomenon, and both are inter-related and mutually inclusive. Thus, class is a group of persons bound together by occupational, economic and stratificatory bonds.

Keeping in view the different definitions of the middle class, it has been defined as a composite intermediary layer of the society occupying the central position between the two extremes of capitalists and workers and consisting of a wide range of occupational interest but bound together by a common style of living and behaviour pattern. Ideologically the new social order stood for intellectual freedom and social mobility, liberal individualism and political democracy. A middle class, thus, becomes identified with a stratified social order representing new standard of values which its members or groups impress upon the entire society in which they live.

The middle class started emerging under the British rule in such fields as trade and commerce, industry, land, education and the learned professions. Their growth proceeded in the main from a change in the political system and its institutional arrangement based on the supremacy of law and legislative authority. The spread of Western education also brought a process of social change.

The new middle class became visible at first in the three presidency towns of Calcutta, Bombay and Madras. Calcutta was, in fact, the first among the presidency towns to be effectively influenced by the Western ideas and institutions. These filtered downward to provincial and district levels through the agency of the Company's courts and factories. To these must be added cultural diffusions from the Christian missionaries, free merchants, European traders and European planters, who, likewise, carried liberal traditions to the interior of the Bengal Presidency where schools and colleges came later. These constituted the various nuclei for the growth of a modern middle class on the basis of money, economy and Western education.

The modern middle class, which owed its birth as well as its prosperity to European commercial enterprise in Bihar, originally, was purely commercial in character. It was the exigency of the European traders, who neither knew languages nor customs and trade practices, that forced them to seek mediation of local people who could help them secure supplies of local merchandise from producers and sometimes financial accommodation from local bankers or 'Sahukars'. Thus there emerged a commercial middle element of agents, 'gomashtas', munims, brokers, paikars, dallas, moneylenders, baniyas, shroffs, poddars or cashiers, who constituted the spring-board of a raising middle class in the latter part of the 18th century when they, on the strength of their accumulated fortunes, established themselves as independent businessmen, such as, traders, merchants aad also as landlords.

The emergence of the industrial middle class took place slowly in Bihar. The poverty of the industrial workers and their social disabilities operated as serious handicaps to the growth af industrial middle class on European lines. Moreover, an industrial occupation was not a respectable one. The abolition of the trade monopoly of the East India Company in 1833 and the end of its rule in 1858 was the real beginning of the era of laissez-faire of free enterprise in commerce and industry. The flow of European capital and skill contributed to the agricultural and manufacturing industries in Bihar facilitating the introduction of the managing agency system, which provided a pattern of industrial organisation leading to the emergence of new functional groups as well as expansion of the existing ones. Besides, the establishment of institutions imparting technical knowledge and skill created a group of technicians. These developments increased the avenues and scope of industrial employment covering directional, managerial, technical, supervisory and clerical elements constituting the industrial middle class. Emergence and growth of small independent industrial entrepreneurs also added to the number of the industrial middle class in Bihar.

The middle class landed interest, which comprised of under-tenures (raiyats). small zamindars and peasant proprietors, grew both from the disintegratian and partition of old estates as well as from the increase of under-tenures. The farming out of the revenue collection by auction to the highest bidders under Warren Hastings, the recognition of smaller zamindars and holders of under-tenure called 'Mukarraridars' in Bihar by settlement of revenue direct to them, the settlement of rent-free lands resumed under Regulations II and III of 1819 and 1828, 'the sunset law', the provision for the partition of estates among heirs, led to the growth of sub-feudation comprising a number of intermediate proprietary layers constituting the nuclei for the growth of the landed middle class in Bihar as elsewhere in India.

The educated middle class, which signifies a group of persons who received English education and engaged in various professions, emerged a bit late in Bihar. It was because of the fact that the Biharies wese not so enthusiastic as the Bengalies to learn English due to several factors. But till the end of the 19th century the number of its members began to swell due to the establishment of colleges for higher education. This class comprised of lawyers, public servants, doctors, teachers, writers, newspaper editors, clerks, assistants, and university students.

Thus by 1912, a strong middle class had emerged in Bihar which came forward to successfully transform the simmering discontent of the people into a movement against the British rule. As in the case of other provinces, the middle class in Bihar sharply reacted against the racial arrogance and reactionary administration and recruitment policy of the Britishers. The curtailment of freedom of expression and liberty resulting in stringent Press Laws greatly infuriated the middle class in Bihar. Moreover, the revenue administration, labour laws and other aspects of British economic policies created a gulf between the middle class and the British administration. The tackling of the communal problems by the Britishers also hurt the sentiments of the middle class in Bihar. Such grievances made the middle class in Bihar restive and so it actively participated and assumed the leadership in various phases of India's struggle for freedom.

From the early Congress days, Bihar witnessed modern political consciousness and national awareness under the leadership of the middle class. Rajendra Prasad, Ramdayalu Singh, Sachchidanand Sinha, Satish Chandra Chakravarty, Kamleshwari Charan Sinha, Deep Narayan Singh, Mazharul Haque, Sarfaraz Husain, Ali Imam, Kuwar Nandan Sahay, Parmeshwar Lal, Braj Kishore Prasad, Nand Kishore Lal and others played a leading role in arousing national consciousness and organising institutions and organisations furthering the cause of nationalism. Most of them belonged to the landed middle class families and, later on, turned professionals after taking Western education.

After the creation of Bihar as a separate province, the educated middle class of Bihar became more vocal in their demand for a separate University and their chief organ, The Biharee, campaigned for the establishment of a University in Bihar. Mazharul Haque, Purnendu Narayan Sinha, Kedarnath Sinha, Dwarakanath, Sachhidanand Sinha, Rajendra Prasad, Krishna Sahay, Braj Kishore Prasad, Jadunath Sarkar and others, whose efforts led to the establishment of the Patna University in 1917, belonged to the educated middle class of Bihar.

In course of the Home Rule Movement in Bihar we see that the middle class dominated the political scene in participation and leadership. Prominent persons who organised and propagated the Home Rule Movement in Bihar were Mazharul Haque, Purnendu Narayan Sinha, Chandra Bansi Sahay, Sarfaraz Husain, Tarini Prasad Sinha, Manindra Nand, Balmukund Bajpai and Puranchand. All, except the last five, were lawyers constituting the most dominant group of the educated middle class.

As regards Gandhiji's Champaran Movement, the middle class of Bihar played the leading role. Since the day Gandhiji started from Calcutta to Champaran till the end of this mission, he was assisted by lawyers. Important among them were Gorakh Prasad, Braj Kishore Prasad, Janakdhari Prasad, Dharnidhar Prasad, Bindeshwari Prasad Verma, Mazharul Haque, Ramnavami Prasad and others of the same profession. Besides them, Raj Kumar Shukla (a peasant), J.B. Kripalani (a professor), Ramdayalu Sahu (a Banker), Shyamnandan Sahay (a student of G.B.B. College) and others played an important role in the movement.

With the arrival of Gandhiji on the political scene of India, there was a marked change in the character of the movement for freedom. Now participation of the masses increased. Yet the middle class remained in the vanguard. This class of Bihar played the dominant role in furthering the cause of Indian nationalism by enthusiastically responding to the new urge for freedom on the 6th April, 1919, the Satyagraha Day. The meetings to educate and prepare the people to make the Satyagraha Day a success were organised and addressed mainly by the educated middle class. Prominent leaders belonging to the class were Rajendra Prasad, Mazharul Haque, Purnendu Narayan Sinha, Hasan Imam, Chandra Bansi Sahay, Gorakh Prasad, Raghunath Lal and Narayan Tammaji.

Turkey's tragic fate after the World War I fanned the flame of discontent among the Muslims of India including Bihar. Under the leadership of the middle class, this discontent was transformed into a vigorous movement to pressurise the British Government to change her policy towards the Khailfa. Important persons belonging to the middle class of both the communities, who contributed immensely to the Khalifat Movement, were Hasan Imam, Mazharul Haque, Rajendra Prasad, Maulvi Nurul Hasan, Mohammed Zubair and Krishna Prakash Sen Sinha.

The middle class of Bihar played the pivotal role in the Non-Cooperation Movement, which stood for five boycotts—

boycott of elections and legislatures and of law courts and educational institutions, of foreign cloth and drinks. It was due to the leaders belonging to the middle class that the Non-Cooperation Movement was transformed into a mass movement. Earnest zeal and persistent efforts of the middle class imbued the general mass with consciousness and moral faith in the righteousness of their cause, which were supremely important factors for the progress of the freedom movement. Besides, this class played a significant role in the establishment of the Swarajya Party and its working. Composition of the office-bearers of the Swarajya Party shows the predominance of the educated middle class. This class also played a remarkable role in organising vehement protest to the Simon Commission. When the Simon Commission visited Patna on the 12th December, 1928, the leaders of this class played a leading role in mobilising a great assembly at Patna Railway Station with black flags and loud slogan, "Simon, go back." One significant development of the period between the Non-Cooperation and the Simon Commission was that the number of the members from the groups other than the educated middle class increased remarkably.

Another phase of the Non-Cooperation Movement, known as the Civil Disobedience Movement (1930-34), was soon initiated by Gandhiji and it was fully implemented in Bihar under the guidance of the middle class. This class directed its fullest attention towards educating and preparing the people for the coming Civil Disobedience Movement. Bihar, under the leadership of the persons belonging to the middle class, enthusiastically responded to the Salt Satyagraha formally launched on the 6th April, 1930, by Mahatma Gandhi by violating the monopoly of the British on salt at Dandi, and salt law was broken at several places in Bihar by preparing salt in spite of highly repressive measures employed by the Government. Besides, other forms of the Civil Disobedience Movement were also observed with same zeal and enthusiasm. A host of lawyers had given up their practices and many teachers rendered their resignation in obedience to the clarion call of the Mahatma. Picketing of foreign cloth and intoxicants had been going on with immense vigour throughout the province and preparations had been made at several places for non-payment of chaukidari tax. In this period components of the middle class other than the educated middle class became more active and participative and in small urban centres and rural areas even leadership was shared by them.

The year 1934 started with an unprecedented calamity for Bihar. In the afternoon of the 19th January, 1934 there occurred a terrible earthquake which devastated a vast area of Bihar. A Bihar Central Relief Committee was formed with Rajendra Prasad, a member of the educated middle class, as Chairman.

The revolutionary movement between 1912 and 1933 also penetrated into Bihar. The persons who carried on the revolutionary or terrorist movement, were mostly the members of the educated middle class. This movement was held in saluting position mainly by lawyers, college teachers and students. A few from the commercial, industrial and landed middle class also took part in it. Prominent persons belonging to the middle class, who played a leading role, were Sachchindra Nath Sanyal, Raghuvir Singh, Sudhir Kumar Sinha, Raj Narayan Basu, Kamta Prasad, Ram Binode Singh, Yogendra Sukul, Gyan Saha, Suraj Nath Chaubey and Chandrama Singh.

The middle class played a significant and inspiring role in mobilising the masses in favour of the Congress and it was mainly due to its earnest efforts that the Congress got victory with absolute majority in the provincial elections of 1937. The role of the leaders coming from the middle class was remarkable in the propaganda against the War Policy of the British. Their contribution was highly commendable in making the session of the Ramgarh Congress and the Satyagraha Camp at Sonepur a success by participating and mobilising the masses to attend these two occasions. The Individual Civil Disobedience was mainly a movement by chosen leaders coming, in most cases, from the middle class.

The Quit India Movement was a mass movement. But it was the middle class which played the leading role in educating and preparing the masses for this irresistible mass upsurge against the British imperialism. Besides, the members of the middle class, who remained outside the prison bars, played the role of a guiding force in this movement. Students, mainly college students, remained in the vanguard. It is because of this fact that this movement is called as a movement of students.

The underground revolutionary movement was carried on under the leadership of Jai Prakash Narayan, a member of the educated middle class. Besides him there were others belonging to the different groups of the middle class who played marvellous role in this movement. After 1943, the leaders coming from the middle class played a commendable role in the national movement and political development leading to the attainment of independence in 1947.

Besides, the middle class of Bihar played an important role in making successful observance of hartals, Independence Day and other national occasions. They organised meetings at which demands were made for the release of national leaders.

Indian nationalism has not been a mere political phenomenon. It aimed not only at securing political freedom of the country from the alien domination but also sought to affect a potent socio-economic revolution. And it was the enthusiastic and persistent efforts of the middle class that charged the masses with consciousness for successful consumnation of a creative and constructive revolution. From the Non-Cooperation to Independence constructive programmes, which stood for production and use of khadi, establishment of Panchayats, removal of untouchability, establishment of national schools and consolidation of the Congress Organisation, were carried on under the guidance of the leaders belonging to the middle class of Bihar.

One highly disquieting feature of the period under study was the growing tension between the Hindus and Muslims and consequent outbreak of communal riots in post-Non-Cooperation Movement. Bihar did not escape the infection of communal frenzy and, in Septemer-October 1924, Hindu-Muslim riots occurred at several places in Bihar. Communal riots re-occurred in April-May of 1926. Role of the middle class in spreading communalism was shown at a meeting of the Muslim representatives of Bihar in the Anjuman-a-Islamia Hall at Patna in May 1927 where demand for separate electorate was upheld.

Besides, the Muslims held a Conference at Chapra on the 13th and 14th April, 1940, where resolution about partition of India was passed. Observance of Pakistan Day and decision of the Hindu Mahasabha to observe anti-Pakistan Day led to serious communal outbreaks at Biharsharif. Delegates of the League, after their return from the League Conference at Karachi, showed enthusiasm in observing Urdu Day on the 4th February, 1944. A Pakistan Conference and a Pakistan meeting were held in the same year at Gaya and Monghyr respectively demanding Pakistan for the Muslims. These actions of the League further led to communal bitterness, which found expression in widespread communal disturbances in 1944 and 1946 in Bihar. Thus we see that during the period under study communal politics in Bihar, under the guidance of some of the members of the middle class, led to communal separatist forces strengthening the hands of Jinnah, whose slogan was 'Divide and Quit'.

Under the leadership of the persons of the middle class, the Kisan Movement gained momentum during post-Non-Cooperation Movement. It enjoyed full support of the Congress and the Socialist members too were actively helping. Under the guidance of their leaders, Kisans played a significant role in the struggle for freedom from the foreign yoke.

Thus we see that the middle class in Bihar played a significant role in India's struggle for freedom. Among the various components of the middle class in Bihar, the middle class educated elites played the most dominant role. This class not only provided leadership at the various stages of the movement but also contributed greatly in spreading consciousness among the people and mobilising mass support for the Congress in fighting the British imperialism. This greatly helped Gandhiji in transforming the character of the national movement into a mass movement, thereby increasing the pressure on the British to quit India.

Bibliography

Books

Aarnovitch, S., *Monopoly : A Study in British Monopoly Capitalism.*

Andrews, C.F., *The Renaissance in India*, Bombay, 1956.

Azad, A.K., *India Wins Freedom*, Bombay, 1959.

Bhatia, B.M., *History and Social Development*, Vols. I & II, Vikas Publishing House, New Delhi, 1974, 1977.

Buchanan, *A Journey from Madras*, Vol. I, 1813.

Baines, *Cotton Manufacturers of India.*

Ball, V.A., *Manual of the Geology of India.*

Bamford, P.C., *Histories of the Non-Cooperation and Khilafat Movements*, Government of India, 1925.

Bannerjee, S.N., *A Nation in Making*, Calcutta, 1964.

Bhagwan, Vishnu, *Constitutional History of India and National Movement*, 1972.

Bolts, Williams, *Considerations on Affairs of East India Company*, 1765.

Chibber, Y.P., *From Caste to Class.*

Cole, G.D.H., *Studies in Class Structure.*

Chirol, Valentine, *Indian Unrest*, London, 1910.

Chopra, P.N. (ed.), *Who is Who of Indian Martyrs*, Vol. I, Government of India Publication, New Delhi, 1969.

Diwakar, R.R., *Bihar Through the Ages*, Orient Longmans, Bombay, 1959.

Datta, K.K., *History of the Freedom Movement in Bihar*, Vols. I, II & III, 1957, 1957 and 1958.

Datta, K.K. (ed.), *The Comprehensive History of Bihar*, Vol. III —Parts I, II, Patna, 1976.

Desai, Mahadev, *Gandhiji in Indian Villages*, Delhi, 1959.

Datta, Bhupendra Nath, *Dvitiya Svadhinatar Sangram* (Bengali), Calcutta, 1949.

Elwin, V., *The Story of Tata Steel.*

Fredrick, John Shore, *Notes on Indian Affairs*, Vol. I, 1837.

Ghurye, G.S., *Caste and Class in India.*

Gadgil, D.R., *Industrial Evolution in India in Recent Times*, 1860-1930, OUP, 1971.

Hoebel, E.A., *Man in the Primitive World.*

Hiller, E.T., *Social Relations and Structure.*

Henry, Maine, *The Early History of Institutions.*

Holwell, *India Tracts.*

Houlton, Sir J., *Bihar—The Heart of India.*

Heimsath, Charles, H., *Indian Nationalism and Hindu Social Reform*, Princeton, 1964.

Haque, Mazharul, *The Great Trial of Mahatma Gandhi.*

Joseph, Schumpeter, *Class, Status and Power.*

James, Mill, *History of India*, Vol. III.

Jha, J.S., *Education in Bihar* (1813-1859), (Thesis), unpublished.

Sarkar, J.N. & Jha, J.C., *History of Patna College.*

Kornnauser, R., *Approach to Social Stratification.*

Karunokaran, K.P., *Religion and Political Awakening in India.*

Lelis and Maude, *The English Middle Classes.*

Lewis, Corey, *Class, Status and Power.*

Max, Weber, *Economic and Social Organisation.*

MacIver & Page, *Society.*

Mills, C.*W*., *White Collar*.

Marx, Engels, *Collected Works*, Moscow, 1950.

Marx, Karl, *A Contribution to the Critique of Political Economy*, Moscow, 1970.

Mahatma Gandhi, *Autobiography*, Ahmedabad, 1956.

Mahatma Gandhi, *Young India* (1919-22), Madras, 1922 (1922-24) and (1924-26), Madras, 1927.

Majumdar, B.B. & Majumdar, B.P., *Congress aud Congress-men*, Calcutta, 1967,

Majumdar, R.C., *History of the Freedom Movement in India*, Vols. I, II, III.

Martin, *Eastern India*, Vol. II.

Memoir, *Geological Survey of India*, Vol. XXXIV, Part II, 1902.

Misra, B.B. (ed.), *Mahatma Gandhi's Movement in Champaran*, 1960.

Misra, B.B., *Bureaucracy in India*, Oxford University Press, London, Bombay, 1977.

Misra, B.B., *The Central Administration of the East India Company*, 1959.

Misra, *The Indian Middle Classes : Their Growth in Modern Times*, London, 1961.

Mitra, Shishir Kumar, *Sri Aurobindo and Indian Freedom*.

Narayan, Baldeo, *August Kranti* (Hindi), Patna.

O'Mally, L.S.S., *History of Bengal, Bihar and Orissa under British Rule*, Calcutta, 1925.

Page, C.H., *Class, Status and Power*.

Hill, Christopher, *Puritanism and Revolution*, London, 1958.

Pandey, S.N., *Educational and Social Changes in Bihar* (1900-1921), Delhi.

Prasad, Rajendra, *Atmakatha* (Hindi), Ahmedabad, 1948.

Prasad, Rajendra, *Mahatma Gandhi and Bihar*, Delhi, 1957.

Prasad, Rajendra, *Gandhi in Champaran*, Delhi, 1955.

Prasad, Rajendra, *Satyagraha in Champaran*, Delhi, 1955.

Prasad, Rajendra, *Autobiography*, Bombay, 1957.

Prasad, Rajendra, *Champaran Mein Mahatma Gandhi* (Hindi), Delhi, 1955.

Prasad, Janakdhari, *Kuch Apni Kuch Desh Ki* (Hindi), Muzaffarpur, 1970.

Prasad, Janakdhari, *Autobiography*, Part I.

Pal, Bipin Chandra, *Swadeshi and Swaraj*, Calcutta, 1954.

Rudolph & Rudolph, *The Modernity of Tradition*, Bombay, 1967.

Revolution & Revolution, *Collection of Karl Marx's articles*, published in New York, Tribune, 1851-52.

Roy Chaudhary, P.C., *Inside Bihar*, 1962.

Roy Chaudhary, P.C. (ed.), *B.R.D.G. Champaran.*

Singh, Baljit, *Urban Middle Class Climbers.*

Sinha, H., *Early European Banking in India*, 1927.

Sen, P., *Western Influence in Bengal Literature*, Calcatta, 1932.

Stanley, W. Moore, *The Critique of Capitalist Democracy*, New York, 1967.

Sastri, Sivanath, *History of the Brahmo Samaj*, 2 Vols., Calcutta, 1911.

Srinivas, M.N., *Social Changes in Modern India.*

Sinha, Sachchidanand, *Some Eminent Bihar Contemporaries*, 1944.

Sarkar, J.N. & Jha, J.C., *History of Patna College* (1885-1963), Patna, 1963.

Sitaramayya, B. Pattabhi, *History of the Indian National Congress*, Vols. I & II, Bombay, 1935, 1947.

Shrikrishna, *Abinandan, Granth* (Hindi).

Singh, Arjun Prasad, *Bihpur Satyagraha*, 1930.

Speeches and Writings of Mahatma Gandhi (Fourth Ed.).

Tara Chand, *History of the Freedom Movement in India*, Vols. I, II, III, Ministry of Information and Communication, 1967, 1972.

Tripathy, Amlesh, *Trade and Finance in Bengal Presidency* (1793-1833), Orient Longmans, Calcutta, 1966.

Trevelyan, C.E., *On the Education of Peoples of India*, London, 1838.

The Civil Disobedience Movement, Government of India Press, New Delhi, 1956.

Tendulkar, D.G., *Mahatma*, Vol. III, V, Vol. 1-8, Bombay, 1951-54.

Vachaspati, Indira Vidya, *Arya Samaj Ka Itihas* (Hindi), Vol. II.

Verma, Kamla Prasad, *Bhulti Bhagati Yaden* (Hindi).

Journals and Newspapers

The Beharee, Patna.

The Behar Herald, Patna.

The Balak.

The Bihar Darpan, Muzaffarpur.

The Bihar Times.

The Bengal, Past and Present.

The Kayastha Samachar.

The Calcutta Review.

The Express, Allahabad.

Friend of India.

The Leader, Allahabad.

The Searchlight, Patna.

The Pataliputra.

The Indian Nation, Patna.

The Tribune.

The Times of India.

The Young India, Ahmedabad.

The Yugantar.

The Hindustan Review.

The Modern Review.

Journal of Bihar & Orissa Research.

Society (Subsequently Bihar only).
Man in India.

Reports and Other Government Publications

Bihar, Year to Year : Bihar Government Administration Reports.

Bihar and Orissa, Year to Year.

Bulletins of the Indian National Congress.

Presidential Address of the Indian National Congress from 1912 (Annual).

Proceedings and Reports of the Indian National Congress from 1912.

Proceedings and Reports of the Bihar Provincial Congress Committee (Annual).

Proceedings and Reports of the Indian Social Conference (Annual), 10th, 1887.

Montague-Chelmsford Report, 1918.

Report of the Sedition Committee, 1918.

Proceedings of the Bengal Legislative Council.

Proceedings of the Bihar & Orissa Legislative Council.

All Parties Conference, 1928 : Report & Supplementary Report of the Committee.

Report of the Land Revenue Commission : *Floud Commission.*

Report of the Civil Disobedience Enquiry Committee, 1922.

Indian Statistical Abstract (Annual).

The Moral and Material Progress : Reports.

The Indian Annual Register.

Bihar District Gazetteers.

Imperial Gazetteers of India.

Bengal Directory (Commercial), 1835.

Sketch of Commercial Resources.

Quinquennial Review of the Mineral Production of India.

Reports on the Census of India, Vol. V (Bengal, Bihar, Orissa, Sikkim, 1913).

The Bengal Administration Report of 1872-73.

Annual Rural Bengal, 1897.

Bengal Education Report, 1862-63.

Bengal General (Education) : Annual Proceedings, 1861, 1871, 1906, 1917.

Bengal Appointment : Annual Proceedings.

Bihar Regional Records Committee's Report.

Report of the Patna University Committee : Nathan Committee.

Proceedings, Government of Bihar & Orissa (Education Department), 1913-14.

Quinquennial Review on the Progress of Education in Bihar and Orissa.

Proceedings of Imperial Legislative Council.

First Decennial Review (1912-22) : *Bihar & Orissa.*

The Indian Year Book, 1914.

The Annual India Quarterly Register.

All India Congress Committee's Annual Report.

Bihar Provincial Congress Committee's Annual Report.

Annual Report of the Congress Secretaries.

Weekly Report of the Provincial Congress Committee.

Bihar Political Conference Report.

Reports on Political Events in Bihar : Fortnightly Reports, Bihar.

Bihar Police Administration Reports.

Reports of the Superintendent of Police of Districts.

Fortnightly Reports of Patna Commissioner.

Police Reports.

The Non-Cooperation and the Khilafat Movements in Bihar & Orissa, etc.

Report of the Bihar Vidyapith and its affiliated Institutions, Patna.

Bihar Gazette, Extra-ordinary, August, 1942.

Proceedings Book of Bihar Provincial Congress Committee, Sadaqat Ashram, Patna.

Census Reports for 1921, 1931 *and* 1941.

Unpublished Records

Unpublished Records of National Archives, New Delhi.

Unpublished Records of State Archives, Bihar, Patna.

Unpublished Records of Bengal, Calcutta.

Unpublished Records of the Divisional and District Offices of Bihar.

Proceedings,

Consultations,

Reports,

Diaries

and Correspondence of various officers contained in Confidential Files of Bihar Political (Special) Department;

Home Political Department Files; and

Bihar & Orissa Police Abstract of Intelligence.

Index

Aaranovitch, S., 9
Acharya Narendra Deva, 209
Adam, 34
Agrarian system, 16
Ahmad, Sayed, 40
Ahmad, Wasi, 99
Ali brothers, 127
Ali, Imam, 121
All-India Muslim League, 71
Arif, Yukub, 188
Arya Samaj, 38-40
Asaf Ali, Aruna, 296
Atkinson, W.S., 36
Attlee, 304
Azad, Maulana Abul Kalam, 105, 113, 121, 141, 260, 264
Bajaj, Jamuna Lal, 126, 139, 143
Bajpai, Balmukund, 77
Banerjee, B.B., 122, 161
Banerjee, Surendra Nath, 51, 71
Basu, Bribhangsu, 225
Bentick, William, 17
Besant, Annie, 72-74, 78
Bhatta, K., 122
Bhattacharya, S.B., 192
Bihar, middle class in, 5, 18-19, 20-22, 54, 70-71, 79-80, 98, 103-104, 107-110, 153-154. 217
Bihar and Bengal, separation of, 37, 51
Biharis, 33
co-workers, 81
students, 35
Biswanand, Swami, 121
Biswas, Prafulla Kumar, 221
Bolpur Conspiracy Party, 225
Bose, Khudiram, 219
Bose, J.C., 146
Boycott, 126, 172
Brahmachari, Ram Raksha, 81
Brahmins, 18, 43
Brahmo Samaj, 38, 40
British political supremacy, 20
British power, rise of, 17
British rule, 1
Broomfield, C.N., 136

Capitalism, 6
Caste, class sections of, 1
Catholic outlook, 39
Chakravarty, Prabhat, 233
Chakravarty, Satish Chandra, 51
Champaran mission, 79-80, 90-91
Champaran movement, 54
Chattopadhya, Bankim Chandra, 219
Chaube, Hazari Lal, 231
Chaube, Suraj Nath, 232
Chaudhary, Jaglal, 248
Chaudhary, Luxmi Narayan, 162
Chelmsford, Lord, 103

Christian missionaries, 20
Churchill, Winston, 271
Civil disobedience movement, 124, 134-135, 136, 172, 209
Civil disputes, 15
Class, concept of, 1-5
Class, middle (see middle class), 18-19, 29, 33, 98, 153-154
Cole, G.D.H., 13
Columbus, 19
Congress days, 51
Congress-League Scheme, 72, 77
Cornwallis, 15
  policy of, 31
Cowasjee, Rustomji, 24

Das, C.R., 138
Das, Deshbandhu, 138
Das, Jitendra Nath, 229
Das, Gangadhar, 99
Das, Tarak Nath, 225
Dayal, Raghubir, 99
De Costa, E.P.W., 10
Delhi Congress, 78
Deshpande, 143
Diwani of Bengal, adquisition of, 13
Ducarel, G.G., 30
Duradh, 41
Dwarkanath, 69

East India Company, 13, 18, 26
Education, 14
Education, System of, 18
European capital, 26
Exploitation, 6

Fabian socialism, 78
Fascism, 269
Feudal lords, powers of the, 19
Flag, National, 173
Francis, Philip, 30
French revolution, 4

Gadar Party, 225
Gandhi, Kutir, 151
Gandhi, Mahatma, 54, 71, 82-85, 88-89, 111, 113-114, 126, 135, 142, 175, 240-241, 258, 288
  appeal of, 90
  champaran mission of, 79-80
  illness of, 301
  salt law broken by, 177
  tours of Bihar of, 148-149
Ghose, Phanindra Nath, 232
Ghosh, Aurobindo, 222
Ghosh, Barindra, 221
Ghosh, Ganesh Chandra, 220
Ghosh, Naresh Chandra, 225
Gokhale, Gopal Krishna, 52, 72
Gowalas, 39, 41

Hakim Abdul Hai, 162
Haque, Mazharul, 52, 53, 69, 71-72, 83-86, 101, 107, 125, 143, 151
Hashmi, Zakaria, 111
Hasnain, Muhammad Khurshed, 143
Hastings, Warren, 15, 29-30
  administration, 32
Heycock, W.H., 86
Hexter, 5
Hindu, 77, 152
Hindu-Muslim riots, 146
Hindu-Muslim Unity, 130
Hoebel, E.A., 3
Home Rule Movement, 54, 70-71
  appraisal of, 78-79

Imam, Ali, 52, 54, 153
Imam, Hasan, 74, 77, 86-87, 91, 101, 107
Imam, Nafir, 101
Independence Day, celebration of, 1/3
Indian middle class, 18-19
Indian National Congress, 52, 71, 98-99, 172, 217
Industrial middle class, emergence of, 25

Industrial revolution. 23-24
Industry, Indian, ruinous for, 14
Ismail, S.M., 53

Jallianwalla Bagh, massaere of, 79, 101, 177
Jankins, R.P., 36
Jha, Jainandan, 162
Jha, Ram Avtar, 295
Jinnah, Muhammad Ali, 53
Judicial administration, 15

Kayasthas, 18, 37, 40, 43-44
Khadi, 148
  wearing of, 145
Khan Bahadur Sarfaraz Hussain, 73-74
Khan, Mahboob Hasan, 101
Kkan, Mohammad Ismail, 144, 153
Khilafat Movement, 103-106, 144
Koff, Nim, 3
Kriplani. J.B., 82, 91, 114
Kriplani, Sucheta, 297
Krishna, Gopi, 53
Kurmis, 39

Labour conspiracy, 229-230
Labour, landless, 17
Lahore session, 173
Lal, Dasrath, 53
Lal, Nand Kishore, 53
Lal, Parmeshwar, 53
Lal, Peary, 40
Lala Jagat Narayan, 111-115
Lala Lajpat Rai, 53, 108, 117, 218
Lohia, Ram Manohar, 293
Lucknow movement, 90

Macaulay, minute of, 17
Maharaja Mitrajit Singh, 34
Majumdar, Ambika Charan, 67
Mallick, Basanta Kumar, 137
Malviya, Balgovind, 31, 102
Malviya, Kedar Nath, 234
Malviya, Pandit Madan Mohan, 63
Marwari Community, 139
Marx, Karl, 1, 6
Marxian, capitalism, 6
Marxian petite bourgeoisie, 12
Maulana Abdul Bari, 105
Maulana Abdul Majid, 106
Maulana Abdul Qadir Azad Sohhani, 110
Maulana Muhammad Ali, 145
Maulavi Muhammad Safi, 144
Maulavi Khursheed Hasnain, 101
Maulavi Narul Hasan, 105-106, 145
Mehta, Deo Narayan, 125
Mehta, Pherozeshah, 72
Middle class (see in Class) 5, 18-19
  Champaran mission and, 79-80
  constructive works and the, 155
  definition of, 5-8
  development of, 19
  groups of. 9
  movements and, 98-130
  revolutionary nationalism and, 217-219
Middle class, educated, 33
Middle class, landed, 29
Middle class in Bihar, 20
  commercial, 21
  growth and composition of, 20-21
Miller, Lady, 146
Mishra, Bharat, 133
Mishra, B,B., 19
Mishra, Prajapati, 302
Mishra, S.C.. 107
Misser, Laxshmi Narain, 125
Montagu Mission, 98
Montford Report, 78
Morshead, L.F., 83
Mudholkar, R.N., 52

Mughal rule, 15
Mushars, 39
Muslim, 40, 52-53, 153
Muslim League, 267, 300

Nair, C., Sankaran, 62
Nandkeolyar, R.K.L., 116
Naqvi, M. Saiyid Sulaiman, 144
Narayan, Jai Prakash, 290-291, 295
National Movement, 98, 278-279
Nawab Sarafaraz Hosain Khan Bahadur, 52
Nazism, 269
Nehru, Jawaharlal, 11, 176-178, 244, 257
Nehru, Kamla, 176
Nehru, Motilal, 126, 139, 154
Nizamuddin, Khwaja. 300
Non-cooperation movement, 98, 99, 107
Non-violence, 130

Ogburn, 3
Ojha, Shanti, 256

Pal, Bipin Chandra, 211
Panchayat, 130
Pant, Govind Ballabh, 244
Paranjapay, R.P., 67
Patel, Vallabhbhai, 139, 142, 159
Patna University
  caste organisation and, 61-65
  establishment, 54-56
  journals of, 65-66
Patna University Bilt, 67-68
Patna University Committee members, 58-59
Plato, 1, 6
Population, pressure of, 17
Prasad, Baldeo Rai, 72
Prasad, Braj Kishore, 69, 81
Prasad, Damodar, 77
Prasad, Gorakh, 84
Prasad, Jaleshwar, 177
Prasad, Janakdhari, 75, 77
Prasad, Mathura 156, 173
Prasad, Murli Manohar, 192
Prasad, Rajendra, 51-52, 59, 69, 72, 77-79, 86-87, 89, 110-112, 116-117, 147-149, 173, 178-179, 280, 304
Prasad, Ramnavami, 84
Prasad, Sri Krishna, 51
Prasad, Tajeshwar, 52
Premchand, 77
Prince of Wales, 131, 133
Protestant movements, 4
Purna Swarajya, 172

Quit India movement 278

Rai Bahadur Edal Singh, 42
Rajgopalachari, 139
Rajputs, 43
Ram, Jagjiwan, 280
Ram Rrishna Mission, 39
Renaissance, 4
Revolutionary Nationalism, 217-220, 225-226
Right, natural and political, 4
Roy, Manindra Narayan, 229
Roy, Prakash chandra, 38
Russeo-Japanese War, 218

Sabhas, 40-41
Sahai, Bahu Chandra Bansi, 73, 100-101
Sahai, Krishna, 91
Saiyid Muhammad Shafi, 16,
Sahay, Bikramjit, 88
Sahay, K.B., 224
Sahay, Kuar Nandan, 52-53
Sahay, Madan Mohan, 88
Sahay, Shyam Nandan, 82
Sahay, Sri Krishna, 63, 69
Sahu, Debi Lal, 126
Sahu, Kedar Nath, 126

Sahu, Ramdayal Prasad, 126
Sahu, Ramdayalu, 91
Salt Law, 138-140
Salt Satyagraha, 172
Samarth, N.M., 53
Sapru Bahadur, 63
Saran, Mahavir, 99
Sarkar, Jadunath, 69
Satyagraha, 98, 103
Schumpeter, Joseph, 2
Sen, D.N., 70
Sen, J.B., 173
Sen, S.P., 99
Setalvad, C.H., 63
Settlement of land, 14
Settlement, permanent, 31-32
Seva Samiti Movement, 128
Sharma, R.N., 53
Shukla, Raj Kumar, 81-82, 89-91, 162
Shukul, Shashi Bhushan, 245
Simon Commission, 98, 153-154
Singh, Bisheshwar, 41
Singh, Chait, affair of, 30
Singh, Deep Narayan, 52, 120
Singh, Langat, 41
Singh, Ram Binode, 224
Singh, Ramdayalu, 51
Singh. Ram Narain, 173
Singh, Saligram, 41
Singh, Suraj Narayan, 297
Singh, Tej Narayan, 41
Sinha, Badri Narain, 296
Sinha, Krishna Prakash Sen, 161
Sinha, Madhava, 99
Sinha, Mahamaya Prasad, 259, 280
Sinha, Nalini Ranjan, 73
Sinha, Purnendu Narayan, 39, 69-70, 73, 100
Sinha, Sachchidananda, 52, 57, 67, 77, 86, 91, 153-154, 161
Sinha, Sudhir Kumar, 221
Swadesh movement, 51
Swami Dayanand Saraswati, 38
Swami Satya Deva, 223
Swarajya Party, 98
  formation and working of the, 138-140

Tammaji, Narayan, 101
Tata Iron and Steel Company, 28
Thakkar, A.V., 267
Tilak, Lokamanya, 126, 217-218
Tinkathia, 80
Tiwari, Ramdeo, 119
Tiwari, Suraj Prasad, 119
Turkey, tragic fate of, 103

Upadhyaya, Bachcha, 88
Untouchability, 244

Vakil, 99
Varma, Arunjay Sahay, 132
Varma, Badri Nath, 114, 156
Varma, Bindeshwari Prasad, 91
Varma, Bipin Behari, 156
Varma, Phulan Prasad, 247
Varma, Sambhu Saran, 91
Vaswani, 158
Vidyalankar, Jaichand, 229
Vijayaraghavachariar, C., 117
Vosco-da-Gama, 19

Wavell, Lord, 304
Weber, Max, 2, 8-9
Weberian, 2
Western education system, 18, 33
Wilson, J.M., 83
Wood, Charles, 33
World War, First, 26, 70, 103, 225, 269
  Second, 278

Zahiruddin, K.B., 99, 162
Zamindars, 14-15, 29-30, 41-42
Zerait system, 80
Zubair, Shah Muhammad, 108, 120, 192